Future Studies and Counterfactual Analysis

"Ted Gordon is a pioneer in future studies with a deep history of developing methodological innovations. This is a book I would enthusiastically read and keep on my shelf for reference. It is an extremely important contribution to the futures/forecasting domain. I thus recommend it with enthusiasm."
—Paul Saffo, *Professor of Engineering at Stanford University and Chair of Future Studies at Singularity University, USA*

"This should be read for the sheer pleasure of it; it distills Gordon's lifetime of futures research into an extraordinarily diverse set of vignettes to solve very serious and well documented problems. His uniquely well informed imagination is matched only by the depth of research and citations."
—Jerome C. Glenn, *Director of the Millennium Project, Washington, DC, USA*

"Futurists Theodore Gordon and Mariana Todorova dare to extend forecasting tools to explore the deepest questions about the future survival of our human species. They explore beyond the now imminent self-inflicted external threats to our life-supporting planetary home caused by our limited perception. They also courageously examine our same human cognitive and emotional disabilities which inadvertently allowed deployment of social information technologies that now blind us and may limit our capabilities for self-governance and future cultural evolution. Must reading for all concerned with our common global future."
—Hazel Henderson, *CEO of Ethical Markets Media Certified B. Corporation, USA, and author of* Mapping the Global Transition to the Solar Age *and other books.*

"Aware of the inherent limitations to our mental vision, Mariana Todorova and Theodore Gordon understand both the relativity of historical perspectives and future outlook which are continuously being recast based on current knowledge and changing attitudes. They remind us of the relativity of all knowledge, both of the past and future. This a precious endowment for it tells us that both our sense of fatalism and blind optimism are poorly grounded in reality. The real reality depends not on what will happen to us, but on the choices we will make."
—Garry Jacobs, *Chair of the World Academy of Art and Science, India*

Theodore J. Gordon · Mariana Todorova

Future Studies and Counterfactual Analysis

Seeds of the Future

Theodore J. Gordon
Millennium Project
Old Lyme, CT, USA

Mariana Todorova
Bulgarian Academy of Sciences
Sofia, Bulgaria

ISBN 978-3-030-18436-0   ISBN 978-3-030-18437-7   (eBook)
https://doi.org/10.1007/978-3-030-18437-7

© The Editor(s) (if applicable) and The Author(s), under exclusive license to Springer
Nature Switzerland AG 2019
This work is subject to copyright. All rights are solely and exclusively licensed by the
Publisher, whether the whole or part of the material is concerned, specifically the rights
of translation, reprinting, reuse of illustrations, recitation, broadcasting, reproduction
on microfilms or in any other physical way, and transmission or information storage and
retrieval, electronic adaptation, computer software, or by similar or dissimilar methodology
now known or hereafter developed.
The use of general descriptive names, registered names, trademarks, service marks, etc. in this
publication does not imply, even in the absence of a specific statement, that such names are
exempt from the relevant protective laws and regulations and therefore free for general use.
The publisher, the authors and the editors are safe to assume that the advice and
information in this book are believed to be true and accurate at the date of publication.
Neither the publisher nor the authors or the editors give a warranty, expressed or implied,
with respect to the material contained herein or for any errors or omissions that may have
been made. The publisher remains neutral with regard to jurisdictional claims in published
maps and institutional affiliations.

This Palgrave Macmillan imprint is published by the registered company Springer Nature
Switzerland AG
The registered company address is: Gewerbestrasse 11, 6330 Cham, Switzerland

This book is dedicated to the pioneers of futures research who break new ground with each new method and speculation they explore. It takes courage to open boxes that have no apparent boundaries. Futurists ask what might be in store and how destiny can be shaped to make lives better forever. What seems inevitable is not always immutable; to futurists, adventure comes in discovering what opportunities lie ahead.

Preface

In our time, the atom has been made to fission, the human gene has been decoded defining the instructions of life, genetic instruction that shapes a fetus into a human being have been amended before birth, and the moon has been host to Earth-based humans. We have launched mechanical emissaries beyond the solar system and captured a close-up photograph of a comet crashing onto another planet. We have shattered time into billions of a second and measures of distance into portions of an angstrom. We've extended time back to within femo-seconds of the big bang and into space with light year dimensions beyond our ability to comprehend. And there's more to come, much more.

Yet we are at heart still aborigines, living atavistically in a glass and steel world but still with a jungle mentality. The mismatch between what we have made and understand and how we behave is astonishing. It is a measure of our youthfulness and naivety, an indication of how far we have yet to go. We fight, hate, distrust, cheat, and abuse as though our near-term survival depends on it. Perhaps it does. But long-term survival really depends on getting over it and finding modes of behavior that accommodate, empathize, and focus on the common good. We need systems of justice that go beyond national interests as our national systems of justice go beyond individual interests.

If we could plot the status of science and technology as an index, beginning near zero in deep antiquity of civilization, 30,000 years ago, rising slowly, oscillating with good ideas and bad. Beginning of the seventeenth century, the curve would slowly begin to swoop upward, then

viii PREFACE

accelerate with Newton, Mendel, Darwin, Laplace, Freud, Einstein, and Watson and Crick. Despite the false starts and the wrong ideas (alchemy, phrenology phlogiston, for example), science and technology as we know them are very recent and cover 300 years or so out of the 30,000 years of time that we call civilized. This momentum will continue, we think, and will define—for better or worse—the world in which our children, their children, and all others to follow will surely find themselves.

There is a comparable plot for moral achievement. It begins earlier, because civilization itself is based on a set of rules about acceptable behavior, so when we say civilization began 30,000 years ago, certainly some forms of morality began then as well. There are also names on this second chart: Aristotle, Moses, Christ, Mohammed, Kant, and Gandhi. But their ideas did not extinguish the fog of atavism and egocentricity that the instinct of the jungle provided to us. This second graph rises and falls as the forces of civility battle: the sacred and profane, the moral and the evil, the selfish and the empathetic.

Perhaps as important is understanding whether the gap between the first graph of scientific and technological achievement and the second graph of civilized behavior is growing or shrinking. If the gap is growing, science and technology and powerful decision makers of the world may be addressing the wrong problems; if it is shrinking then the future is bright indeed. Hard to tell which it is. We hope that this book provides a bit of clarity, but we have no illusions that it will lift the veil of uncertainty very far. If it stimulates some new thinking, we will be satisfied.

The authors of this book have worked on it for three years. Todorova converted the historian's tool of counterfactual analysis to its mirror image for use in future studies. Gordon wrote the book.

Old Lyme, USA

Theodore J. Gordon

Sofia, Bulgaria

Mariana Todorova

CONTENTS

1	**Introduction**	1
	References	8
2	**True or False**	11
	References	30
3	**Proliferation: Doomsday or Politics?**	33
	References	49
4	**The Bounds of Humanity**	51
	References	59
5	**The Beginning and Hereafter**	61
	References	68
6	**Immortality**	69
	How Long Can We Live?	78
	References	81
7	**Religion**	83
	References	89

x CONTENTS

8 Decision Making: The Talent for Decisions   91
References   106

9 Dealing with Bio-terrorism   107
References   116

10 Our Computer Overlords   119
References   126

11 What Constitutes Progress?   127
Seeking Happiness   127
References   139

12 Political Chaos   141
References   150

13 The Perfect Human   153
References   157

14 Conclusions   161
References   167

Appendix   169

Index   185

ABOUT THE AUTHORS

Mr. Theodore J. Gordon is the author of many client reports, peer-reviewed technical articles, and five books dealing with topics associated with the future, space, and scientific and technological developments and issues. He is the author of the *Macmillan Encyclopedia Article on the Future of Science and Technology*. He is currently on the editorial board of *Technological Forecasting and Social Change*.

He was also Chief Engineer of the McDonnell Douglas Saturn S-IV space vehicle (he ran a 3000 person department); director of Advanced Space Stations and Planetary Systems, the advanced design function of the division. He was also in charge of the launch of early ballistic missiles and space vehicles from Cape Canaveral. His career at Douglas spanned a 16-year period, from 1952 to 1968.

He was Regents Professor at the UCLA Graduate School of Business (1968), and a Woodrow Wilson scholar at Bowdoin (1975). He has lectured at several other universities in business, planning, innovation, forecasting and engineering, including Columbia, University of Texas at Austin, University of Houston, Duke University, University of New Haven, Universidad Simon Bolivar, Singularity University, and the Turku School of Economics and Business Administration (Finland). He has been a consultant to the RAND Corporation math and policy department. He is senior author of the first publicly available Delphi study (1964) and has developed several forecasting techniques including

xii ABOUT THE AUTHORS

Real-Time Delphi, Cross Impact Analysis, Trend Impact Analysis, and State of the Future Index. His current research has focused on terrorism prospects.

Mr. Gordon holds several patents in space vehicles, acoustics, automated collection of voter judgments, and speech recognition. His degrees are in aeronautical engineering from Louisiana State University and Georgia Institute of Technology.

Mr. Gordon is the co-founder of the Millennium Project and continues to serve on the Board of Directors. He also started the consulting firm, The Futures Group in 1971. As CEO, he led that firm for 20 years. The company performed contract research in economic and social development and strategy for private organizations and government agencies. Prior to forming The Futures Group, Mr. Gordon was one of the founders of the non-profit organization: The Institute for the Future. Mr. Gordon has served on the Board of several organizations including the Institute for Global Ethics, The Futures Group, Apollo BioPharmaceutics, (a start-up firm in the field of anti-aging pharmaceuticals), Rolodex Corporation, Registry Magic (a start-up company in the field of speech recognition). He also served as Chairman of the Connecticut Product Development Commission Loan Board, and Acting Chairman of the Connecticut Commission on the Future.

He is a radio amateur (W1FAR) and flies his own Light Sport airplane.

Dr. Mariana Todorova is an assistant professor at the Bulgarian Academy of Sciences and has been a Member of Parliament of the National Assembly of the Republic of Bulgaria.

Mariana is a researcher in the field of future studies and strategic planning. She is building a new methodology of scientific forecasts combining counterfactual analysis and scenario building. She is an analyst, futurist, strategist, and trend tracker.

She earned her Bachelors Degree in cultural studies and cultural anthropology at Sophia University St. Kliment Ohridski in 2002. She completed an Executive Program in political leadership at Harvard University, John F Kennedy School of Government in 2010. She completed the International Visitors Leadership Program at the US State Department in 2012. She earned her Ph.D. in futurology, future studies at the Bulgarian Academy of Sciences in 2013. She completed an Executive Program in Political Leadership at the Chinese Academy of Governance in 2013.

CHAPTER 1

Introduction

Historians study the paths that have led from paradise or fearful despair to the present; futurists study the paths that lead from the present to a promised paradise or fearful despair. One profession looks back and learns from past successes and mistakes; the other looks forward to find a route to a desired future. One tries to find truth about what happened and the other conjectures about what may happen and how to improve on a future based on random chance and weak decisions.

Looking backward from the present shows a network of intersecting and branching paths that got us here. Looking forward shows extensions of those paths, each a network of its own with unnamed branch points and decisions yet to be made. Like a GPS, we can trace the single route that got us here, and uncover the many, perhaps infinite, number of routes that will get us to the next waypoint. In answering the question about how best to get to the waypoints, GPS algorithms can find the shortest, the fastest, the one with least cost, or the one with the grandest scenery or the least traffic, and then tell us to turn right then go ½ mile down the road and so on until we arrive at where we want to be. There are tens, maybe thousands of routes to the same destination, some that make good sense, others are senseless, like going from Boston to Times Square by way of the Ginza. Throw away the bad routes and you are still left with an infinity of routes to the future.

So we have in our minds a mental picture of a map that measures time not distance. We are in the center of the page. To our left is a network of roads starting from a great number of past beginnings; the antebellum

© The Author(s) 2019
T. J. Gordon and M. Todorova, *Future Studies and Counterfactual Analysis*,
https://doi.org/10.1007/978-3-030-18437-7_1

South, slavery, the beginnings of our country, the Crusades, religions, the big bang, World wars: everything imaginable that makes up history, making turns and twist to get us to where we are now. To our right is an even more complex network of roads starting from where we are in the center of the map out to the right-hand margin. Each branch point offers dozens of turns and twists of their own and they in turn spawn more turns and twists down the road. Some branch points result from new technology: invisibility, quantum phenomena, flying cars, and even increased life span. Other intersections raise the possibility of social and political changes: wars and treaties, financial bubbles and compromises. Many roads are indistinct, only dotted lines really. And as we look further to the right or left, all of the lines, solid and dotted, become less distinct, fuzzy, out of focus. The scales of time are exponential: near the center, a year is the width of a thumb; near the outer margins, a thumb covers a century.

The roads to the left trace the historians' time lines of history (Brownstone and Frank 1996; Grun 1991), the roads to the right are the futurists' scenarios of the future.

This time-map analogy is a vast oversimplification. The past is also indistinct, even if we have lived through those times, we have different recollections and records of what really happened. Our images of the past and future are shaped by our own predilections, anticipations, and biases. The map in reality is not just 2 dimensional and flat but n-dimensional. We may not be at the center of the map at all, but at one edge or the other. Further, there may not be edges at all. We may not move continuously from left to right but sometime in the future, the time vector may jump discontinuously to the right or left or move in some other direction. Perhaps a better analogy would be a 3D picture of the brain with 90 billion or so interconnected neurons.

The intersections of paths on this conceptual time-map imply decisions that have been made in the past or may be required in the future. Should we go to war or not? Should I take this road or that one? Should I open the door that leads to the East or the West? Should I marry this smart man or woman or that handsome or beautiful one? Should I take this high paying job, with all its risks or let well enough alone, stay satisfied with my old Ford and not aspire to an Aston Martin? There is a nineteenth-century short story called *The Lady or the Tiger* that captures the drama involved in deciding among choices under conditions of high uncertainty. In this tale, a trial takes place in a room with two doors: A beautiful woman is behind one, and a hungry tiger is behind the other. The accused is forced to choose and his guilt or innocence will be demonstrated by his survival or death (Stockton 1882). This is the dilemma that repeats in greater or lesser degree at each future path intersection; this is the dilemma of decision making in uncertainty.

We will find out the results of some of our choices because we will live through them, but we will never know for sure what we missed. How will we ever know what might have been? The doctor asks "is that pain medication working?" How can you tell? You have no pain now, but would there have been pain if you hadn't taken the pill? You say, "I'm feeling great, Doc, so it must be working," But neither you nor your doctor can know what might have been.[1]

This is a book about a few important unresolved issues, their origins, their paths to the present, and the outlook for their futures. We define an important issue as one that affects or promises to affect many people, deeply, for long periods of time. Many involve decisions that are irreversible. Ten such issues form the chapters of this book. These are issues we recognize now but have not solved: We have put them aside for now because they are difficult, expensive, and divisive. We have, in effect, left them to be solved later by our children or grandchildren or even more distant descendants. Perhaps by then there will be new tools, new approaches, new values that ease the task of deciding. But in the meantime people may die or suffer, costs of solutions may escalate, and rage over our inadequacies and timidity grows. Examples in this book include control of nuclear weapon proliferation, death and dying, and the definition and necessity of progress. But to be fair we should recognize that trying to cure problems before their time may result in chaos and worsen the situation.

The cases we examine in this book were derived from suggestions made by a Real Time Delphi panel of European experts who were asked to identify important issues of the present that had, for various reasons, been overlooked or deliberately "kicked down the road," to be addressed later but inevitably. We were aided in nominating the issues for this group

---

[1] The lyrics of a song from the 1971 Broadway show *Follies* captures the yearning to know what might have been. "You take one road, you try one door, there isn't time for any more. One's life consists of either/or. One has regrets, which one forgets, and as the years go on, the road you didn't take hardly comes to mind," from the song, "The Road You Didn't Take" Lyrics by Steven Sondheim, *Follies*, 1971.

by a taxonomy of issues developed by one of the authors (Todorova) who proposed that issues worth considering could be of three types:

1. dormant facts (sleeper issues like the conflict that divides religious groups),
2. reinterpretation or reinvention of facts (as political demigods are apt to do through propaganda), and
3. rumors, gossip, and hypotheses, imagined realities that may be as strong as real facts such as stereotyping.

We selected ten of the issues that came from the experts on the basis of what we perceived to be their importance to the future and the richness of the alternatives they presented. For these we studied the left side of the time-map to establish the nature of the issue and answer if we could, how we got here. Then we asked where we might be headed by illustrating some of the paths open to us in the future, the right side of the time-map.

We used an application of counterfactual analysis to explore some of the possible future evolutions of these issues, and a more readable and instructive form of scenarios to describe some of the paths on the right side of the time-map. Where most scenarios written by futurists are built on cause/effect narratives or depend on numerical models derived from historical relationships, ours are mostly point descriptions, a form that we found allowed more imaginative presentations. Author Biographies give much more detail about all of the methods we employed.

Real Time Delphi and scenarios are well-known futures techniques; counterfactual analysis is a technique known to historians but new to futures applications. In "classic" counterfactual analysis, the historian asks what if we had opened a different door and gone down a different road in the march to the present? In their use of counterfactual analysis historians and novelists pose questions such as "How would history have been different had Y happened instead of X?" Take for example, Pascal's philosophical question, "Cleopatra's nose, had it been shorter, the whole face of the world would have been changed," meaning, of course, that she might not have been so attractive to Marc Antony or Julius Caesar, and one thing leads to another and thus a different world ensues (Pascal 1669). The science fiction novelist, Ray Bradbury, wrote a short story about travel back in time in which a time traveler from the present is sent back to the Late Cretaceous, and contrary to instructions steps off the safe path and inadvertently crushes a butterfly. When he returns to the present, he finds a different world: a different President, words spelled differently, language changes (Bradbury 1952). Or consider how the world might be different if Count von Zeppelin had chosen helium rather than hydrogen in the design of his rigid airships. The gas leak in the Hindenburg would not have led to the explosion at Lakehurst and we might still have luxurious lighter than air travel. Another example is in the novel by Philip Roth, *The Plot Against America*, in which he supposes that the aviation hero Charles Lindbergh wins the 1940 election by defeating Franklin Roosevelt. Charles Lindbergh was believed to be sympathetic toward Nazi Germany and Hitler, and in the imagined scenario of Roth's book, after being elected, Lindbergh reaches a political accommodation with Hitler, and establishes grotesque anti-Semitic policies in the USA.

What if Hitler had invaded Britain in the Second World War in the fall of 1940? The German military had planned Operation "Sea Lion," the invasion of Britain, and was awaiting the order to proceed. Hitler had said: "As England, in spite of the hopelessness of her military position, has so far shown herself unwilling to come to any compromise, I have decided to begin to prepare for, and if necessary to carry out, an invasion of England." France had fallen and morale was very low in Britain. The evacuation at Dunkirk had taken place a few months earlier. Some historians think the invasion might well have been successful, but instead Hitler directed that the manpower massed for Sea Lion be transferred to the East to join Operation Barbarossa, the invasion of Russia. Why? What was he thinking? The Nazi Luftwaffe under Göring who came to France to take personal control of the air attacks on England was to supposed to have gained air superiority in a prelude to Sea Lion but the RAF in the Battle of Britain put up stiff resistance that denied this goal to the Germans. Churchill later famously said, "Never in the field of human conflict was so much owed by so many to so few" (*Guardian* 1940).

But suppose (counterfactually) that Spitfire production had lagged just a bit and the RAF had fewer aircraft or that a few of the RAF aces were not there or that Churchill was not resolute, what then? Suppose that Germany gained air superiority by winning the Battle of Britain, then Sea Lion might have launched, with the Nazi's attacking Poole, Portsmouth, Brighton, and Dover simultaneously. The obsolete destroyers of the Royal Navy were no match for the German naval forces, the home guard crumbled in front of the invaders, the lend-lease plan of the USA to strengthen Britain would not have taken place and with this demonstration of force and the lack of an ally in Western Europe, the USA might not have been disheartened as well. Franklin Roosevelt would have been discredited, and the world would have looked very different today.

Tetlock, Lebow, and Parker served as editors of a series of essays that also used a counterfactual approach to explore history. In describing their work, they asked:

> What if the Persians had won at Salamis? What if Christ had not been crucified? What if the Chinese had harnessed steam power before the West? Disparaged by some as a mere parlor game, counterfactual history is seen by others as an indispensable historical tool. Taking as their point of inquiry the debate over the inevitability of the rise of the West, the eminent scholars in *Unmaking the West* argue that there is no escaping counterfactual history. ...
>
> Whenever we make claims of cause and effect, we commit ourselves to the assumption that if key links in the causal chain were broken, history would have unfolded otherwise. Likewise, without counterfactual history we all too easily slip into the habit of hindsight bias, forgetting, as soon as we learn what happened, how unpredictable the world looked beforehand, and closing our minds to all the ways the course might have changed.

Tetlock and his colleagues defend the concept of counterfactual analysis as a legitimate pursuit of historians (as indeed it is); they call it "an essential addition to the real history" (Tetlock et al. 2006).

Counterfactual analysis of history requires comparisons between the real world and a world constructed with at least one historical distortion, a false decision, or a real event that did not occur, for example, that leads to a fictitious world. The differences between the real and the fictitious worlds are, logically enough, attributed to the false step. Tracing the effects of this insertion can be done analytically if there is a model, but more often judgmentally through a reasoned step-by-step cause-effect analysis. By comparing the real world to a world changed by the insertion of an alternate decision or some other changed circumstance allows the analyst or novelist to show the consequences of the imagined change. For Bradbury, a time traveler stepping on a Late Cretaceous butterfly led to a present with a different President and strange words.[2] Of course this explanation glosses over many difficulties because such analyses are never "clean." There are issues in describing what is real (as dealt with here in a later chapter), cause/effect reasoning is often faulty, and the causal chain from the crushed butterfly to last year's election is highly speculative and even if a model were available, there are causal factors involved that cannot be anticipated by any model.

In this book, we also view counterfactuals in the future tense. Much as the historian compares a constructed world to the real world, the futurist using counterfactual thinking compares two or more forecasted worlds, one might be called a reference world, built by extrapolation and "sure thing" forecasts and the other a similar world with a change like the crushed butterfly. Comparing the two would ideally show how the death of the insect changed the outcome of a contemporary election and the evolution of language. We call the inserted difference, the crushed butterfly, for example, a counterfact, although it is not a fact at all, any more than the reference world is most likely. It is the irritant that changes a "most likely" future to one that explores possibilities for change and sensitivity to accidental or deliberate manipulation. It can be and has been the heart of policy analysis.

In this book, we deal with the unfinished business of the present.[3] Unresolved issues of the present are our "gift" to the future. In effect, we say to our children—or theirs—"Here is an agenda, some issues left over from our time; sorry we couldn't solve them. We hope you have better luck." And when we consider how these "holdover" issues could be resolved we might choose to perform counterfactual analysis on future issues just as historians apply counterfactual analysis to past turning points.

Crises tend to focus the mind; in the absence of crisis, many unresolved issues are simply set aside "like kicking a can down the road." But many of these issues will need to be addressed in the years ahead and

---

[2] It is a remarkable that Bradbury used the unnatural death of butterfly in his 1952 short story. The "Butterfly Effect" was used as a metaphor by Edward Lorenz to help explain Chaos theory in 1972. In non-linear systems, very small disturbances can lead to gigantic changes in the downstream performance of complex systems.

[3] This topic was introduced to the futures community by one of the authors of this book (Todorova 2015) in the article Counterfactual Construction of the Future: Building a New Methodology for Forecasting, *World Future Review*, Sage, 2015.

we can recognize some of them now. What kind of issues? How about sovereignty in the Arctic Ocean and South China Sea, the ending of nuclear proliferation, rekindling of the cold war, employing people who are made obsolete by technology, and curing destructive terrorism without undue impingement on civil liberties? In short, we have considered some legacy issues that have been held over for future resolution, to open the can that was kicked down the road, and to examine the branch points they will create.

***

In short, this book is a collection of essays about how today's unresolved issues might be resolved in the future, about the doors that might exist then that do not exist now, and the unexplored paths and their intersections where tigers and beautiful ladies wait on the other side of closed doors. We have applied counterfactual analysis to identify some important future possibilities and constructed scenarios, some deadly serious and others tongue in cheek, that describe a few of the many possible decisions and their possible outcomes.

A word of caution: Scenarios are neither true nor forecasts. They are no more or less than plausible descriptions of what might, or could happen under the right circumstances. "Plausible" is tricky word: 20 years ago an accurate description of today's world would have almost certainly seemed implausible. Because scenarios are often complex and involve many component forecasts, their likelihood is also vanishingly small. They are, in effect, short fictional stories, presented as future histories ("one thing leads to another") or as point scenarios ("a day in the life of...") to illustrate how we think some pending issues might mature in the future. They are meant to show the wide variety of possible outcomes. We have used present tense in all of our scenarios, so in order to avoid any possibility of confusion between true history of the facts in the issues we discuss, and speculation, we have placed the scenario narratives in italics throughout this book. They are not true.

References

Bradbury, Ray. 1952. *A Sound of Thunder and Other Stories*. New York: Paperback.

Brownstone, David, and Irene Frank. 1996. *Timelines of War*. New York: Little Brown.

Ferguson, Niall. 1999. *Virtual History: Alternatives and Counterfactuals*. New York: Basic Books.

Grun, Bernard. 1991. *The Timetables of History*. New York: Simon and Schuster.

Guardian. 1940. Never in the Field of Human Conflict Was so Much Owed by so Many to so Few, August 21. https://www.theguardian.com/century/1940-1949/Story/0,,128255,00.html. Retrieved March 29, 2019.

Pascal, Blaise. 1669. *Pensees*. Paris. https://birminghamhistorycenter.wordpress.com/2011/05/19/cleopatras-nose/. Retrieved November 20, 2018.

Roth, Phillip. 2004. *The Plot Against America*. New York: Houghton Mifflin.

Stockton, Frank. 1882. *The Lady or the Tiger*. A short story that first appeared in the magazine *The Century*.

Tetlock, Philip, Richard Ned Lebow, and Geoffrey Parker (eds.). 2006. *Unmaking the West: "What-If?" Scenarios That Rewrite World History*. Ann Arbor: University of Michigan Press.

Todorova, Mariana. 2015. Counterfactual Construction of the Future: Building a New Methodology for Forecasting. *World Future Review* 7 (1): 30–38. Los Angeles: Sage.

CHAPTER 2

True or False

Issue: How can we know what is true when it is difficult to tell fact from lies, when social media replicate unverified assertions and imagined truths a thousand-fold, when lies interfere with decision making, when popular opinion and democratic voting lead to answers that are unappealing or demonstrably wrong? History shows that propaganda can be based on lies masquerading as facts. Social media provide a new way to disseminate stories and amplify them, whether true or false. Confirmation bias is a quirk of human thinking that tends to make us more readily accept stories that confirm beliefs we already hold and reject those that challenge those beliefs. The consequences as we have seen can be catastrophic.

Fact checking has grown and may eventually be accepted as a means for validating statements made by politicians and others in public settings and politifact.com is an example of one organization that attempts to identify the levels of truth of statements of politicians and the media. Their research leads to classifications of statements as true, mostly true, half true, mostly false, false, and "pants on fire" (meaning a blatant lie).[1] Similarly the Washington Post awards multiple "Pinocchios" for statements offered as true but are in fact not true; for example, President Trump was awarded four Pinocchios for his false claim that "that Clinton only won the popular

---

[1]A current example of this site can be found at http://www.politifact.com/punditfact/statements/. Retrieved February 1, 2018.

© The Author(s) 2019

T. J. Gordon and M. Todorova, *Future Studies and Counterfactual Analysis*,
https://doi.org/10.1007/978-3-030-18437-7_2

vote because millions of people voted illegally"[2] (Kessler 2016). Hopefully systems such as these will unmask propaganda, bogus statistics, and fake news stories that are attempts to sway opinion. Social media users echoed and amplified stories that validated their biases, and not incidentally, the clicks they generated on the spreading stories were profitable to the media.

The intensity and apparent validity of falsehoods will make them more dangerous in the future and camouflaging technology will become even better so the falsehoods will be better masked and harder to detect. Curing the problem may compromise freedoms that are basic to free societies. The longer we wait, the more difficult the resolution.

Time: October 30, 1994.

Place: At home, after dinner, a quiet time.

We're settled in front of the TV to watch what we hope will be an exciting prime-time program. We've been promised a TV version of Orson Welles's *War of the Worlds*, the radio show that panicked the East Coast 56 years earlier.

Orson Welles' famous radio program was based on H. G. Wells' science fiction story about Martians who, with superior intelligence and firepower, and plain ugly shock value, invaded the earth. Some people knew it was radio theater, some panicked, and others said, "Hey, it's only New Jersey." The play was very realistic: The program began as though it were a mild-mannered musical half hour. Just minutes into the program, the music was interrupted by a news announcer with a special bulletin: An eruption on Mars resulted in a large meteorite following a trajectory toward earth. A few minutes later, the meteorite turned out to be metal, cylindrical in shape; in fact, a strange alien craft. "Stay tuned for further reports." Things went from bad to worse. "We take you now to the landing site for an eye witness account." Sirens in the background. Breathless announcer and a scientist on the scene telling of Martian monsters coming out of their spacecraft and zapping every one in sight. The roads out of New Jersey clogged with refugees fleeing the advance of the monsters of Wells' imagination.

---

[2] Glenn Kessler a fact checker for the Washington Post awarded President Trump "The Biggest Pinocchios of 2016." In describing their finding about President Trump, they said, "He not only consistently makes false claims but also repeats them, even though they have been proven wrong. He always insists he is right, no matter how little evidence he has for his claim or how easily his statement is debunked."

2 TRUE OR FALSE   13

Now, in 1994, 56 years later to the day, we are in our living room, waiting for the TV version on CBS. The program is titled "Without Warning," and as we are soon to find out, the plot also involves asteroids approaching the earth, a topic that was then much in the news. Four months earlier, the comet Shoemaker–Levy had actually crashed into Jupiter. It was, by any measure, a spectacular astronomical event, unique in civilized history, and perhaps something like the collision between a comet and the earth 65 million years ago that killed the dinosaurs.

The topic was also in the news because a group of scientists (including Dr. Edward Teller, who was known as "the father of the H Bomb") met some months before Shoemaker–Levy to discuss a new program designed to guard the earth from asteroid impacts, that could—if extreme—upset the balance of life on earth (Worsnip 1984).[3] They proposed to fire nuclear-tipped ballistic missiles at any astronomical body on a collision course with the earth. A hit on an incoming asteroid would vaporize it or at least make small asteroid s out of big ones, and a lot of small hits are much better than one massive one.[4]

The 1994 TV show begins. It starts low key, like the radio program 56 years earlier. A routine news broadcast. The news anchor, Sander Vanocur, is recognizable and immediately legitimate. Then, "I've just been handed a special bulletin." Vanocur says that a new asteroid has been detected approaching the earth. "We'll bring you more on this story as it breaks." Back to the ordinary program. Then, "Here's more on that asteroid. Let's go to Kitt's Peak in California for an up-to-the- minute report...." Mild-mannered astronomers talking about the extraordinary body approaching the earth, and, incidentally referring to the real Shoemaker–Levy comet and its impact on Jupiter.

Coverage shifts to Air Force command, tracking the body. We recognize the graphics—straight out of the Gulf war. More real time coverage. A collision is virtually certain. News shots follow showing President

---

[3] This suggestion was made as early as 1984 by US and Soviet scientists. See: Patrick Worsnip, "U.S., Soviet Scientists Urge Pooled Effort Against Nuclear War," Reuters North European Service, August 23, 1984. This news article reported on a suggestion attributed to Joseph Knox of Livermore Laboratories and Joseph Smith of the University of Chicago.

[4] Some 2000 asteroids larger than 1 km cross the earth's orbit; these have an impact equivalent of 10,000 megatons of TNT. A 100-meter asteroid might hit the earth every 100–200 years, but 2–3 new earth orbit crossing asteroids are discovered every month. See *Science News*, February 5, 1994.

Clinton—the real President Clinton—at a meeting in the far-east (he really had been at such a meeting). He is leaving hurriedly to come back to the USA. This footage is indistinguishable from real news coverage.

So realistic, in fact, that a yellow crawl band at the bottom of the screen reminds us that this is fiction, that what we are seeing on the screen is not really happening. Out of concern for panic, the crawl band was inserted by local TV stations. CBS also makes announcements during the commercial breaks, telling us that the plot is fictional. It's riveting anyway. Why? We recognize the format. We fall into the routine of believing, watching the comet, just like the scenes of Bosnia, of Somalia, of the Gulf War, of Iraq, of Afghanistan, of terrorist attacks, of Syria. It's unfolding for us, this bizarre plot, in front of our eyes. We are party to it, part of it.

The message on the yellow crawl band at the bottom of the screen changes. Now there is a warning of a thunderstorm in the area. Dangerous lightning and wind. Right where the "don't believe it, it's only fiction" sign had been a second before. Do we believe the lightning warning or is it part of the program? Only the thunder outside tells us that at least this message is true.

"Without Warning," resulted in 1300 calls to CBS, most of them from viewers who took the program as fact. Some non-CBS stations were called and asked why they were not reporting on the big story. A local news anchor in Minneapolis went on the air to apologize for the anxieties raised by the program.

Distinguishing reality from fiction is the subject of this chapter. Somewhere in the not too distant future the confusion between what is really happening or has happened and what might have been or might be, envelops us in a fog of artificial truth and we will have to ask, every so often, is it really a thunderstorm or is it the stroke of an artist's digital brush?

As the Nazi propagandist Joseph Goebbels taught the world in the Second World War, lies repeated with emphasis and insistence come to be believed by listeners; the illusion of truth can be constructed. Psychologists have shown that lies can come to be believed even when the true facts are generally known; repetition makes lies seem more believable and generally accepted as truth. It worked for Hitler; it continues to work for politicians even in democracies (Stafford 2016).

The state of the art of artificial realism is now so advanced that human senses can no longer determine whether pictures are real and untouched, real but manipulated or wholly artificial. Truths can be half-truths or of the "it depends" type. Faces can be sketched from DNA fragments.

Voices can be modified and constructed to fool friends, relatives, and even one's self. Machines looking for telltale signs of manipulation can sometimes pick up subtle clues to artificiality, but the modification techniques are improving and it won't be long before all traces of manipulation are invisible to humans and sensors alike.

When an image is captured in digital form, it is relatively easy to change its shape and color, to shrink it or enlarge it, to move it to another place in the frame, to another picture entirely, or to save it for future use. When an old image is moved to a new frame, it is not just "pasted on" but rather is integrated electronically with the original picture so that pixels that comprise the image flow continuously. A new television commercial shows Humphrey Bogart, long dead, alongside and talking to living actors. This isn't makeup; this is really Bogie's image, teleported to the present. The movie *Forest Gump* uses images of Presidents and historical clips in the same way. Brandon Lee died during the shooting of the film *The Crow*. The movie was completed anyway, by inserting digitized images of Lee into the incomplete scenes. Clint Eastwood, in *Line of Fire*, was inserted into a newsreel of a real presidential motorcade.

Computers can "morph" two images; that is given one picture of say a shoe, and another of an old woman, a computer can be instructed to create a series of images that begin with the shoe and transition smoothly, frame by frame, pixel by pixel, into the old woman. *Terminator II: Judgment Day* used this technique with spectacular effect to show the emergence from the floor of a "liquid-metal cyborg." In Japan, an arcade game called *Love, Love Simulation,* uses "morphing" to combine images of two would-be parents to create an image of a baby that they might have, based on the features of both. Or if one prefers, the Japanese machine can merge your picture with a monkey, a flower, or a painting.

Computers can also create natural images from scratch. Using fractals, very complex images of nature—clouds, mountains, plants, trees—can be constructed with simple formulas. Ten lines of Basic computer program code can construct the picture of a fern using fractals. It is hard to imagine how figures so complex can emerge from so few instructions.

The industry that produces special effects for games, movies, television, and advertising is growing rapidly. Small wonder. Using digital, composite, and model techniques, sequences indistinguishable from reality can be made at very low cost, on site, without high salary film stars. Why is this important? Because the director can move characters with a computer mouse, compose on the screen. *ET* and *Jurassic Park* flow from the monitor. Because films can be created without the help of established unions, without grips, without best boys, without sets, without conventional lighting. Because computer operators can digitally insert actors shot against a black backdrop, as they really appear or in distorted or enhanced form, onto real or artificial scenes, from the present, from the past, or from the imagined future. The products are more exciting and cheaper than their conventional counterparts. The tools of this industry come from companies like Silicon Graphics and are used by companies like Industrial Light and Magic. The new companies not only hint at the future, they are creating it visually and they can create a false and imagined reality.

Fade in: The international design team of an automobile manufacturer meets to consider the design of their next automobile platform. The displays that surround the group show the tools that the next generation of designers will use. On the wall hang holograms of Ming vases. Set in wooden frames these vases are so real that they seem to be museum displays mounted in shadow boxes behind the wall. Only when they are touched does their depth give them away as two-dimensional reproductions. Down the wall a few feet away hangs a holograph ic bust of President Trump smiling and as challenging as in real life, mounted like a trophy moose, so real you'd like to say "Hello." On a nearby table, floating in air, the prisoner of an optical illusion, are scale model cars that you can walk around and view from all angles, but they are chimeras, ghosts that pass through the hand. On the large scale TV monitor is a 3D picture, visible without special glasses, showing a futuristic car, perhaps the precursor of the showroom of the future. This is not the CAD 3D line drawing that can be rotated to assume any aspect on a flat screen, this appears to be a real car, you see its depth as you see a car on the road, you focus on the scene, your eyes see life in the image. And if one sits in the ghost car's cabin, the illusion becomes even more realistic: You can dive the car, feel the road, corner like a professional driver, and win the Le Mans.

When it is so easy to construct images and pass them off as real, how will we know what is true? How do we know now? *Item*: A group of disbelievers say that the Apollo moon landing happened on a movie studio's back lot. What data do they have? These three pieces of evidence:

- The very realistic film "Capricorn One" in which actor/astronauts James Brolin, Sam Waterston, and O. J. Simpson were forced by NASA to fake a moon landing under threat of harm to their families.

2 TRUE OR FALSE   17

- The statement made by Neil Armstrong, who was asked about the "hoax theory" after his Apollo 11 splashdown. Instead of denying it he said, "I think that one would find that to perpetuate such a hoax accurately and without a few leaks around would be very much more difficult than actually going to the moon."
- The incredible and ill-conceived presentation by the then NASA press secretary Julian Scheer at the 10th annual meeting of a drinking club called Man Will Never Fly Memorial Society, after the Apollo 12 mission. He showed a film of astronaut training exercises on a simulated moonscape in Michigan and said, "The purpose of this film is to indicate that you really can fake things on the ground-almost to the point of deception." He invited the audience to come to their own conclusions "about whether or not man actually did walk on the moon" (Peterson 1989).

Of course we landed there and the footprints and the debris we left on the moon are there for a future space archeologist to discover and reconfirm our landings.

Item: In a 1994 survey of people in the USA about the Holocaust, some 22% agreed that it "was possible that the Holocaust had not happened"[5] (Lipstadt 1994; Brennan 2018). One conclusion to be drawn from such surveys is that establishing truth by popular vote is not very reliable.

At the end of the war, General Dwight Eisenhower, seeing that so monstrous a deed might not be believed in the future, went to the camps himself. At the entrance to the Holocaust Museum in Washington, DC

---

[5] In her 1999 book Dr. Deborah Lipstadt reported on knowledge of the Holocaust in the USA, she said. "In April, 1993... the Roper Organization conducted a poll to determine the extent of American's knowledge of the Holocaust... When asked 'Do you think it possible or impossible that the Holocaust did not happen?' 22 percent of American adults and 20 percent of American high school students answered, yes, it was possible." There was, of course, a possibility that the double negative phrasing of the question misled the participants, but as Dr. Lipstadt points out, a similar question, asked in England and France, received a seven percent positive response. The survey was run again in the USA but this time with the double negative removed. To this newer study, "83% said the Holocaust definitely happened, 13% said it probably happened, and 4% said it did not or had no opinion." David Brennan reporting in a 2018 Newsweek article said, "31 percent of the Americans surveyed, and 41 percent of millennials within that group, do not believe that 6 million Jews were killed during the Holocaust and think the real death toll is at least 2 million lower."

18 T. J. GORDON AND M. TODOROVA

there is an engraved sign quoting General Dwight Eisenhower, on his visit to a German concentration camp after the Second World War. It reads:

> The things I saw beggar description... The visual evidence and the verbal testimony of starvation, cruelty, and bestiality were... overpowering... I made the visit deliberately in order to be in a position to give first hand evidence of these things if ever, in the future, there develops a tendency to charge the allegations merely to propaganda...

Think about the Holocaust for a moment. What hard evidence exists? The survivors' eyewitness testimony, speeches of German leaders, particularly Himmler boasting of the near extermination of the Jews, documents that survived the war including methodical German records of the transport of the Jews to the camps.

Nevertheless, the deniers raise the question. Deborah Lipstadt author of *Denying the Holocaust* refuses to appear in debates with deniers arguing that to do so would indicate their position was worth discussing. In trying to convince her to appear, the producer of one show said, "I certainly don't agree with them, but don't you think our viewers should hear the other side?" (Lipstadt 1994).

Stay tuned. David Duke, the former Imperial Wizard of the KKK from Louisiana who won 43% of the vote in his race for the Senate in 1991, and was subsequently a presidential candidate, "described the Holocaust as a 'historical hoax' (and) wrote that the 'greatest' Holocaust was 'perpetrated on Christians by Jews. Jews fostered the myth of the Holocaust, he claimed, because it generates 'tremendous financial aid' for Israel and renders organized Jewry 'almost immune from criticism.' Mr. Duke stood for election in the Louisiana governor's race in 1991 and lost with 32% of the vote. He announced for the presidency as a Republican in 1992 and garnered 120,000 votes in the primaries. He ran again in 1996 for the US Senate and received 140,000 votes but lost. In 1999, he ran for the US House and received 19% of the vote and lost again. He ran for the US Senate again in 2016 but was roundly defeated, having received only 3% of the vote. In the run-up to the presidential election he endorsed Mr. Trump and after the election and his aborted attempt to enter the Senate, he applauded the first picks by Mr. Trump for staff and Cabinet as "great first steps" (Blake 2016) but left to our imaginations what those steps were toward. What if people like David Duke could master the future false art of recreation of history?

Stay tuned a little longer. Let's imagine that paranoiac time when reality is routinely forged for financial or political purposes. This is a time when the tools to manipulate news, images, statistics, and data are cheap, easily obtained, and widely available; when these tools can be used to enhance photographs, make money, create scenes, teach, manufacture movies, sew distrust in government, credit or discredit political figures, undermine elections; when people reach out for the new dimensions of artificial experience in entertainment and education.

Social media acts as an amplifier through re-tweeting true or false news without discrimination. One tweet about anti-Trump protesters being bussed into Austin after the 2016 elections was false but generated over 300,000 re-tweets and shared messages (Maheshwari 2016). The Russians are suspected of enlisting trolls, and bots to re-transmit false stories in the 2016 US presidential election to create a divided electorate, undermine democracy, and to sway public opinion; in a close race not much swaying is necessary. Seventeen intelligence agencies in the USA agree that Russia interfered in the 2016 election. In examining the effect of Russia's "active measures" one source said:

> Russian propaganda on social media can be divided into four themes: political messages intended to foster distrust in government (e.g. allegations of voter fraud, corruption), financial propaganda (i.e. create distrust in Western financial institutions), social issues (e.g. ethnic tensions, police brutality), and doomsday-style conspiracy theories…

> White or overt channels include state-sponsored pro-Russian news outlets such as Sputnik and RT, the grey less-overt outlets include data dump sites, such as Wikileaks, and more sinister black channels involve covert operations such as hacking. The agents disseminating the information include bots (automated web robots), and real people, often presenting themselves as innocuous news aggregators. These agents form the key engine for distributing misinformation and disinformation.

> Black or covert measures—once highly risky and dangerous to carry out—are now easily and efficiently carried out through social media. Our security agencies tell us that Russia, China, North Korea, Pakistan, Iran are now able to remotely coordinate an army of hackers, honeypots (in this instance, social media profiles used to bait other users into giving compromising or embarrassing information), and hecklers or internet trolls (individuals who purposely create discord or provoke). (Weisburd et al. 2016)

20 T. J. GORDON AND M. TODOROVA

Hypothetical Scandal 1

The satellite news media interview the oil ministers of the three major oil- producing countries. The interviews create market turmoil: the ministers from Iran, Iraq and Saudi Arabia say, in effect that there has been a secret agreement among the countries to restrict petroleum production and the data of the past few weeks indicates that the cartel has been effective once again. Oil prices quickly move up by 20% and then 50%.

Something is peculiar but outside observers can't put their finger on it. In fact what happened is that all of the interviews but one were fake. The Iranian interview was legitimate and well planned, but the others were constructed and fed into the wire networks as though the real interviews were happening. The news agencies, of course, followed up with more detailed reporting, but by that time the duped oil producing countries realized that the fraud was to their great economic benefit. Despite their original discomfort, they went along with the fait accompli.

Two weeks later, it becomes clear that the interview was faked by a cartel- not the oil countries- but by some futures traders. As much oil as ever is flowing around the world, and the bubble bursts. The markets are in disarray and collapse, Paranoia sets in.

Hypothetical Scandal 2

In a Miami neighborhood, a man goes on trial for killing his neighbor's dog. The plaintiff has a home video showing the whole thing. The video is bought by the local TV station to be shown on the 10 o'clock news. The defendant says in court, the next day: "It's a fake." Photogrammetry experts are no help; half say it's a real un-doctored record, half agree that it's a fake. The defendant sues the neighbor and the station and wins. In trial after trial, recorded information- audio, camcorder, motion picture, still picture, TV, u-tubes, electronic or silver halide, images are no longer accepted as evidence. Paranoia sets in.

Hypothetical Scandal 3

The Department of Defense issues secret contracts for the development of computer viruses that can be used to invade the enemy's databases and computers to destroy selected records. In addition, a mutant variety of this virus is designed to interrupt the enemy's command and control systems and substitute commands of our choosing. In one of the biggest scandals of the early 2020's, a similar computer virus is used by unknown third parties to destroy criminal incarceration records in 23 states. Paranoia sets in.

2 TRUE OR FALSE 21

Hypothetical Scandal 4

> *The Satellite Global News Network receives footage showing a meeting between the President of an Eastern European country and a known Mafia kingpin. The video shows the two meeting at the airport, entering a building and ostensibly talking about plans for bringing drugs into the country. Being responsible and fully aware of the possibility of photographic fraud, the network sets out to trace the authenticity of the video. They find that experts cannot detect any manipulation of the tape, that the person in question had actually flown to the country two days before the suspected meeting and that drugs are indeed showing up at customs in increasing quantity. Not enough evidence to run the video. Paranoia sets in.*

So we go into the future not knowing how to recognize truth, using systems that spread truth and falsehood with equal ease. The first amendment comes under scrutiny once again. What worked in the era of print and silver halide pictures may not work now. Can anyone publish anything? Can anyone fake anything? Can anyone challenge the collective memory? Do the old fraud laws still work? Some media sources argue it is proper to "illustrate" and "reconstruct" past scenes to make their stories more "accessible" to the public.

A branch point occurs when the search for positive means to identify what is true intensifies. Here three scenarios flow from that fork in the road to the future: *Market Madness, Bureaucratic Truth, and the Courts of Supreme Wisdom.*

Scenario 1: Market Madness

Congress decides that the market place can solve the problem. They avoid making any new legislation that impinges on the First Amendment and half the country applauds. The Supreme Court supports this view. Tapes and photographs are inadmissible if there is proof that they have been doctored. As for the suppliers, re-tweeters, and consumers of news, let the media work it out. Pornography is still defined by what offends society. What else is new?

In this chaotic time, fraud takes new dimensions. Land is sold by hologram, some images are real and others are not. "Buyer beware" has new significance. Electronic corruption abounds. Augmented reality becomes a new channel for injecting distorted truths. A virus is sold on the black market that postdates contracts, changes credit records, fixes bids, and awards scholarships.

From this chaos come some free market responses. First, several new "members only" media channels comes to life. They are an amalgam of purportedly valid information sources, digital country clubs, and secret societies. As a group they are known as the "cognessetti." They keep a quiet and below the surface presence. Applications are by invitation only and are carefully vetted to insure that the applicants have values consistent with the organizations' and a yearning to avoid the idiocy of the broader social media. A few are listed on the New York Stock Exchange and their IPO's are generally successful. Joining costs tens of thousands of dollars, and monthly fees are a few thousand dollars. Two thirds of people who apply for membership are turned away. What do they get for their money: access to blogs and other forms of publication that present current news with a guarantee of accuracy. All sources of information are documented and double or triple authenticated. Members can also buy concierge services to protect their on-line identities and third party cutouts for transmitting and receiving private messages. Like the Masons, some of the groups have secret signs of recognition and rituals, and like the Masons their secrecy and privacy raise suspicions and jealousies. They say they are a political but their influence is surely felt and welcomed by governments.

In addition, a new profession of Certified Public Authenticator is born. It grows from today's "fact checkers." At first, the province of small entrepreneurs, these new CPA's test the validity of data and images, of claims and counterclaims. Like Good Housekeeping used to be. Like Consumer Reports is believed to be today. Big accounting firms and the most astute consulting firms join these early innovators. Their field is data forensics: collecting, analyzing, synthesizing, and drawing inferences about validity and risk. Like financial CPA's of today, they issue opinions about truth; newspapers headlines carry ratings that indicate the likelihood that a statement is true. Advertisements, TV news broadcasts, realistic fictional programs: all rated. This solves a lot of the problem.

It works until the corruption scandal breaks in the CPA industry. Some firms are on the take. Who can we believe? Paranoia sets in.

Scenario 2: Bureaucratic Truth

Congress decides that the market place can't solve the problem. They pass new legislation known as The Truth in Imagery Law. It is co-authored by 45 members of the Senate and the President has a Rose Garden ceremony when he signs the bill. In essence, the bill establishes a new independent

2 TRUE OR FALSE 23

department with the responsibility of watch-doging. It is known as the Data Watch Agency (DWA) and charged initially with exposing false news sources, but soon in the wake of the infamous anonymous New York Time op-ed editorial and those that followed, sources of all news stories: true or false.[6] *The mission of the Data Watch Agency is parallel to the mission of the Food and Drug Administration (FDA). The FDA has the responsibility of assuring that the information about food and drugs is complete and accurate and that the foods and drugs available to the population of the US are pure and safe. The DWA has a similar responsibility: assuring that the information offered to the public by news agencies is true, pure, and safe. The FDA has its nutrition research labs; the DWA has its discovery labs looking for fake photos and stories. The work of the FDA is rarely challenged these days, and neither are the pronouncements of the DWA. And the DWA publishes the National Gazette that now replaces the older and obsolete newspapers that could not distinguish fake from real news.*

No one is really happy, but the Supreme Court supports the validity of this new agency. The Court says that tapes and photographs are admissible only if a "preponderance" of supporting non-electronic evidence is available. As for the suppliers of news, the court allows the DWA to check sources. "It's like truth in advertising, after all," the argument goes. Pornography is still defined by what offends society. What else is new? There are objections to "big brother" getting bigger yet, but what else can be done? Liberals complain that this is a first step toward government efforts to take control of the news media.

Subsequent events seem to support this position. A draft of a revision to the First Amendment has been submitted to the states for ratification. The new version has its supporters but the initial response is sluggish: in three years only 5 states have signed up but 35 more are inclined favorably.

The tide changes after a kidnap situation develops in Houston. The victims are twins, 6 months old, children of the mayor. The mayor releases photographs of the children. The local news is picked up by the networks, the wire-services and national newspapers. The kidnappers show, on the screen, the torture of the babies. The nation is riveted, enraged. The DWA finds

---

[6]A self identified but anonymous Trump administration official wrote an extraordinary op-ed for the *New York Times* in which he or she said: "I am part of the resistance", *CNBC*, 5 September, 2018. https://www.cnbc.com/2018/09/05/i-am-part-of-the-resistance-anonymous-trump-white-house-official-writes-in-extraordinary-nyt-op-ed.html. Retrieved September 8, 2018.

nothing wrong with the tapes but warns it may still be a hoax. No matter, the country wants action. What do the kidnappers want? Money, transportation, immunity, release of people they call political prisoners in the Middle East and Guantánamo, and most importantly, publicity for their cause: independence of an obscure island tribe on a distant continent. All demands are duly satisfied, delivered and paid for. The babies, as promised, are found safe, unharmed. The babies were taken as reported, but their torture by the kidnappers- as shown on the video- was a fake, manufactured imagery. The reaction is uproar. The mayor himself is suspected as being one of the kidnappers, but is exonerated. It is the trigger to action. He gets reelected with the biggest majority in history.

The remainder of the states ratify the amendment in short order. Now, in the United States, the Constitution does not guarantee freedom of the press or expression under certain circumstances. Kidnapping and terrorist activities that involve hostages cannot be reported until the issue is resolved. It is unlawful to report an event as truthful if in fact it is false. Paying by the click is outlawed to help prevent sensationalism. Other democracies follow. Most people feel that there is some semblance of order at last.

Five years later young children who learn this history ask, "You mean there was a time when you could say anything?" There is a nagging suspicion that we have lost something important but we can't quite remember what it was.

Scenario 3: The Courts of Supreme Wisdom

The Supreme Courts in countries around the world remain powerful and for the most part, the seats of honest jurisprudence. But now there is another kind of court that functions alongside these Supreme Courts: the Courts of Supreme Wisdom. These courts are made of wise men and women who have been identified systematically and to a degree, scientifically, as people who "get it right." Some are distinguished and well known, others are bright star mavericks, as yet "undiscovered." They are our modern Solomon's to whom the public turns with issues of monumental importance that will get worse if unanswered.

The parable of Solomon comes from the ancient Hebrew bible. The story as told is:

> Now two prostitutes came to the king and stood before him. One of them said, "Pardon me, my lord. This woman and I live in the same house, and I had a

baby while she was there with me. The third day after my child was born, this woman also had a baby. We were alone; there was no one in the house but the two of us.

During the night this woman's son died because she lay on him. So she got up in the middle of the night and took my son from my side while I your servant was asleep. She put him by her breast and put her dead son by my breast. The next morning, I got up to nurse my son—and he was dead! But when I looked at him closely in the morning light, I saw that it wasn't the son I had borne."

The other woman said, "No! The living one is my son; the dead one is yours."

But the first one insisted, "No! The dead one is yours; the living one is mine." And so they argued before the king.

The king said, "This one says, 'My son is alive and your son is dead,' while that one says, 'No! Your son is dead and mine is alive.'"

Then the king said, "Bring me a sword." So they brought a sword for the king. He then gave an order: "Cut the living child in two and give half to one and half to the other."

The woman whose son was alive was deeply moved out of love for her son and said to the king, "Please, my lord, give her the living baby! Don't kill him!"

But the other said, "Neither I nor you shall have him. Cut him in two!"

Then the king gave his ruling: "Give the living baby to the first woman. Do not kill him; she is his mother."

When all Israel heard the verdict the king had given, they held the king in awe, because they saw that he had wisdom from God to administer justice.[7]

But where are the Solomon's of today? If only we had a group of such wise men to guide us in decisions that are seemingly unsolvable, like deciding whether it would be better to punish drug offenders or to try to rehabilitate them, or giving priority for research to curing a disease or to life extension, or balancing the rewards of tax reform between the wealthy and the average citizen.

[7]Kings 3:16–28; quoted in: https://www.biblegateway.com/passage/?search=1%20 Kings%203:16-28. Retrieved October 25, 2017.

Where are today's Solomon's? Researcher Phillip Tetlock Annenberg University Professor at the University of Pennsylvania described how in the course of his work on forecasting future events, he and his colleagues discovered that in groups of people there are usually a few who seem to anticipate the dates of occurrence of future events much more accurately than chance or than the group as a whole[8] (Tetlock and Gardner 2015). Some people are simply better forecasters than others.

Following Tetlock's research, groups of people were asked (in this scenario) to forecast the short-term outcomes of recently enacted policies and they were scored on the accuracy of their predictions. And, as in the case of event forecasting, some people always seemed to "get it right." These were people of superior insight, the post-modern version of wise King Solomon (although neither they nor Tetlock would put it that way).

And so the testing began of the committees of wise persons that came to be known as Courts of Supreme Wisdom, to whom we now turn to give guidance in answering the unanswerable. Has it worked? Are decisions any better than chance or than they used to be? The jury is still out.

On February 17, 2017, US President Donald Trump said in a Tweet, "The FAKE NEWS media failing @nytimes, @NBCNews, @ABC, @CBS, @CNN) is not my enemy, it is the enemy of the American People!" (Trump 2017) 51,000 people re-tweeted it and 154,000 "liked" it. On August 5, 2018, he tweeted, "The Fake News hates me saying that they are the Enemy of the People only because they know it's TRUE. I am providing a great service by explaining this to the American People. They purposely cause great division & distrust. They can also cause War! They are very dangerous & sick!" (Smith and David 2018) 118,000 people "liked" that tweet. At the annual convention of the Veterans of Foreign Wars, President Trump said: "Stick with us. Don't believe the crap you see from these people, the fake news" (Cochrane 2018). Boos from the crowd. When Sarah Sanders the White House press secretary was asked if the President really believes the press is the enemy of the people, she said he has "made his comments clear" (Phillips 2018).

This rhetoric incites to violence. One reporter wrote that he had received threatening voice mail; one caller left this message:

---

[8]Tetlock required precision in defining the future event, the ability to tell in retrospect if an event had happened or not, and scoring the accuracy of prediction by each participant. In general, superforecasters were found to be quantitatively oriented, generally young, smart, newsjunkies, open-minded, and self-critical.

"Hey Bret, what do you think? Do you think the pen is mightier than the sword, or that the AR is mightier than the pen?" He continues: "I don't carry an AR but once we start shooting you f—ers you aren't going to pop off like you do now. You're worthless, the press is the enemy of the United States people and, you know what, rather than me shoot you, I hope a Mexican and, even better yet, I hope a n— shoots you in the head, dead." He repeats the racial slur 10 times in a staccato rhythm, concluding with the send-off: "Have a nice day, n— lover." (Stephens 2018)

Earlier, in Annapolis Maryland, a killer with a shotgun killed five people at the offices of the *Capital Gazette*, a local newspaper.

The dystopia of George Orwell, the book 1984, was built on the principals of "doublespeak" and characterized by three "pillars": "War is Peace," "Freedom is Slavery," and "Ignorance is Strength." Had Orwell lived in our time perhaps he might have added a fourth aphorism "The Media Are The Enemy of the People." His world also had a Ministry of Truth (would we be surprised to hear a suggestion for such an institution to cope with fake news?) Orwell warned about excessive power that the media could express; we live in the opposite reality: The media are not the bullies; they are being bullied. The "two minute hate sessions" of the Orwell book surfaced as early as the 2016 presidential campaign; reporting on one of his rallies they said:

> And by Monday night, Trump iterated his anti-media script, indulging the crowd's hate for reporters by letting supporters scream for two minutes at the press penned into the venue. (Stokols 2016)

The Washington Post masthead carries the motto "Democracy disappears in darkness"; can we keep the lights on?

Scenario 4: Enemy of the People

"Shit" said the owner of the network.
 "Shit" said the network news director.
 "Shit" said the network auditor,
 "Shit" said the news anchor.
 They are all reflecting on the new anti-fake law, known as AFL by those in the news industry. Members of Congress call this legislation H.R. 777: The Federal Truth in Reporting Act, drafted on a bi-partisan basis, passed by both houses with a comfortable margin, and tested at least in preliminary

form in the Supreme Court. Why now? Because people in high places used every opportunity to call the press "The Enemy of the People." The opposition wrote op-ed pieces calling this "the big lie" and recalled that the technique of repeating a lie often enough creates its own perceived truth. It had to be big and repeated time and again. It was a tactic used by Hitler, Goebbels, Stalin, Mao, Peron, and Pinochet and other masters of this propaganda technique.

Goebbels is often quoted as saying;

A lie told once remains a lie but a lie told a thousand times becomes the truth. (Quotes 2019)

It was Goebbels, not Orwell who said "Think of the press as a great keyboard on which the government can play." *Hitler said in Mein Kampf:*

… in the big lie there is always a certain force of credibility; because the broad masses of a nation are always more easily corrupted in the deeper strata of their emotional nature than consciously or voluntarily; and thus in the primitive simplicity of their minds they more readily fall victims to the big lie than the small lie, since they themselves often tell small lies in little matters but would be ashamed to resort to large-scale falsehoods. It would never come into their heads to fabricate colossal untruths, and they would not believe that others could have the impudence to distort the truth so infamously. Even though the facts which prove this to be so may be brought clearly to their minds, they will still doubt and waver and will continue to think that there may be some other explanation. (Hitler 1939)

In the United States, in the run-up to enactment of the AFL, President Trump used every opportunity to berate the media, calling them dishonest and accusing them of printing fake news, blacklisting some but favoring other media outlets that were in some way complimentary, saying at some rallies "I hate some of these people", and "horrible, horrendous people," condemning satire like Saturday Night Live as being "totally one-sided," threatening to sue for libel for printing factual reports, and by bypassing the media and communicating directly with the public through extensive tweeting where he can say anything, even obvious falsehoods. He has well over 50 million followers and says "the media are the enemy of the people."

Now, at last count, 52 nations including France, Russia, Denmark, Singapore, Egypt, and Brazil have laws against fake news (Funke 2018). *A careful reading of these actions shows that many may have been*

*introduced to limit dissent and encourage support for controversial govern-
ment policies, and others to preserve truth in media. But who can tell the
difference?*

The AFL in the US has these features:

- *Allows for blocking websites and entire social media platforms if they
  deliberately spread false information or impinge on national security.*
- *Requires that any factual reporting not witnessed by the reporter have
  two corroborating sources.*
- *Establishes penalties for deliberate falsification of news including fines,
  jail terms, and barring from future publishing activities.*
- *Blocks hate speech, pubic incitement to violence, and symbols associated
  with either.*
- *Initiates public programs to help people recognize misinformation,
  through brochures, new high school courses, and public broadcasts.*
- *Requires social media to publish the names of purchasers of sponsored
  content and the prices they paid.*
- *Establishes a database of violators of these policies including names
  of their followers to facilitate tracking and future intervention in
  their activities. This widely cited as a primary example of pre-crime
  legislation.*

"Shit," say the liberals, "we have lost freedom of speech."

"Shit," says the far right, "we should have locked 'em up."

In the years to come, the technologies that now provide the ability
to manipulate and create false images of reality will improve and make it
even more difficult to distinguish fact from fiction. These technologies
include artificial intelligence that will enable the machines themselves to
learn how to trick humans into believing new but false realities, and falsi-
fying records on a global scale without leaving a trace, confounding history and making collective memories untrustworthy.

The technology of counterfeiting reality will become essentially perfect. Despite parallel improvements in detection methods, fakes will
proliferate, will be cheaper and easier to produce, and the fakers will be
almost impossible to identify. As a result rules of evidence will have to
change. Hard evidence and firsthand experience will become invaluable,
at least until experience also becomes fakeable.

We have imagined several approaches to this problem. First, the invention of a new profession: truth certification. The second path places the

responsibility for validating truth in a government agency. The third imagines a panel of wise people who, like umpires at a ball game or a supreme court of truth, use their judgment to judge what is true. Assuring that they are incorruptible is another looming issue. And the fourth approach anticipates legislation to punish truth counterfeiters. But we need another invention, a DNA for facts that authenticates them as surely as DNA distinguishes and identifies an individual.

Statues show Lady Justice blindfolded and carrying a scale and sword. The scale reminds us of the need to balance mercy with punishment; the sword, the power of justice; and the blindfold, that all people who seek justice should be treated equally. But facts must be known and true for justice to function, so maybe there should be a fourth symbol: light. Statues of Lady Justice should shine and reflect the sun to remind us that she works best in the open fields of truth.

References

Blake, Andrew. 2016. David Duke, Former Clan Leader, Applause Trump Staff, Cabinet Pics as Great First Steps. *Washington Times*, Washington, November 19. https://www.washingtontimes.com/news/2016/nov/19/david-duke-former-klan-leader-applauds-trumps-cabi/. Retrieved November 20, 2018.

Brennan, David. 2018. One-Third of Americans Don't Believe 6 Million Jews Were Murdered During the Holocaust. *Newsweek*, New York, April 12.

Cochrane, Emily. 2018. Trump Talks Likes (Tariffs) and Dislikes (Media) in V.F.W. Speech. *New York Times*, New York, July 24. https://www.nytimes.com/2018/07/24/us/politics/trump-vfw-veterans.html. Retrieved August 7, 2018.

Funke, Daniel. 2018. A Guide to Anti-misinformation Actions Around the World. Poynter, July 24. https://www.poynter.org/news/guide-anti-misinformation-actions-around-world. Retrieved August 11, 2018.

Quotes, AZ. 2019. Quoting Goebbels, Joseph. *Quotes, AZ.* https://www.azquotes.com/quote/1419276. Retrieved May 23, 2019.

Hitler, Adolph. 1939. *Mein Kampf*, trans. James Murphy. London: Hurst and Blackett Ltd. https://archive.org/stream/MeinKampf_483/HitlerAdolf-MeinKampf-VolumeIIi1939525P._djvu.txt. Retrieved August 7, 2018.

Kessler, Glenn. 2016. The Biggest Pinocchios of 2016. *The Washington Post*, Washington, December 16.

Lipstadt, Deborah. 1994. *Denying the Holocaust*. New York: Plume (Penguin Press).

Maheshwari, Sapna. 2016. How Fake News Goes Viral: A Case Study. *New York Times*, New York, November 10. http://www.nytimes.com/2016/11/20/business/media/how-fake-news-spreads.html?_r=0. Retrieved January 8, 2017.

2 TRUE OR FALSE   31

Peterson, Clarence. 1989. Moonstruck. *Chicago Tribune*, Chicago, July 20.

Phillips, Amber. 2018. Sarah Sanders Presents the Official White House Policy: The Media Is the Enemy of the People. *The Washington Post*, Washington. https://www.washingtonpost.com/news/the-fix/wp/2018/08/02/sarah-sanders-presents-the-official-white-house-policy-the-media-is-the-enemy-of-the-people/?utm_term=.c919c03f0f9c. Retrieved August 7, 2018.

Smith, Graham, and Javier E. David. 2018. Trump Launches Another Attack. *CNBC*, August 5. https://www.cnbc.com/2018/08/05/trump-steps-up-his-media-feud-saying-press-are-dangerous-and-sick.html. Retrieved August 7, 2018.

Stafford, Tom. 2016. How Liars Create the Illusion of Truth. BBC Future, London. http://www.bbc.com/future/story/20161026-how-liars-create-the-illusion-of-truth.

Stephens, B. 2018. Trump Will Have Blood on His Hands. *New York Times*, New York, August 3. https://www.nytimes.com/2018/08/03/opinion/trump-fake-news-enemy.html. Retrieved August 7, 2018.

Stokols, E. 2016. Trump Unbounded. *Politico*, October 11. https://www.politico.com/story/2016/10/donald-trump-campaign-republicans-229577. Retrieved August 7, 2017; Retrieved August 7, 2018.

Tetlock, Philip, and Dan Gardner. 2015. *Superforecasting*. New York: Crown Publishers.

Trump, Donald J. 2017. A Tweet: The Fake News Media. Washington. https://twitter.com/realDonaldTrump/status/832708293516632065?ref_src=twsrc%5Etfw%7Ctwcamp%5Etweetembed%7Ctwterm%5E83270 8293516632065&ref_url=https%3A%2F%2Fabcnews.go.com%2F-Politics%2Ftrump-calls-fake-news-media-real-enemy-people%2Fstory%3Fid%3D56687436. Retrieved August 7, 2018.

Weisburd, Andrew, Clint Watts, and J.M. Berger. 2016. Trolling for Trump: How Russia Is Trying to Destroy Our Democracy. University of Texas, National Security Network. https://warontherocks.com/2016/11/trolling-for-trump-how-russia-is-trying-to-destroy-our-democracy/. Retrieved November 20, 2018.

Worsnip, Patrick. 1984. *U.S., Soviet Scientists Urge Pooled Effort Against Nuclear War*. Reuters North European Service, August 23, 1984. This news article reported on a suggestion attributed to Joseph Knox of Livermore Laboratories and Joseph Smith of the University of Chicago.

CHAPTER 3

Proliferation: Doomsday or Politics?

Issue: We know that the major nuclear countries have very large stockpiles of strategic and tactical nuclear weapons and that other nations, primarily North Korea and Iran, want to acquire such weapons too. We know as well that weapons tend to be used and that there is no shortage of possible flash points and confrontations among nuclear powers in the near future. President Trump has warned North Korea in terms rarely heard in international discourse that "fire and fury and frankly power" would be unleashed by the USA if North Korea does not stop threatening the USA with the possibility of a nuclear ballistic missile attack. People of good will everywhere would de-escalate if they could, but we have not found a way to take us back to a less threatening world. So we hand to our successors a problem we have not been able to solve, a counterfactual situation with many branch points carried into the future for later resolution. Will we blow ourselves up? Can we yet save ourselves?

Time: November 20, 1983

Place: At home, after dinner, a quiet time. It is Sunday at the height of the cold war and tensions are high between the USSR and the USA

We're settled in front of the TV to watch what we hope will be an exciting prime time special program on ABC called *The Day After*. We are looking forward to it because there has been much advanced on-air speculation that this program could be important. The Christian Science Monitor newspaper said, a few days before the program ran that it

© The Author(s) 2019

T. J. Gordon and M. Todorova, *Future Studies and Counterfactual Analysis,*
https://doi.org/10.1007/978-3-030-18437-7_3

was "liable to have as much effect upon the people who watch as the evening news coverage of the Vietnam war seemed to have on viewers in the 1960's and 1970's" (Unger 1983). The real world was tense. A few months earlier, in March 1983 President Reagan had labeled the Soviet Union "an evil empire," in September a Korean airliner had been shot down by a Soviet fighter when it strayed into Soviet airspace, and NATO was conducting war games that were later revealed to have brought the world very close to actual war (Foreign Intelligence Advisory Board 1990).[1]

The Day After was set in a midwestern Kansas town with characters that looked like they were taken from an ordinary sitcom. It showed in disturbing detail the exchange of intercontinental nuclear missiles, the rush to shelters that offered no protection from the holocaust, the burning of cities and people, and what life might be like for the survivors. Close to 100 million Americans saw it on its first run. The film left people stunned, depressed, and frightened. In the days following, ABC carried a live discussion led by the commentator Ted Koppel in which the scientist Carl Sagan, former Secretary of State Henry Kissinger, former Secretary of Defense Robert McNamara, General Brent Scowcroft, and conservative commentator William Buckley discussed the concept of nuclear deterrence and whether mutual assured destruction (MAD) was enough to keep distrustful nuclear-armed nations from destroying themselves and the world. Sagan said, "Imagine a room awash in gasoline, and there are two implacable enemies in that room. One of them has nine thousand matches, the other seven thousand matches. Each of them is concerned about who's ahead, who's stronger" (Allyn 2012).

Since that time, Russia and the USA have managed to wind down their stockpiles a great deal. At its peak, the Soviet Union had about 40,000 warheads and the USA about 30,000. Today both the USA and Russia are down to about 4500 warheads each. Other nuclear powers include France (300 warheads), China (260), UK (215), Pakistan (130), India (120), and Israel (80) (Baker 2016). In moments of sanity, key nations of the world signed the nuclear Non-Proliferation Treaty (NPT) in 1968 and in 1996, the Comprehensive Nuclear Test Ban Treaty (CTBT). North Korea withdrew from the NPT in 2003 and may have

---

[1] This report was declassified in October 2015. It describes the Able Archer 83 exercise that was, among other things, designed to test "new nuclear weapons release procedures." The Soviets strongly (and incorrectly) suspected that the West might be about to attack.

some 6–8 warheads and material for half a dozen more at present (2018) (Davenport 2018). They have conducted five underground atomic bomb tests, once in 2006, 2009, 2013, and twice in 2016 (Hun and Jane Perez 2016) and have not been shy about their intent to use nuclear weapons at least as a political bargaining chip.

The reductions in the size of the stockpiles are impressive, but even with these past reductions, the weapons have the potential for massive overkill. Furthermore, other nations would be delighted to join the party; these apparently include Syria which is preoccupied with its civil war and Iran which is currently deterred from developing its nuclear arsenal as a result its 2016 multilateral agreement with USA and other nations to cease its enrichment program.

In the run-up to the US presidential elections, Mr. Trump made several statements, orally and in tweets, that hinted at his future nuclear policy. With respect to North Korea, he said on a morning talk show: "I would get China to make that guy (Kim Jong Un) disappear in one form or another very quickly," Trump said on CBS This Morning. Was he suggesting assassination? He didn't clarify whether disappearing was equivalent to being assassinated but said, "Well, I've heard of worse things, frankly."

> "I mean, this guy's a bad dude, and don't underestimate him," Trump said, referring to North Korean leader Kim Jong Un, whom he didn't mention by name, but later called him Rocket Man. "Any young guy who can take over from his father with all those generals and everybody else that probably want the position, this is not somebody to be underestimated." (Mccaskill 2016)

After Kim Jong-un announced that North Korea was making preparations for launching an intercontinental ballistic missile, Mr. Trump tweeted:

> North Korea just stated that it is in the final stages of developing a nuclear weapon capable of reaching parts of the U.S. It won't happen! (Trump 2017)

Did he mean that he did not believe that North Korea was ready to explode a hydrogen bomb in an underground test or that he was prepared to intervene in process by which they would do so? The point is now moot: NK exploded a hydrogen bomb on September 3, 2017.

In an even more far-reaching tweet, he said:

> The United States must greatly strengthen and expand its nuclear capability until such time as the world comes to its senses regarding nukes. (Fisher 2016)

Did he mean the country should produce new nuclear warheads, move stockpiled weapons to active standby status, withdraw from START treaty, increase the yield of newly manufactured bombs? We are left a bit in the dark. There is a sentiment in the press and among many nuclear and arms control experts that talking about weapon policies requires more than a tweet. In a March 2016 interview on CBS, he said he would:

> "... like to see Japan and South Korea develop nuclear weaponry in order to combat North Korea. Unfortunately, we have a nuclear world now," Trump said. "Would I rather have North Korea have [nuclear weapons] with Japan sitting there having them also? You may very well be better off if that's the case. In other words, where Japan is defending itself against North Korea, which is a real problem." (Flores 2016)

Was he talking about promoting proliferation?

In the late 1950s, the USA and Soviet Union had become locked in a deathly embrace called "Mutually Assured Destruction (MAD)." Each country had its ballistic missiles in underground silos, mobile launchers, submarines, or aircraft aimed and ready to launch at the other's major cities. The argument was that as long as we have retaliatory capability that can survive a first strike, the enemy's destruction is assured and therefore they will never attack.

MAD assumes rationality on the part of political and military decision makers. Surely no same person would decide to launch an attack when they were fairly certain such an action would bring down their enemy's bombs on them. There are at least two things wrong with this reasoning. The enemy may not be rational, and there may be circumstances not under control of decision makers that cause a launch. We have examples in the behavior of Lone Wolf terrorists that seems irrational to an observer that may seem quite rational and ordinary to a terrorist. And we have seen seemingly irrational behavior decision-makers: witness the bizarre behavior of Kim Jong-un. In addition to the possibility of irrationality, there are other triggers that military strategists have considered: including bad intelligence (in 1995, Boris Yeltsin, then the Russian President, activated the nuclear briefcase in preparation for a launch when a Norwegian science rocket was mistaken for an attack rocket) (Hoffman 1998), misinterpreting the intent of the enemy (war games vs. real mobilization), and accident (like the mistaken drop of two nuclear bombs in 1961 from a B52 as a result of a structural failure) (Lacey-Bordeaux 2014).

Suppose that the answer to N Korea's new status as a potential hydrogen bomb deliverer is neither military nor economic deterrence, but acceptance of the country as a new nuclear power. It's a case of "sweet lemons," the opposite of "sour grapes"; we couldn't realistically do anything about it, so we accept a modern version of MAD in which three interacting powers have overwhelming deterrent capacity.

Unlike a three-legged table that stands stable no matter how uneven the floor, a three-party version of MAD is a world of uncertainty and pain. The argument will run: If we see an ICBM coming over the horizon, we will know if it comes from Russia or N Korea and we could launch a crippling attack on the appropriate country. But are the two in cahoots? Launch against both? And how do mobile launchers affect the game? Or submarine-launched missiles where the country behind the weapon is not obvious. Think of the permutations: the USA and Russia against NK, NK and Russia against the USA, and (do we dare?), the USA and NK against Russia.

The old two power MAD world was paranoiac. The future "n- body" MAD world is hyper paranoiac. And this maze does not even consider India, Pakistan, Iran, China, UK, France, Israel, or, we hasten to add, ISIS.

This kind of thinking led to the ultimate MAD-world idea: an impregnable nuclear warhead in orbit, under the control of one nation so that its response time would be less than ½ that of an earth-launched missile, and since it could be maneuvered to attack any point on earth, all geography under its orbital track would be a possible target.

In a holdover from the MAD strategy of the cold war, the big nuclear powers tend to keep at least some ICBM's at the ready so that they can be launched in minutes in response to an attack. Back in the 80's and 90's, designers of ICBM launch sites were careful to build redundancy into their launch systems and protocols; primarily, they wanted to be sure that if a launch command were ever sent that it would get through and launch the missile to deliver its deadly payload. Launching by mistake was a threat to be avoided at all costs. But mistakes could come from equipment failures resulting in an unintended launch command, false signal of an impending attack such as mistaking a meteorite for an incoming missile, and from human failures resulting from misunderstanding of an enemy's intent. To cope with the possibilities of equipment failures, the design principle was: Make sure failure rates were as close to zero as human design could be. To cope with the possibility of some human failure, rigid protocols were established, and to the extent possible, decisions were pre-made. There have been no unintended nuclear explosions so far; the safety provisions that guard against these types of failure have not failed. But they might.

So far, mistaken alerts—and there have been dozens—have been quelled before catastrophe. For example: In 1983, Soviet early warning satellites were operating correctly but were fooled by sunlight reflected from clouds and sent data that erroneously reported an incoming attack by US nuclear missiles. All the systems checked out in the short time available to make a decision. At that point, had the officer on duty, Stanislav Petrov, followed procedures he would have recommended launching Soviet missiles (see more detail later in this chapter). In this case, the strongest, and one of the few, safety links in the chain were the judgment of the officer in command of the early warning center. Had a different officer been on duty, the situation could have ended very differently.

Failures of equipment are another risk. Take loss of communications for example. In October, 2000, the US Air Force lost communications with 50 nuclear ICBM's that taken together had enough firepower to kill 20 million people. For almost an hour, the safeguards that protect against unauthorized launch of America's missiles were compromised. And that elevated the risk of the world being plunged into a nuclear war that none of the nuclear-armed states intended (Bair 2010).

This episode illustrates another kind of threat: a terrorist hacker takeover of a missile system, a situation reminiscent of the 1983 movie War Games. In this movie, a US supercomputer used in war gaming is activated innocently by a young computer whizz who thinks it's a game, but the computer thinks it's real.

Today with smaller numbers of nuclear weapons capable of being launched from silos, from aircraft, or from submarines, autonomous or controlled remotely from the USA, Russia, China, or other countries, the nuclear powers are still standing at the ready and are improving their delivery capability.

3 PROLIFERATION: DOOMSDAY OR POLITICS? 39

We present four scenarios leading to peace or war. The first postulates an equipment failure that results in an apparent attack. The second imagines a case of inadvertence in which human reasoning averts nuclear catastrophe. The third begins the exploration of nuclear weapons in the hands of terrorist. Finally, the fourth describes a route to a world without nuclear weapons, even if for the wrong reasons.

Scenario 1: A Mouse on the Road to Hell

The little mouse runs down the tunnel and sniffs at something that smelled vaguely like Swiss cheese. She turns and in the dim light found the yellow wire that was giving off the smell. She takes an experimental bite thinking about her family and how glad they would be to learn about this new source of food. Two slivers of electrical insulation disappear, exposing the wire electrical conductors. One bright spark jumps between them and then all hell breaks loose. Flame comes rushing down the tunnel.

This is a Soviet silo housing an R-12 multiple warhead ICBM aimed at the multiple cities and towns around Los Angeles. It is ready to launch, fueled, pressurized, and with gyros spinning, aimed but inert for a decade. Now it is underway with no means to call it back.

The Soviets are known for direct, no-frills, straight-forward engineering designs but because of their sensitive role, these installations are designed with safeguards and redundancies. The electrical flash between the mouse-stripped wires ordinarily would not have been enough to trigger the launch but the day before a drill had required that a micro-switch be closed to simulate lift-off and, as luck would have it, the switch remained in the closed position after the drill. The closed position told the missile's guidance system that it had lifted off and that its proper configuration was to keep the propellant valves open. Was the closed switch human error? Was it the failure of a two-dollar part? It hardly mattered since the missile was now up and out of the launch tube and heading for Los Angeles.

Soviet designers had calculated the probability of failure of every critical part in the system and the micro-switch was estimated to have a failure rate of one in 10,000,000 operations, far beyond the number of operations anticipated for the switch's lifetime.[2] Furthermore for a failed switch to energize

---

[2] The US Federal Aviation Administration, for comparison, requires a minimum of one billion hours between failures of critical parts in a passenger-carrying airliner.

the rocket, the design required one other circuit condition of the electrical system: it had to be turned on, alive. A double, simultaneous failure had a vanishingly small probability of occurrence: About one chance in 10 billion operations.

But there it was: the mouse shorted the wires when the switch was closed. Today we would have called this coincidence a Black Swan.

As improbable as it is, there is no calling the missile back, no fail-safe. No possible radio destruct command. No country is very angry with another as is often the case. No one is expecting war. No country is mobilized. No country believes they would somehow gain by war, yet destruction is on the way to Los Angeles.

MAD kicks into full operation and the inadvertent missile flies on. Its trajectory is unmistakable and defensive and offensive systems in the US are activated. Bombers are scrambled, submarines prepare their Minutemen for launch. Leaders are awakened, sirens wail. Red phones ring. This is not a drill; WW 3 is underway and it is because of that damned mouse.

Scenario 2: The Decision Maker

The following is a true story. It is different from most scenarios in this book; because it is more than plausible, it actually happened. This is not false news, it is true. Look it up. We know what you're thinking: The authors say it is true, but that is only part of the scenario, a trick to make us readers think it could really happen in the future. No, we assure you it happened. It is in this book about possibilities and conjectures because it has happened more than once and could happen again. Really, believe us.

On September 12, 1986, at the height of the cold war, a Soviet Molnya observation satellite alerted the missile defense system of the Soviet Union that a fleet of US intercontinental ballistic missiles seemed to be in flight and aimed at Moscow. The officer in charge of a Soviet missile launch bunker outside of Moscow, Lieutenant Colonel Stanislav Petrov, age 44, talked about that incident decades later. He is now known as "The man who stopped World War III and sacrificed his career" (Shima 2013).

Picture the chaotic scene. It is just after midnight. Until now it had been a quiet watch now the sirens were blaring. The TV screens were alive and warning that and attack was in progress. 15 minutes to respond, that's all. As Petrov is quoted as saying in an interview

3 PROLIFERATION: DOOMSDAY OR POLITICS? **41**

to the Voice of Russia, "For 15 seconds, we were in a state of shock. We needed to understand, what's next. It was not for nervous people. There was such shock, bewilderment and confusion that it could have easily grown into panic." He used his head and did not respond as his orders instructed. He continued, "When people start a war, they don't start it with only five missiles. You can do little damage with just five missiles, Second, the computer is, by definition, brainless. There are lots of things it can mistake for a missile launch" [ibid.].

It had happened before. During the 1962 Cuban Missile Crisis, the commander of a Soviet submarine, Vasili Arkhipov, refused to fire nuclear torpedoes against American ships blockading Cuba and war again depended on the frail decision of one brave man. He was awarded the Future of Life Prize (Davis 2017).

> Petrov's decision wasn't entirely based on a mental roll of the dice.
>
> It was subsequently determined that the false alarms had been caused by a rare alignment of sunlight on high-altitude clouds and the satellite's highly eccentric orbit.
>
> Petrov saved the planet that day but he exposed the flaws in a system that had been built at great cost. In the dystopia n Soviet system, to reward him would be a slap in the face of the elite Soviet forces. So he was punished. During his audit, Petrov was asked stupid questions such as to why he did not maintain a log. He was not sacked but was never made full colonel upon retirement, which impacted his pension significantly. However, after the end of the Soviet Union, Petrov's superiors publicized his heroism and he became a celebrity in the West. In February 2013 he got the Dresden Prize. (Shima 2013; Vasilyev 2013) He died on 18 September 2017, still an un-promoted lieutenant colonel but known as the man who saved the world. (Sewell 2017)

The following is fiction and did not happen, but might:

Dave Ackerman is an airman first class (E3) in the Air National Guard. He is affable, liked by almost everyone, and stays out of trouble. He is stationed at the Minuteman launch facility at Minot Air Force Base, North Dakota and intends to make the Air Force his career. Ackerman was part of the most recent Alert Mission inspection performed when a team from the Inspector General's office at NORAD arrived unannounced to test the unit's "readiness." Their unit passed with flying colors. Ackerman had been only a small part of a big machine but he is proud, nevertheless that their unit received the highest rating of "Mission Ready" for 24/7 Alert units in the United States Air Force and U.S. Air National Guard.

Most nights he is assigned to boring duty at a communications monitor console, watching for hot messages from Air Force bases around the world, serving as part of a relay network ready to acknowledge any traffic that requires receipt verification. But tonight, he is actually at a Minuteman launch console serving as a last minute replacement for the NORAD launch officer down with the flu. This is one the 400 Minuteman III ICBM's that are still in the arsenal of the US. He has one of the two launch keys required to launch "his" Minuteman. He is happy with this assignment; this "honor" means that his career is about to take off.

He reads the message on his screen three times: "BALLISTIC MISSILE THREAT INBOUND TO HAWAII THIS IS NOT A DRILL."

Holy shit.

Ackerman knows that Hawaii had just reactivated their siren warning system a few days earlier and that President Trump and Kim Jung Un have been trading insults for months. The situation brought warnings of nuclear war that had not been heard in decades. In response to joint military exercises involving the US and South Korea, North Korea said: "This is a grave provocation and will escalate the situation to the brink of nuclear war." And President Trump said, with intended sexual innuendo, that his nuclear button was bigger and more powerful than Un's and that the US "would use whatever means" it could to de-nuclearize the Korean peninsula, including as the President had said in a tweet, "to rain down fire and fury like the world has never seen." North Korea had lobbed ICBM's into the Pacific to demonstrate their existence and capability to hit the US mainland. A few nights ago Ackerman watched a TV news magazine 60 minutes segment that conceded that, North Korea had packaged a fission bomb small en0ugh to fit into one of its ICBM's and that a thermonuclear H Bomb payload was about ready as well. And the President's sanity had been questioned (Liptak 2018).

Ackerman's partner said, "Let's go buddy. Put the key in the slot. This is it." But there was not a red alert on any of the screens facing them, only shots of panic on the streets of Honolulu and repeats of the warning message. "This is not a drill," repeated again and again. He picks up the red phone to talk to headquarters. The line is down (is this part of the plot?); they are isolated.

3 PROLIFERATION: DOOMSDAY OR POLITICS? 43

Decision time. They had been trained to act, not decide. But this is peculiar- why no red alert from NORAD? Where is the U.S. Pacific Command? Why is there no word from Homeland Security? Yet the words "This is not a drill" keep repeating on the screen. If they act and are wrong, they start WW III. If they act and are right they would be remembered as patriots. If they fail to act and are wrong they could be shot as traitors. If they fail to act and are right, their heroism would be unrecognized. At most they have five more minutes.

In those five minutes, the President is briefed at his vacation hotel in Florida (turns out it has hardened rooms but not nuclear bomb proof rooms for the President's entourage). He says: "Go red; We'll show those f—bastards," and the missile shields at a dozen locations slide back, submarines are alerted and prepare to launch their payloads, dozens of stealth bombers take off, sirens wail, world leaders are awakened, and other war preparations, some visible, some not, are automatically triggered by the red alert.

Ackerman and his partner hesitate. Then the all clear appears on their screens: it was a false alarm.[3]

Nations today are beginning to provide weapons with autonomous decision making, self-determination algorithms about whether or not to launch even (or maybe particularly) when human life is involved, pre-determining the actions triggered in certain situations, to avoid the kinds of decisions faced by Ackerman in the scenario or by Petrov and Arkhipov in real life. Call these self-determining systems the "steel decision makers." Their algorithms offer no room for mind changing and are therefore dangerous in the extreme. We have been warned in real life and in fiction: For example, the movies Fail Safe and Dr. Strangelove and the books Command and Control all illustrate how systemic instructions can make machines designed to avert war, cause them instead. If the machines had been in control instead of Ackerman, Petrov and Arkhipov, and scores of others, we would probably not be here to discuss it.

---

[3]Although this story is fictional, it is based on a real occurrence. In January 2018, when tensions with North Korea were at a peak, an employee mistakenly sent out this message to all cell phones in the state: "BALLISTIC MISSILE THREAT INBOUND TO HAWAII. SEEK IMMEDIATE SHELTER. THIS IS NOT A DRILL." The situation was not corrected for 38 minutes. https://www.washingtonpost.com/news/the-switch/wp/2018/01/30/heres-what-went-wrong-with-that-hawaii-missile-alert-the-fcc-says/?utm_term=.53c37f599d07. Retrieved July 29, 2018.

Scenario 3: In the Fruit Garden of Pakistan

Wikitravel says, "If you are taking the overland route from Istanbul to New Delhi without going through Afghanistan you will have to pass through Quetta." It is known as the fruit garden of Pakistan because a combination of weather and soil has resulted in an abundance of fruits (peaches, pomegranates, apricots, and cherries) and nuts (pistachios and almonds) being grown there in what seems endless, fecund, sweet smelling groves. It is also a terrorist sanctuary.

We listen into an audio recording made by REDACTED that was an undiscovered eavesdropping witness to a planning session of the local ISIS chapter, in an unassuming house in the outskirts of the city.

Unidentified voice 1: It is clear that our heroic brothers have shaken up the Christian community. There will be more to come.[4] But tell me. Where do we stand on the nuclear matter?

Unidentified voice 2: We have made contact with our friends in North Korea during the Olympics, it was easy to remain anonymous in that crowd. They need foreign exchange as a result of the Western sanctions, and have accepted our offer of 500 million rupees, payable 50 million now, and the rest on delivery. God is great and brings together in our time what we will need to be successful and fulfill his instructions in the Koran. Our North Korea friends will deliver the materials, packaged for our use in about 3 months.

Voice 1: Yes, by then we will have the 450 million, promised to us by the syndicate and I believe them. They are deeply involved in the poppy traffic from Afghanistan and the money is a pittance to them. And if the crops fail, there is always kidnapping… If it were God, they'd steal from him, too (Tavernise 2009).

Laughter and indistinct comments.

Voice 2: But I wonder what's in it for the syndicate?

Unidentified voice 3: I believe they are operating under the assumption that times of chaos always bring fresh opportunities for them to make a euro or a buck, and they are hoping that we will cause enough chaos- but not only us, the US will come as they say, unglued, run helter- skelter, and add to the chaos and the syndicate's opportunities. They see it as a business proposition, likely to give an excellent return on investment. They do not yet understand that they themselves may be our next target for surely they have no sacred motivations.

---

[4] He is probably referring to the suicide bombing that took place in the city the week before Christmas, 2017. See: Salman Massod (2017).

3 PROLIFERATION: DOOMSDAY OR POLITICS? **45**

Voice 1: So what will we have? A 20 kiloton bomb in a backpack. Remarkable. We should target something, some infidel or group, who will be instantly recognizable and whose destruction will be interpreted properly by the rest of the world. Who? Where? When?
Murmuring becomes indistinct.
Voice 3: There has been some work in the West on pre-detection of our activities, our planning in progress. Tactics such as installing robots who act as security guards for high value infrastructure and conduct automated crowd surveillance to identify who is inappropriately nearby, using facial recognition, license plate readers, gait, and REDACTED for preliminary identification. We must warn our brother who will deliver our present to take appropriate steps. And of course they still believe, mistakenly, that they can infiltrate our core (Gordon et al. 2017).
Unidentified voice: What's this? This little spec looks like an insect, a REDACTED but it's mechanical and electronic. Step on it. Crush it.
The feed goes dead, but the questions "Who? Where? When?" still echo in the analysts' ears.

Scenario 4: The True Story Behind Trump-Putin Day

Let's imagine that Putin and Trump meet in Washington midway through the President's term, as Putin has suggested. They are clearly on friendly terms, but the atmosphere is charged and they are on guard. There are no witnesses to the meeting that took place at the Trump International Hotel although both believe hidden cameras are rolling and tiny microphones are listening. The redacted transcript from a recording of the 20-minute meeting reads as follows[5]:

> *DT: Hello Vlad, Please ask your bodyguards to clear out; we are safe enough here. How do you like my new place? Cost 200 million: And it's on Federal land, an old Post Office, almost rent-free: 60 thousand a week. Here, have a drink. We call this place Trump Tower. Very Popular. Trump Tower. Beautiful.*
> *I hope you had a good trip over. Next time I will send Air Force One.*

---

[5] This is a satirical scenario. It is not true. It is not false news because it is not news at all. To be useful, scenarios can be far fetched but must be at least plausible (and this one may come close to violating this criterion. This one raises the question could neophyte Trump engineer a universally applauded arms reduction?

We have a few things on the agenda, so what do you say we get started? First, there's the matter of Ukraine and Crimea and why you're building up troops on the border again. I thought all of that was settled.

VP: *Good to see you again Donald. Yes, I'd love to get into that with you and when we discuss it let's also talk about the little matter of NATO and all those anti missiles launching sites sprouting up around Europe.*

DT: *That reminds me. We really ought to talk about all the nukes you and I have sitting there in silos. Terrible waste don't you think? We have to maintain them, make sure the propellants aren't leaking and that the guards stay awake. One of our guys dropped a socket wrench down a Minuteman silo and the damned thing went right through the tank walls. Damn near blew it up. What a mess. A mess.*

DT: *We both keep them manned and ready to fire although we both know that that's like the old Russian proverb "Eto tak zhe maloveroyatno, tak kak prikhlopnul mukhu na sobstvennoy zadnitse (translation: unlikely as swatting a fly on your own ass-). You have the same problems, too, I think.*

VP: *Ha, Donald. You're learning Russian. What do they think of that in the Foggy Bottom? Yes we do, in fact, have the same issues. You must already know. What's on your mind, old friend?*

DT: *My guys have told me that twenty years ago we (and the UK) agreed to let Ukraine go its own way, if they agreed to become a non-nuke state, so I think all your saber rattling on the borders is in bad taste to say the least and it gets NATO and the rest of Europe all excited. And for its part Ukraine agreed to sign the non-proliferation treaty and get rid of your left over missiles and materials. They did both. And how do you pay them back? You take the Crimea. Tsk tsk.*

VP: *Well, you don't know the pressures I have, and I have an election coming up soon. The people in Crimea, they wanted to be part of Russia, anyway. So I helped them out. What's up your sleeve Donald?*

DT: *I think what we have to do is change the name of the game. What say we surprise everybody and drop the number of warheads we have. You and I know we're not going to use them and they are just a pain in the neck. And nobody is expecting that. Will make a hell of a news flash. Hell of a media headline. We will go down in history for the right reasons.*

VP: *Let's see. We both have about 4500 warheads. I'll go for 2000. That still leaves plenty of firepower and will keep my generals happy.*

DT: *I'll raise you 1000 more. Don't be a piker.*

VP: *I'll call. So we eliminate three thousand warheads each. What's your price?*

DT: *Well it would be a nice gesture if you took our Guantanamo prisoners and sent them to one of your Siberian gulags. We don't have many left and you're keeping your Chechen guests there anyway. And thinking out loud,*

3 PROLIFERATION: DOOMSDAY OR POLITICS? 47

maybe I could build a golf course there. Could be good for the Siberian economy. We could drop the sanctions a bit, quid pro quo- wise. But seriously, imagine the headlines. And let's not go through the UN or make treaties or anything like that- we' just do it ourselves, bi-laterally. Make the world safer and all that. That will sure rile up the liberals. Call it the Trump Accord.

(Tape has indistinct muttering at this point. VP seems to be saying "But, but...")

DT: Statues for both of us. Validation and immortality. Diplomacy is simple, just like business. Oh, and by the way please destroy the "golden shower" tape. You know which one I mean?

VP: I will of course (but you'll really never know if I kept a copy, so watch out my friend).

DT: Think we can get the Chinaman to join us?

And the Chinaman did and brought North Korea into the accord, and pressure and promises from Russia led to Iran's participation, too. A time of lasting peace came to the world- well, not exactly peace, but at least a time when the of threat nuclear war, of proliferation, and of MAD were no longer on list of 10 worst problems facing the world. The doomsday clock of the Bulletin of Atomic Scientists was turned back 10 minutes.

Here's how ex- Secretary of State Aaron Marshal described the evolution of our time of peace in an interview on the TV series Remember When.

The UN Non Proliferation (NPT) treaty of 1970 came after Herman Kahn wrote some startling white papers in the 60's at RAND warning against the dangers of proliferation of nuclear weapons. The NPT was designed to prevent the spread of nuclear weapons and by any measure it was largely successful. It helped keep the number of nuclear powers to a handful and proliferation was a rare event. India and Pakistan got the bomb, of course, and N Korea, and Iran were trying mightily to achieve that status. N Korea succeeded. But statesmanship and economic sanctions helped shape the outcome.

Not only did the NPT require nations to agree that they would not pursue the development of nuclear weapons, but it also required them to stand in the way of transferring nuclear technology to what we then called rogue states and guard against the acquisition of nuclear material by non-state actors. It didn't work.

Without nuclear weapons you were just another country; with nuclear weapons you could join the debates- whatever they were - around the world on any issue, nuclear or not. You were a member of the nations that shaped the world order. There were nations that had nukes and those that didn't, and the

NPT was seen by most nations as a means of keeping the number of have's to a minimum by those that already had. After a half dozen well publicized near accidents that would have killed millions of people and made major cities uninhabitable for centuries, and an ugly confrontation between North Korea and a hard-to-anticipate (some said deranged) US President, as every school-child knows, development of nuclear weapons was outlawed, stockpiling was made an international crime with severe punishment. And that, my friends is why we celebrate Trump-Putin day. Ultimately, as in the case of Reagan and Gorbachev, it had been a game of personalities. The Black Swan of Glasnost has been matched by the Black Swan of the Trump Putin Accord.

Scenario 5: Putting the Genie Back in the Bottle

The Chairman of the House Intelligence Committee was speaking to a closed classified session. This was a particularly crucial and intensely antic-ipated meeting because two would-be terrorists had been apprehended three weeks earlier with 2500 grams of highly radioactive cobalt 60, apparently an accumulation of material salvaged from a hospital waste disposal stream. They were preparing to turn it into a mass of ultra fine particles, a nano powder that could float on the wind. They planned to distribute the powder from rented planes flying at less than 1500 feet over the city.

Chairman: So, ladies and gentlemen we have heard from various experts this morning. As far as is known this is the first theft of this kind. It is par-ticularly worrying because as you have heard, the half-life of this material is over 5 years. If they were successful in this attack it would have made large portions of the city uninhabitable. This was no fly-by-night, spur of the moment operation. It was well planned and it was only through luck that we learned about it in time to stop it.

Let's stop teaching foreign students how to build nuclear stuff. Let's find all of the publications that document the processes and burn them. Let's make actions that promote proliferation a capital offense. Let's harden defenses we use in the disposal streams of nuclear wastes, let's seal up the stor-age sites too, like the Waste Isolation Pilot Plant (WIPP) where a massive amount of nuclear waste is stored and I understand that some of that mate-rial is really hot- half life of 10,000 years.

Any other ideas?

So what do we conclude from this dangerous history and threatening outlook? While some problems may diminish in scope over time, the prob-lems of proliferation can only grow and become more complex because as time passes the technology of nuclear bomb making "improves" and

3 PROLIFERATION: DOOMSDAY OR POLITICS? 49

diffuses, and with sufficient capital, motivated nations and non-state groups can build or acquire nuclear devices or construct weapons made from production wastes. What has been learned about building nuclear capability cannot be unlearned. The Genie cannot be put back in the bottle. We can restrict access to the technology, burn books and files that describe it, and invest in the destruction and protection of nuclear wastes: None of these paths eliminate the threat. We have been lucky so far, but how long can our luck hold out?

REFERENCES

Allyn, Bruce. 2012. *The Edge of Armageddon: Lessons from the Brink*. New York: RosettaBooks.

Bair, Bruce. 2010. Could Terrorists Launch America's Nuclear Missiles? *New York, Time Magazine*, November 11. http://content.time.com/time/nation/article/0,8599,2030685,00.html. Retrieved February 24, 2017.

Baker, John. 2016. *Arms Control in the Age of Trump: Lessons from the Nuclear Freeze Movement*. Ploughshares Fund, December 14, from http://www.ploughshares.org/issues-analysis/article/arms-control-age-trump-lessons-nuclear-freeze-movement. Retrieved January 10, 2017.

Chan, Sewell. 2017. Stanislav Petrov, Soviet Officer Who Helped Avert Nuclear War, Is Dead at 77. *The New York Times*. New York. https://www.nytimes.com/2017/09/18/world/europe/stanislav-petrov-nuclear-war-dead.html. Retrieved November 21, 2018.

Davenport, Kelsey. 2018. *Nuclear Weapons, Who Has What*. Washington, Arms Control Association. https://www.armscontrol.org/factsheets/Nuclearweapons-whohaswhat. Retrieved November 21, 2018.

Davis, N. 2017. "Soviet Submarine Officer Who Averted Nuclear War Honored with Prize. *The Guardian*. London. https://www.theguardian.com/science/2017/oct/27/vasili-arkhipov-soviet-submarine-captain-who-averted-nuclear-war-awarded-future-of-life-prize. Retrieved February 22, 2019.

Fisher, Nax. 2016. Trump's Nuclear Weapons Tweet, Translated and Explained. *New York Times*. New York. http://www.nytimes.com/interactive/2016/12/22/world/americas/trump-nuclear-tweet.html. Retrieved January 10, 2017.

Flores, Renna. 2016. *What Donald Trump's America First Vision of the World Looks Like*. CBS News, New York. http://www.cbsnews.com/news/donald-trump-america-first-vision-world-election-2016/. Retrieved January 11, 2017.

Foreign Intelligence Advisory Board. 1990. *The 1983 War Scare Declassified and for Real*. http://nsarchive.gwu.edu/nukevault/ebb533-The-Able-Archer-War-Scare-Declassified-PFIAB-Report-Released/. Retrieved January 10, 2017.

Gordon, Theodore, Yair Sharan, and Elizabeth Florescu. 2017. Potential Measures for the Pre-detection of Terrorism. *Technological Forecasting and Social Change* 123 (May): 1–60.

Hoffman, David. 1998. Cold-War Doctrines Refuse to Die. *Washington Post Foreign Service*. Washington. http://www.washingtonpost.com/wp-srv/inatl/longterm/coldwar/shatter031598a.htm. Retrieved January 12, 2017.

Hun, Choe Sang, and Jane Perez. 2016. North Korea Tests a Mightier Nuclear Bomb, Raising Tensions. *New York Times*, September 8. https://www.nytimes.com/2016/09/09/world/asia/north-korea-nuclear-test.html?_r=0. Retrieved January 10, 2017.

Lacey-Bordeaux, Emma. 2014. Two Nuclear Bombs Nearly Detonated in North Carolina. *CNN*, June 12. http://www.cnn.com/2014/06/12/us/north-carolina-nuclear-bomb-drop. Retrieved January 12, 2017.

Liptak, Kevin. 2018. Trump Defends His Sanity Amid Questions About His Mental State. *CNN*. New York. http://www.cnn.com/2018/01/06/politics/president-donald-trump-stable-genius-smart/index.html. Retrieved January 15, 2018.

Mccaskill, Nolan. 2016. *Trump: "China Should Make Kim Jong Un disappear."* Virginia, Politico. https://www.politico.com/story/2016/02/trump-kim-jong-un-219068. Retrieved November 21, 2018.

Salman, Massod. 2017. Pakistan Church Attacked by Two Suicide Bombers. *New York Times*. New York. https://www.nytimes.com/2017/12/17/world/asia/pakistan-quetta-church-attack.html. Retrieved February 7, 2018.

Shima, Rakesh. 2013. The Man Who Stopped World War III and Sacrificed His Career, Russia Beyond. https://www.rbth.com/blogs/2013/09/12/the_man_who_stopped_world_war_iii_and_sacrificed_his_career_29317. Retrieved January 31, 2019.

Tavernise, Sabrina. 2009. Organized Crime in Pakistan Feeds Taliban. *New York Times*. New York. http://www.nytimes.com/2009/08/29/world/asia/29karachi.html. Retrieved February 7, 2018.

Trump, Donald. 2017. Spotlights North Korean Nuclear Program, Chides China in Tweets. *Washington*. CBS. http://www.cbsnews.com/news/trump-spotlights-north-korean-nuclear-program-chides-china-in-tweets. Retrieved January 10, 2017.

Unger, Arthur. 1983. Controversy Surrounds ABC's Apocalyptic 'Day After' the Christian Science Monitor. November 16, New York. http://www.csmonitor.com/1983/1116/111608.html.

Vasilyev, Yuri. 2004. On the Brink. *The Moscow News*. Moscow. http://www.brightstarsound.com/world_hero/the_moscow_news.html. Retrieved November 21, 2018.

CHAPTER 4

The Bounds of Humanity

Issue: This is the Malthusian question in modern dress. Will population growth outpace the world's ability to support the people who inhabit it? Beginning in the mid-1970s, three forces came together unexpectedly that changed the world for all time. The event was so important that historians of a hundred or a thousand years from now may look back and say that among all of the developments of society before and since this was the most crucial to the social order: These forces were the rise of feminism, availability of contraceptives that were cheap and effective, and family planning. Now that we have some measure of control over population size, we ask, "Should we limit the number of people in the world and if so, how and to what extent?"

The three forces of feminism, contraception, and family planning didn't appear through deliberate forethought; they came on the scene through coincidence. In a momentous instant, the combination of these three independent developments began to slow the rate of growth of world population. World population is still growing of course, but for the last 50 or so years its rate of increase has been diminishing. Good news.

The first of these forces was social: the growth of feminism, first in the West, and then spreading around the world. Anywhere there was a TV set, and a society at least partially open to new ideas, feminism empowered women and made it acceptable for women to begin to exert some control over decisions that affected them, including the size of their families. It happened faster in some countries than others, it was impeded

© The Author(s) 2019

T. J. Gordon and M. Todorova, *Future Studies and Counterfactual Analysis,*
https://doi.org/10.1007/978-3-030-18437-7_4

51

by tradition, poverty, and illiteracy in many places, but its progress was relentless and ultimately global. Women began working, married later, had children at an older age, and wanted smaller families.

The second force was technological: the availability of cheap, simple, and effective contraceptives. In the late eighteenth century, condoms were made of animal bladders and segments of animal intestine; they didn't work very well. Then in the mid-nineteenth century, with the invention of vulcanized rubber, condoms became more effective. By the early 1970s, the inventory of contraceptives included spermicides, sponges, IUD's, the pill, diaphragms, *coitus interrupts*, the rhythm method, and an odd assortment of herbal concoctions and barks in rural societies. But it was the condom and to some extent the pill, available worldwide, distributed through pharmacies and health clinics in third world countries that made the difference. The Agency for International Development (AID), an arm of the US Department of State, subsidized the export of these contraceptives to poor countries and made them available free or at low cost. They were distributed in the cities and villages, by women who talked privately to other women, by clinics and the healthcare network, or by new modes of distribution. In Nepal, for example, remote villages received subsidized condoms and birth control pills as well as medical supplies through a distribution network created specially for this job: detailed men that packed the supplies on their backs and walked the narrow trails to the villages.

The third force was political: the establishment of family planning programs, with government approval and encouragement. By the early 1980's, the governments of most countries of the world saw that it would be to their benefit and the benefit of their citizens to limit population growth. World population growth rate hit a high of over 2% per year in 1970 and dropped to 1.1% per year in 2018 (UN 2017).

Picture yourself as the enlightened political leader of a rapidly growing poor country. Say the rate of growth in your country is equal to that of Niger or Equatorial Guinea, two African countries that had growth rates of about 3% per year.[1] At that rate, population doubles every 25 years

---

[1] A doubling rate of twenty-five years, incidentally, is still the norm for some poor countries including almost all countries in sub-Saharan Africa. But poverty and lack of access to contraceptives are not the only reasons for high national population growth rates. Other reasons include religious beliefs, migration, and culture. Consider these rates of growth in 2016: Bahrain: 3.8%; Qatar: 3.5%; Ireland: 2.0%; Pakistan: 2.0%; Israel: 2.0%.

4 THE BOUNDS OF HUMANITY   53

or so. So as leader of this country, you'd have to find a way to double everything in your country in the next 25 years—you would need twice the number of jobs, roads, schools, food, and water. In your own self-interest, if for no other reason, you'd prepare for the onslaught of people, but you'd probably also look for a way to diminish the population growth if you could. Family planning programs—sponsored by governments and private organizations—existed in a few places in the 1960's, in many places in the 1970's and now in most countries in the world.

Most of these programs have been successful for a simple reason: Women in most poor countries wanted to stop having children and now have the means to do so. Contraception was clouded in folklore, macho tradition, and misinformation. But since 1970, contraceptive use in the world has almost doubled (from 36% in 1970 to 64% in 2015) (UN 2015).

All three of these forces—feminism, contraceptives, and family planning—were in place in the late 1970s and the acceleration in the growth of population slowed. But the number of people responds slowly. Population is still growing despite the diminished acceleration, and the growth is massive. There are about 7.6 billion people in the world as this is written. Population growth rate seems to be stabilizing at 1.1% per year. For the next decade at least, about 90 million people per year will be added to the world's population; this amounts to about 2.5 million added people *per day*. If current trends continue, what level will population reach before it stabilizes? Almost no one estimates less than ten billion. Many guess fifteen and a few guess over twenty billion. It's hard to visualize what twenty billion people mean—that's almost three people for every one currently alive. Just how many people can the earth support? Will food be adequate?

Extrapolation is a poor method of forecasting because the future will not be like the past and many new inventions, technical and social, will create a different future than we imagine. Some of these changes will affect birthrates, death rates, and fertility rates, so to imagine that the past history of fertility, mortality, and population growth rate tells us anything more than the immediate future is misleading. What could happen that will affect population growth? New attitudes toward children and families, the cultural acceptability of suicides, the advent of robots, new leisure enjoyments, increased health and unprecedented life span, disease cures, wars yet unimagined, new dimensions of terrorism, new sorts of epidemics, and abundance for some but starvations for others.

Will population size stabilize? At what level?

Along one branch lies coercion. For four decades, China followed a one-child policy to limit population growth. Control was heavy-handed, using methods that included forced abortion s, mandatory sterilization, and forced insertions of IUD's (Bohon 2013). With such measures, China's annual growth rate dropped from 2.8% in 1971 to 0.50% in 2016. This was roughly half the rate of growth of the world as a whole (1.12% in 2016). Do coercive policies work? Yes but at the expense of freedom and human rights and dignity.

The second branch involves a gentler approach: more intense family planning that provides information, education, encouragement, and effective contraceptives wherever appropriate throughout the world. This is the social marketing branch, delivering information to influence behavior and change what is considered modern. We see social marketing all around us, from anti-smoking ads to the naming of condoms; it's "Tigers" in Mexico to match the local macho image.

In the 1970s, many economists, social scientists, and politicians argued that economic development is the best contraceptive, because with it comes education, improved health care, improved female literacy, increasing presence of women in the labor force, and, diminished birth rates. Therefore, we should stress programs that are designed to improve economies. This was a position that appealed to both the Catholic Church and the Communist Bloc.

Yet there are examples of increasing wealth without diminished population growth, diminished population growth without increased wealth, failed economic development programs and the successes of contraceptive distribution leads most demographers today to reject the economics-first idea. They would say instead, that the best contraceptive is a condom. They would add that in any event, poverty is probably not an aphrodisiac.

In any event family planning that includes abortion as an option, even as a response to rape and incest, is still an issue that has deeply divided policy-makers and the public at large.

The third branch is technological. New techniques of contraception will be available soon. Vaccines are being developed for both genders that will be effective for extended periods of time, perhaps as long as a year. Anti-fertility vaccines cause the immune system to create antibodies that bind to proteins involved in the fertilization of an ovum or its early development process. These vaccines could immobilize sperm or form protective shields around an egg to prevent the sperm from reaching its surface. Female vaccines have already been tested on humans in India. These techniques would yield, in effect, pregnancy immunization.

And the condom is in for improvement. New, specially designed polymers (e.g., polyurethane) that interfere less with sensation and are less likely to leak replace the ubiquitous latex sheath.

It is also plausible to discuss technologies that provide for the selection of the gender of unborn children (Gordon and Glenn 1993). Since boy babies are valued more highly in some societies, gender selection would tend to lower population growth since many families could stop "trying for a boy."

We have these choices. We could let nature take its course, employ coercive measures designed to force growth lower, expand family planning strategies, or foster research into technology that reduces the frequency of conception inexpensively and effectively. Wish for wisdom.

Scenario 1: The China Syndrome

World population stands over 15 billion. Eighty percent of these people live in countries that are called disadvantaged. Most births are natural, but many involve artificial means: frozen sperm or ova, implantation into surrogate mothers, prenatal diagnosis of inherited diseases through analysis of fetus' genomes. A vaccine has been developed for many epidemic diseases, and while the threat from "terrorist" manufactured diseases still exists, detection technologies have reduced the threat. In both rich and poor countries infant mortality is low and life expectancy at birth is about 85 years. Lowering infant mortality and extending life expectancy has given the population curve an upward bump in recent decades. Some people, of course, still live much longer healthy lives than others. Suicide is a growing norm. The population levels of some countries are falling and others are expanding, but overall the world's population growth rate averages 1.1% per year. At that rate some 90 million people are currently added each year, but assuming growth rate remains constant, 150 million will be added yearly in another 50 years. Forecasts show that the number of people in the world will double in just over 60 years, in other words, in our lifetimes. The poor still want to become rich and the rich, richer.

The 15th Cairo Conference on Population has just convened. The question before the house is considered by many people to be the single most important issue of their time: should we—the nations of the world—attempt

56   T. J. GORDON AND M. TODOROVA

to exert direct control over population growth, influence it by indirect means, or let well enough alone?

The speaker from the right side of the isle had the floor. He is on a billion TV screens around the world. He represents the Chinese delegation.

He says: "Ladies and gentlemen, we've heard all of the arguments. We know that high population levels are a drag on world economic development. We know that too many babies condemn us to a mean struggle for more food, water, energy, waste, poverty. We know that more babies condemn us to overcrowding and overcrowding to disease and filth. We all seek sustainability a population consuming at a level that equals the earth's ability to renew and to produce—to keep things in balance. We've seen now for 100 years that population left alone will grow, albeit more slowly than in the past, but grow inevitably and inexorably. So we have no disagreement about the conditions that bring us here, we have only to discuss the means to limit population."

"My plan," he continues, "is simplicity itself. I propose that other countries of the world use the techniques that my nation, China, pioneered over the last 100 years. Social pressure and taxation are the disincentives. These approaches worked. I have a century of data to prove it. If big families cost more- and I mean cost in the broadest sense, the market will produce population stability. We stand ready to instruct in our practices and will send teams of experts to any nation in the world that expresses a deep desire for our help."

There were murmurs of assent and scattered applause.

Scenario 2: Super Saltpeter

The delegate from the United States mow addresses the Conference. He looks and speaks like a Texan, but his words were sharp. "My people," he says, "would never approve that kind of political manipulation. Let me tell you here and now that there are less coercive ways to achieve stability than the Chinese have used. I'm thinking of long-term contraceptives. Costs pennies, lasts for decades. I'm told there is a drug we could add to water supplies or to rain clouds. It drops birth rate in half, and itself has a half-life of ten years. Super saltpeter. If population growth brings suffering, overcrowding, filth, noise, waste, just sprinkle it on. Furthermore, other benefits with it."

In Omaha, a man watching the screen says: "Give me the bottled water concession."

4 THE BOUNDS OF HUMANITY 57

"I can give this conference reasonable assurance," the Texan continues, "that, with your agreement, my government will be willing to provide the B5 bombers required to do this global seeding. There's even a segment of our techno-complex that thinks this can be done with precision from orbit. But I must tell you that there is a counter voice in my country that asks whether it is wise for the United States to become the world's contraceptive agent, so if we are to move in this direction I need unequivocal support."

There were murmurs of assent and scattered applause.

Scenario 3: Birth Certificates

The delegate from the European Union takes the floor. "I'd guess," she says, "we would grow more slowly under either of the plans presented by my distinguished colleagues from China and the United States. But in the end, population stability is achieved only if a birth is permitted whenever someone dies. To achieve stability—and with it sustainability—we need a new form of birth certificate. This certificate would confer the right to a new life, the right to conceive. It would be issued whenever a death occurs. One death, one birth. The scales stay in balance. Absolutely guarantees a stable population."

"The certificates could be traded; there would be a certificate market, maybe even a certificate futures market. If for some reason we saw a decline in population one year, we could issue more the next."

In Mexico City, a business-man watching the screen says, "But what would she do if some good people ignored her piece of paper and proceed in the old fashioned way?"

As if she had heard the voice in Mexico City, she continues: "Almost all children of the world are immunized against infectious diseases today. I propose that young girls receive another kind of immunization just before menarche. A ten-year implanted contraceptive, to immunize against semen. When a new birth certificate is issued- probably by lottery, the contraceptive would be reversed."

There were murmurs of assent and scattered applause.

Scenario 4: Design Discord

Many people in the audience in Cairo and the viewers and participants around the world who were on line had come specifically to hear this paper, delivered by a brilliant bio-scientist from Germany. She began:

"As most of you know by now, we have, in many respects, within the last decade attained the ability to design our progeny." She is choosing her words carefully, aware that this paper could influence the directions of population and bio-ethics policy. "We have already used CRISPR and other gene editing tools to remove certain genetic anomalies that manifest as diseases, and replace them with sequences that are normal.[2] We have already sequenced the genome of 75% of the world's population and entered this information into databases that permit positive identification of individuals (there's no way to counterfeit genome sequences). We are beginning to understand why certain mammalian cells resist disease and others seem to allow or even invite microorganisms to attack. We have decoded several hundred thousand viruses as well and in the process found what we have called positive viruses that help the immune system instead of fighting it. This progress is mirrored in our improved understanding of how bacteria and fungi relate to human health."

She continues: So what is next is a God-like dilemma: we are ready to design a human? If we gain that capacity, and we are close to it, what would the person look like? Would we go for super intelligence, beauty, longevity? Favor one gender over the other? Evolution of the human species (and many other species) has been the result of essentially random processes since the first cell divided. We can now make that process orderly.

Now we can direct our own evolution. So what do we want to be when we grow up? Who is smart enough to answer that question. We don't need to turn this decision over to artificially intelligent machines—we can turn it over to naturally enhanced humans.

Dare I say it: we will soon have the capability to eliminate racial differences and to create a super race.

---

[2] In the real world, "germline editing" has already begun in China, where in lab experiments, a defective gene was edited out in an embryo; see: https://www.wired.com/story/crispr-base-editing-first-china?mbid=nl_082218_daily_list3_p1&CNDID=46249697. Retrieved August 23, 2018.

Public attitudes seem to be changing too: A Pew Research Center study found that in the USA 72% considered gene splicing appropriate to correct congenital defects in babies, but 80% were against using the technology to "make the baby more intelligent." See: http://www.pewinternet.org/2018/07/26/public-views-of-gene-editing-for-babies-depend-on-how-it-would-be-used/pi_2018-07-26_gene-editing_0-01/; http://www.pewinternet.org/2018/07/26/public-views-of-gene-editing-for-babies-depend-on-how-it-would-be-used/pi_2018-07-26_gene-editing_0-01. Retrieved August 23, 2018.

The audience collectively gasped, all inhaling at once. How long had it been since we heard "super race?"

In response, the Pope rises to address the convention. "The course of the human population in this world must remain in God's hands. It is a matter of human dignity. When the individual intervenes in conception: that is a sin. But when the state intervenes, then the sin falls on the state."

"So we have an answer," says a woman watching a screen in Tel Aviv. "When the state tries to direct evolution, it is the state that is damned."

There were murmurs of assent and scattered applause.

The representatives of the Euthanasia Society, the Eugenics Brotherhood, and the Genome Selection Committee are silent.

And at the close, the distinguished moderator from India in her flowing robes, says, "When children are born without a chance for peace or health, into squalor and filth, condemned from the start to an existence of slavery just to survive, do their lives make sense? What do we advise the world? This is a branch point of unparalleled significance. Control or not? And if there is to be control should it be left to the individual or the state or wise men and women? And as to the controls themselves—are they to be gentle or are they to be brusque?"

She said, "Will we ever know enough to decide wisely?"

This is an issue that has loomed for centuries. Every time a population disaster is predicted, it slips way and the problem seems to diminish. But at every cycle its scale expands. Should we act soon or not at all?

REFERENCES

Bohon, Dave. 2013. *New Campaign in China Forcing IUDs, Sterilization of Women, Report Charges.* New American, June. https://www.thenewamerican. com/world-news/asia/item/15796-new-campaign-in-china-forcing-iuds-sterilization-on-women-report-charges. Retrieved October 31, 2017.

Gordon, Theodore, and Jerome Glenn. 1993. *Issues in Creating the Millennium Project.* Washington: The United Nations University.

United Nations. 2015. *Trends in Contraceptive Use Worldwide.* New York. http://www.un.org/en/development/desa/population/publications/pdf/ family/trendsContraceptiveUse2015Report.pdf. Retrieved October 30, 2017.

United Nations, Department of Economic and Social Affairs, Population Division. 2017. *World Population Prospects: The 2017 Revision,* custom data acquired.

CHAPTER 5

The Beginning and Hereafter

Issue: Some of the great, unanswered questions of our time are: "How did it all begin? Is there an afterlife? Why do we exist?" Was the notion of God a creation of man, a product of our idea that everything must have a beginning and an end? Did God come from divine invention, a quirk of wiring of the brain, or is God an invention of ancient man? And why do most of the people in the world believe he (or she) exists in reality or in spirit? In the spirit of counterfactual analysis, answering these unanswered questions open paths to new beliefs, understanding, and meaning.

We are not going to argue here whether one religion is superior to another, whether heaven or hell exists, whether divination with goat entrails can be used to foresee the future, why the God of some sects commands its followers to kill non-believers, whether evolution is a tool of God. Also we do not plan to try to resolve the conflicts between science and religion, whether God is a manifestation of biological chemistry or exists beyond our brains; rather, we restrict ourselves to questions about religion that may become a more urgent part of the decision agenda in the future.

We are interested in this topic because religion and competing images of God have led to conflicts and atrocities we would rather forget, that plague us yet, and will again unless we ask about how these issues can be accommodated in the future.

Survey research has found that given current demographic trends, the percentage of Muslims in the world, will reach about 30% by 2050 (vs. 23% in 2010) while the percentage of Christians is expected to

© The Author(s) 2019

T. J. Gordon and M. Todorova, *Future Studies and Counterfactual Analysis,*

https://doi.org/10.1007/978-3-030-18437-7_5

remain constant at about 30%. The Muslim increase is the largest of any religion. The percentage of unaffiliated—atheists, agnostics, and other people who are not part of any religion is forecasted to increase in countries such as the USA and France but will account for a declining share of the world population, dropping from about 16% in 2010 to 13% in 2050 (Pew Research Center 2015).

> Seventy two percent (72%) of Americans say they believe in heaven — defined as a place "where people who have led good lives are eternally rewarded." ...

> But at the same time, 58% of U.S. adults also believe in hell — a place "where people who have led bad lives and die without being sorry are eternally punished." (Pew Research Center 2008)

In a poll of 1000 people, over 50% of say they believe in ghosts and 28% say they "personally, (have) seen or believed yourself to be in the presence of a ghost?" (YouGov 2012).

Put the question of the existence of ghosts (or God, for that matter) to a crowdsource vote and the ghost world (or God) might win. But fact is fact, and true facts are not determined by majority vote. Michael Shermer, who specializes in debunking superstitions and is editor in chief of the Skeptic magazine, points out that the propensity to believe in supernatural phenomena may be a product of natural selection. Consider this example: Suppose you are in an ancient hunter-gatherer society out hunting for tonight's dinner. You know there are man-eating saber-tooth tigers around. You hear a rustle in the grass that may or may not be a tiger. You have to act NOW. If you believe it is a tiger, you run. If you are wrong and it was only a gust of wind (false positive), there are few consequences for being wrong, except maybe a missed meal and a bit of kidding at the cave. But if you believe that the rustle is only the wind and do not run, and there is really a tiger out there (false negative), you might BE the dinner and your DNA may not join the evolutionary march to the future. So natural selection gives a few extra points to individuals who follow better safe than sorry strategies: this field is known as evolutionary psychology.[1]

---

[1] This paragraph is partially based on: Michael Shermer, "Why People Believe Invisible Agents Control the World." *Scientific American*, June 1, 2009. https://www.scientificamerican.com/article/skeptic-agenticity/. Retrieved December 14, 2017.

5 THE BEGINNING AND HEREAFTER **63**

If you believe in heaven and God and are wrong, you're no worse off than if you had not believed; if you do not believe and are wrong you might regret your error for a long time. Better safe than sorry strategies say "believe." So evolution primes us to believe.

It also primes us to look for reasons why the grass rustles. This may have led to our propensity to find causes, to construct explanations for everything we do not understand. This drive to find causes could be the origin of belief in gods, soul, ghosts, witches, curses, conspiracies in general, heaven, hell, reincarnation, and the supernatural.

Scenario 1: Faust

"Tell me," Faust said to the fog, "I want to know."

"Know what?" said the fog.

"Everything. Creation. About death and the afterlife if there is one. Why we exist. Whether we are really special, and why something as fine and complex as a person like me, dies."

"That's a tall order," said the fog. "You're asking for a trillion years of information, of trial and error. For cause and effect, when there may be no cause, only effects. You're asking about the reality of being, the explanation of consciousness. I know the answers but you must pay my price to learn."

"How much?"

The fog replied: "Don't ask. You can't afford it."

We take pride in knowing about things, yet we know little about creation and existence. Most people in the world believe in a creator that is either benevolent and loving of his living creations or vindictive and jealous of other gods. But even if there were a benevolent creator, the "why" still lingers. Are we some sort of experiment to see how biological evolution turns out? What about the afterlife? Is there a heaven or hell?

These are questions that are unanswerable and therefore lie in the province of imagination and poetry as well as religion and science.

We want to know, not only because the teachings of religion sometime conflict with facts of science. We want to know because the science of creation—of the big bang and of the pre-big bang—is limited. We want to know because most of us live in cultures that believe everything has a beginning and an end. We want to know because we see in the beliefs of what we consider to be primitive societies, the pre-echoes of our own beliefs, because religion has been responsible for crimes yet unpunished (remember the inquisition and the shielding of sex offenders).

We want to know because religion sets rules and speaks with moral authority, is often unforgiving, and creates enduring stereotypes that mold young minds, for better or worse. We seem to have a built-in religiosity, but are often in conflict with the institutions of religion. We want to know, because religions dictate what is good and right and proper for most people in the world and are themselves evolving. Adhere to the narrow path and your reward is heaven and bliss, stray from the path and your eternity is hell. We want to know if faith is a legitimate path to knowledge. What religion becomes and its power over people is the granddaddy of all counterfactual dilemmas.

As for the mystery of death, Mark Twain was once asked if he feared death. He is supposed to have said that he did not, "...in view of the fact that he had been dead for billions and billions of years before he was born, and had not suffered the slightest inconvenience from it."[2]

My father's family came to the USA to avoid the anti-semitic pogroms in Russia at the turn of the last century. In New York, when he was a young boy, my father asked his father, a devout orthodox Jew, "Who made God." His father, my grandfather, became enraged, that his son should ask such a question. He was a gentleman but he took up a wooden stick and chased my father around their tenement intent on punishing him for this blasphemy. This episode lasted in my father's memory; he told me this story 70 years later.

And he and millions of others ask in 150 languages today's heresy: If God is benevolent and omnipotent why was there a Holocaust, an Inquisition, school shootings of young children, thousands of children attacked by priests who knew but were protected by silence of their church; why is there pain and suffering? As we search for answers, here are some other scenarios.

Scenario 2: A Creation Myth: Empiricism

Scene: Mount Olympus (or wherever the gods of creation reside).

One God says to another: "See this little molecule? I call it DNA. I calculate that there are 450 billion ways that DNA can be manifest in humans and that given free will these humans on the average will make 50 million life determining decisions, give or take a few million, in a life time, so the

---

[2] Quote attributed to Mark Twain in *Atheist Empire*. "Great Mind Quotes." http://atheistempire.com/greatminds/quotes.php?author=8. Retrieved February 12, 2018.

5 THE BEGINNING AND HEREAFTER **65**

outcome of the DNA/decision matrix gives us a really huge number possible futures for every person. Give everything that lives a will to survive, some randomness about what they will face—climate, weather, chance meetings, and discoveries and the like, and in the outcomes of their decisions, and this will be a truly rich mix. I think I'm going to turn it loose and see how they fare."

The second God: "Well, you know among all the billions of outcomes there will be many similarities, but there will also be many different views of creation and death, heaven and hell, good and evil, greed and gluttony, love, hate, and objective truth and falsehood. Given the progress we expect to allow in technology, they might try to direct their own evolution. In any event the built in defense mechanisms, fight or flight, they will kill one another, they will cluster around common short sighted beliefs, claim superiority; brutality—not civility—will be the name of the game and....."

First God (interrupting): "Don't get so excited. I can call it off anytime, like I did for the dinosaurs. This is a grand experiment to see how things turn out. Does good triumph over evil? Is it worth doing this again?"[3]

Baked into our brain's wiring is the will to survive, a result of eons of evolutionary honing. We ran from saber-tooth tigers, fought wars, created laws, locked up or killed those who threaten us, invented medicines, formed clans, and civilizations: All in the name of the instinct to survive or to know about causes. Science also pursues causes, but when that well is dry and science has no answers, the pre-wired brain provides them. Sometimes there is a battle between knowledge derived from observations and knowledge that is innate. Sometimes the answers are supernatural.

Supernatural: Ghosts, witches, hauntings, gods, and devils and the like are products of the mind; pre-wiring contributes to the propensity to look for causes of all that can't be easily explained. There are other factors too: hallucinations (e.g., seeing people, objects, insects that aren't there, hearing voices, smelling things that aren't real) and delusions (believing things as fact that aren't true). Such psychoses can come from diseases like Parkinson's or schizophrenia. They may also accompany brain damage from trauma, alcoholism, or drug use.

Mass hysteria might also trigger irrational behavior or beliefs. In Salem Mass, in 1692, more than 100 people were accused of being

---

[3] The brilliant entrepreneur, Elon Musk, and others have theorized that we are pawns in some advanced computer simulation; see: https://www.theguardian.com/technology/2016/oct/11/simulated-world-elon-musk-the-matrix.

witches and 20 executed, burned, apparently victims of an irrational hysteria or the fungus ergot (Smithsonian 2007). Other examples include the panicked public reaction to the War of the Worlds broadcast of 1938, the Hindu milk miracle of 1990 in which sacred statues were offered and believed to drank milk (BBC News 2016), and the penis panics of 1967 mostly in Africa, Asia, and China in which the belief spread that men's penises were being shrunk by an evil force, a delusion known as Koro.

Somewhere deep inside us is a voice whispering "We are special and something as fine and complex as me should not be wasted in death." So we love, create memoirs, most of us, most of the time, seek to live and avoid death. Only when the pain of living overcomes the will to survive does the will falter.

Scenario 3: It Is All About Connections

Professor Albert Jacobson, MD, Ph.D., holder of the Adler Chair of Bio-electric Mapping was recording a holographic video augmented reality (HVAR) lecture for his graduate students. There were, at last count, 800 of them on line at this instant interacting with each other via Twitter XIV, on sub-sites monitored by bored graduate students earning their tuition and daily bread. The HVAR presentation on 800 screens around the world placed the viewers inside a functioning brain, not a live human brain, of course, but a functioning model, chemically and electrically correct. It was the result of years of research on the anatomy and physiology of the brain, funded mainly by the US National Institutes of Health in an overall program known as RAIN (Research in Advancing Innovative Neuro-technology). It cost a few tens of billion dollars but revolutionized our understanding of the human brain. Whenever Congress asked if it was worth it, the justification has been the search for effective means for ending addiction to powerful synthetic psychotropes constructed in thousands of hobbyist labs.

The model could show the brain hearing, seeing, remembering, although previous memories had been deleted from the model. It could show pleasure and pain, although you had to look closely to distinguish between them. To give a sense of scale, there are 100 million synapse connections in the model, "more than the number of stars in the Milky Way" according to one RAIN scientist.

Neurotransmitter chemicals occupy the spaces between the synapses of the model just as in living brains: glutamate, aspartate, D-serine, γ-aminobutyric acid (GABA), glycine, and the like, differing only in their color coding that identified them for the lecture and allowed the students to see which was being triggered. The synapses themselves glowed red, yellow, or blue depending on their level of electrical excitation. When Professor Jacobson said "Watch the prefrontal cortex when I simulate arousal followed by orgasm." Students called this HVARP—the added P for porn; they were amazed by the flashes of conducting synapses, multi colored neuro-transmitter fluids flowing with dazzling displays of color, the electrical signals controlling the synapses were connected to amplifiers so the visual displays were accompanied by a continuous buzz with punctuating pops and chimes, like 1000 xylophones playing at once. The effect was like fireworks inside the cerebellum, continuous and for most of the students erotic and arousing. Professor Jacobson said after a period of silence that followed the climax, "And that, dear students is what it's like from the inside looking out. There's still a lot we still don't understand about brains and orgasms but we know a hell of a lot more than we used to."

LED's flashed showing that on-line students who had just seen the display were generating a lot of comments and questions. He continued, "Everybody calm down. We will see your questions and comments after class and answer before next Thursday. Thanks for the feedback. Now I am going to reset the brain to its resting state." He pushed a button and all was quiet, well not really quiet but clearly less noisy, like a bicycle coasting downhill.

"The purpose of seeing the brain at rest in its original state is to show you that there's no such thing as a blank state. The brain comes with a menu of pre-designed, built-in, connections. Babies after all know how to suckle and have a response to pain and heat. They know how to cry to attract attention of their mother. They know how to laugh. They may even have a sense of rhythm—music appreciation 101. Early brain development is pre-programmed, as well. The instinct to move at first and then to stand and walk: all preprogrammed and timed almost perfectly across variations our species. All such behavior comes from the DNA-directed, inherited layout of the synapse connections and neurotransmitter flow paths. This should not be a surprise; after all the anatomy and physiology are predetermined products of inheritance: elbows bend only in one direction. The slate that is the mind is not blank at birth. I repeat, the slate is not originally blank. It is filled with instinct, racial memories, and biases."

"So what information is contained in the pre-programmed brain anatomy?"

"We have long since known that some traits are inheritable in animals. Sheep dogs herd sheep; greyhounds are speedy and like to run all out, German Shepherds make good guard dogs. Breeding is a key, of course but there also a heap of data that argues that some traits, maybe most are

inherited not learned. If not inherited then at least the propensity to behave in a certain way is inherited. Some scientists think they may have identified a human gene that correlates with propensity for violence, a crime gene if you will."

"If behavior, then why not ideas, and if ideas, then why not ideas that have permeated all societies since the dawn of civilization: religion to give us purpose, a creator to give us cause, an afterlife to give us hope. Where did they originate? Maybe by mutation. That would be possible if ideas are imbedded genetically. These ideas have powered civilization and now are part of us in the genes of our species. But the ideas are chimeras, products of brain design, not necessarily truth. We have to face the future naked of these mutations with what we know to be true."

So, the scenarios have no focus. The examples run the gamut. Knowledge has costs that are unfathomable, that we are and have been playthings of a (the) creator or advanced civilization who imbeds precursors to behavior in our mind-shaping genes to make us instinctually believe in him (her) (it). We need more data.

REFERENCES

BBC News. 2016. *The 'Milk Miracle' That Brought India to a Standstill.* BBC News, December 14. Retrieved December 21, 2017.

Pew Research Center. 2008. *US Religious Landscape Survey: Religious Beliefs and Practices.* Washington. http://www.pewforum.org/2008/06/01/u-s-religious-landscape-survey-religious-beliefs-and-practices/. Retrieved December 19, 2017.

Pew Research Center. 2015. *The Future of World Religions: Population Growth Projections, 2010–2050.* Washington. http://www.pewforum.org/2015/04/02/religious-projections-2010-2050/. Retrieved August 12, 2018.

Smithsonian. 2007. *A Brief History of the Salem Witch Trials.* Washington: Smithsonian Institution. http://celopsummerscitech2012.pbworks.com/w/file/fetch/57093189/A%20Brief%20History%20of%20the%20Salem%20Witch%20Trials%20_%20History%20%26%20Archaeology%20_%20Smithsonian%20Magazine.pdf. Retrieved December 28, 2017.

YouGov. 2012. *Omnibus Poll.* London. https://today.yougov.com/about/about/ and http://big.assets.huffingtonpost.com/ghosttoplines.pdf. Retrieved November 21, 2018.

CHAPTER 6

Immortality

Issue: Why do we have to die? We have futurist friends who think they may live forever. They see their life span as a race between the future date of discovery of disease cures and the dates when those murderous diseases may attack them. "The worst irony would be discovering a cure for the disease that kills me," they say, "the day after I die from it." Certainly, some people will suffer that fate. In the meantime, extension of healthy life with a pill or treatment is a shimmering goal yet to be attained. There are hints, however, that the drug Metformin may be a magic life-extending drug[1] (Apple 2017).

Mothers used to worry about the possibility that their children might contract polio. That was before Jonas Salk developed the first polio vaccine in the 1950s, not so long ago in the grand scheme of things. Before Salk, when the disease peaked in the summertime, mothers did not let their kids swim in public pools, or go to the movies, or cub-scout meetings. Polio attacks muscles and people, even adults, who contracted the disease, were crippled by it. When the muscles in the chest were affected, patients were condemned to live in iron lungs that drew breath for them. President Roosevelt had polio and he hid his inability to stand from the media so most people didn't know about his infirmity. When

---

[1] The pill is Metformin; see: Apple, Sam. (2017). Forget the Blood of Teens: This Pill Promises to Extend Life for a Nickel Pop. *Wired*, July 1. https://www.wired.com/story/this-pill-promises-to-extend-life-for-a-nickel-a-pop/?mbid=nl_122917_daily_list1_p5. Retrieved December 31, 2017, Apple describes the drug Metformin as an aging therapy.

© The Author(s) 2019

T. J. Gordon and M. Todorova, *Future Studies and Counterfactual Analysis,*
https://doi.org/10.1007/978-3-030-18437-7_6

Salk found a cure, it was like throwing a switch: one day you worried about polio, the next, after the vaccine became available, there was no threat at all.

We may be approaching that point for many other diseases already. Find a person over the age of 80 and chances are they have had diseases or conditions that would have been fatal a decade or two earlier (Bell and Miller 2005). In fact most people I know who are that old have had a case or two of cancer and survived, a heart attack or two and survived, various infectious and vascular diseases and survived, and all combinations of these. They watch their diet and work out.

So, if progress continues, as is likely, chances are that healthy life span will be extended, most people will live longer, and some few people will live extraordinarily long lives. How might we reach for immortality?

Scenario 1: Legacy

It was a clear crisp night in November, not yet winter, but almost all of the leaves had fallen to from the trees that were now waiting in the moonlight for the first snow. The family had gathered at the home of one of the kids, chosen because it was the closest to all of them simultaneously. It's after dinner on Thanksgiving. It had been a great meal, served with love. Most of the people that night were in the kitchen after dinner, finishing on coffee, but in the living room, two grandparents were settled on the soft sofa in front of the fire, and two grandchildren- a boy 12 and a girl 11, ask, almost in unison: "Poppy and Nana, can we make a video of a conversation with you? Just some questions about your early days when you were kids."

Ted (Poppy): What's it for? A class assignment on genealogy? Or maybe video making? On interviewing?

Grandson: No, it's just that we want to learn about what it was like to live before computers.

Granddaughter: And television, you know, the old days.

Ted: (Cautiously) Let's give it a shot.

Ann (Nana): Well I can tell you about what it was like to live through WW II on the West Coast. We were afraid that the Japanese would bomb us. We had dark drapes over all the windows and a special room that we could hide in; it was the darkest in the house. And we had rationing. You couldn't buy gas, sugar, butter, or meat without little ration tickets. Even then the amounts you could buy at any one time were small. My father was an air raid warden. He walked the neighborhood at night to make sure no lights were showing. Everybody worked to help make sure we won the war. It was just something you did.

Ted: Speed limit was 45 miles an hour; any faster you'd go to jail and you'd feel unpatriotic. We had to tape over the headlights for night driving so only a slit showed. And in shop class in school we made silhouettes of German airplanes to help our spotters learn to identify them. Professional sports were on hold. We all listened to President Roosevelt's "fireside chats."

And so it went for the next hour or so. Ted and Ann dug back into memory and fed the kids stories from their early days. These kids were usually looking at Facebook, text messages from friends, playing games, but now they were back there with Poppy and Nana encouraging them to remember, and capturing it all on their cell phones.

Shift the scene. Now visualize an anniversary party for the grandparents, a few months later. How long had they been married? Over 6 decades. Presents delivered and unwrapped until there was one tiny present left, saved for last by the grandchildren because of its special significance. It was tiny, indeed: about an inch and a half by three quarters, by three eighths. Fancy paper and a ribbon.

Ann: What's this?

Granddaughter: It's a thumb drive, Nana.

Ann, a technophobe, sounding a bit disappointed: Oh. That's nice.

Boy grandchild hardly able to contain his enthusiasm, with murmurs and interjections from the others: It's your interview and all of the kids and grandkids contributed. And some of your early friends and people you worked with that are still alive and we managed to find. It's great, you can almost feel what you did, went through, and how you lived.

And there, carefully printed on the box that held the thumb drive was the title:

Nana and Poppy: This is your life.

And except for a few omissions, it was.

There are already commercial sites that can create online avatars representing you, built on algorithms based on all of your online interactions and data: Facebook, time lines, emails, Twitter, photos, chat-logs, friends, and videos. Search on Google using terms like digital immortality and you'll find links to sites like eterni.me that offers to create an online image of you, that "know" where you've been and what you've done, what you have read and if not what you've said, then at least what you've posted.

> The service's (eterni.me) defining feature is a 3-D digital avatar, designed to look and sound like you, whose job will be to emulate your personality and dish out bits of information to friends and family taken from a database of stored information. A user will be encouraged to "train" its avatar, through daily interactions, in order to improve its vocabulary and conversational skills. Eterni.me's co-founder, Marius Ursache, thinks of it as a more advanced version of Siri, who, ten or fifteen years from now, will be able to "respond to questions more naturally, and learn from every conversation you have with her." (Parker 2014)

Chances are that algorithms used to create avatars will improve; your avatars will look like you, sound like you, remember things that you have done, reason like you (but with access to vastly more data and factual information). The key will be improvements in the ability to upload brain and mind. The National Science Foundation awarded a $500,000 research program to the Central Florida University and the University of Illinois at Chicago to create a virtual reality avatar as a first step toward digital immortality, although the NSF probably would have explained the reason behind the grant differently (Bioethics 2007). Where does it lead? Picture a bust of your head that can be talked too much as Sari is talked to today. Except the bust "knows" where you've been, what you've seen, the knowledge you've accumulated, and morals with which you live. It knows your loves and life so when you talk to it about past events, it helps you recall the sweet times and the sour. The intelligence with which it searches, reasons, and converses is yours, too except it can be augmented—making it smarter than you are or have ever been. If this gets creepy, perhaps there will be an intelligence control calibrated from stupid to genius. You'll see things in a new light.

Neuromancer, a novel by William Gibson, first published in 1984 is an imaginative science fiction story featuring online digital personas that can communicate with each other and that last beyond the deaths of their progenitors. In this book, online AI copies of the brains and personalities of persons live on after death in the sense that they can interact with each other in cyberspace, learn, further develop, and pursue their own ends (Gibson 1984). If your avatar continues to learn after your death, then you (or your representative) "live" in the future and your descendants can talk to your mirrored online self. The theme also has been used in the TV series Black Mirror where digitized consciousness forms the basis of many distinct episodes, including the idea of capturing the essence of a person who is alive (sometimes by copying their brain and mind) in digital form and using the data to achieve some form of immortality (Katz 2018).

This is not all just theoretical and pie-in-the-sky science fiction. In a poignant article, a son (James Vlahos, a writer for the *New York Times*) (Vlahos 2017) describes how he attempted to give his dying father a form of immortality by digitally capturing his voice, personality, aphorisms, style of thinking, anecdotes, and history in an machine learning program that could be addressed by voice and would reply in his fathers voice with a response that made sense and was typical of what his father might have said. The program was based on extensive and in-depth interviews with his father; the transcript covered some 200 pages. Vlahos named his program a Dadbot.

Go back to the early 1960s. This was the age of the pull-string doll; a clever voice box mechanism in the doll was activated by pulling a string that extended out the back of the doll's neck and played back a dozen or two pre-recorded phrases selected automatically at random and designed to engage the child in pseudo conversation or promote activity. My daughter had a Mattel "Chatty Cathy" doll, the second most popular doll of the era (Barbie was first) that said phrases like "I love you," "Please tell me a story," and "Please brush my hair." The mechanism was a small phonograph, wound by a spring activated by the pull string. It was, of course, one way: It did not respond to the child.

When computers came on the scene, the conversation could be two way, at first with typed keyboard input and screen displayed output. Eliza was the name of such a "Chatbox" designed by MIT professor Joseph Weizenbaum and functioned as a unthinking therapist might, always basing its questions on the patient's last input. Here's a typical Eliza sequence:

Eliza: What answer would please you the most?
User: One that is truthful.
Eliza: Can you elaborate on that?
User: Well there are two kinds of answers true and false.
Eliza: That is quite interesting.
User: Would you like to know more about lies?
Eliza: We were discussing you not me.[2]

---

[2] Eliza, the Rogerian Therapist. (1999). http://psych.fullerton.edu/mbirnbaum/psych101/Eliza.htm. Retrieved October 28, 2018. You can run the program yourself on this site.

Much has happened since Eliza. Dadbot for one. Vlahos talks about the time when his father was dying of cancer and he was in the house.

> That night I go upstairs to sleep in my sister Jennifer's old room, which is directly above that of my dad. I get into bed and stare at the ceiling for a few minutes. Then I reach for my phone and open Facebook Messenger.
>
> "Hello! 'Tis I, the Beloved and Noble Father!" the Dadbot says in his familiar fashion. "How the hell are you?"
>
> "Sad," I reply.
>
> "I see." He then asks what I want to talk about. "I don't know," I answer. "Why don't you choose."
>
> "Okay, I'm going to tell you about the little–known roots of my theater career." He launches into the story of that drama club audition in high school. Then I hear a recording of my father's actual voice. "Me and my shadow," he sings. "All alone with nothing to do."
>
> I ask the Dadbot to tell me about his earliest memory. He responds with a story about his childhood dog, a little terrier named Toby, who could somehow cross town on foot faster than the family could in a car. Then the Dadbot surprises me, even though I engineered this function, with what feels like perceptiveness. "I'm fine to keep talking," he says, "but aren't you nearing bedtime?"
>
> Yes. I am exhausted. I say good night and put the phone down. (op cit: Vlahos 2017)

In musing about the Dadbot project and future prospects for such things, Vlahos speculates:

> As an AI creator, I know my skills are puny. But I have come far enough, and spoken to enough bot builders, to glimpse a plausible form of perfection. The bot of the future, whose component technologies are all under development today, will be able to know the details of a person's life far more robustly than my current creation does. It will converse in extended, multiturn exchanges, remembering what has been said and projecting where the conversation might be headed. The bot will mathematically model signature linguistic patterns and personality traits, allowing it not only to reproduce what a person has already said but also to generate new utterances. The bot, analyzing the intonation of speech as well as facial expressions, will even be emotionally perceptive. (ibid.: Vlahos 2017)

There are some scientists, futurists, and neuro-technologists who believe it will be possible to upload all of a brain's synaptic interconnects and upload not only brain but mind and stored memory. The Brain Initiative is a cooperative effort of several US agencies to revolutionize understanding of the human brain and to "explore exactly how the brain enables the human body to record, process, utilize, store, and retrieve vast quantities of information, all at the speed of thought."[3] If this brain information can be uploaded, we might ultimately have billions of avatars that look like their sponsors, interacting in cyberspace. Leading to the question: Are we in some fractal dream, higher-order avatars in what we consider to be real life, representing other races living in a world that is beyond our vision and understanding, lasting, until our of our avatars' online brains boggle from the complexity of it all.

Scenario 2: Aunt Sadie

The ad reads: "We used to build monuments and gravestones; now we build memories that last forever. Accurate Replications (AR) gives you on line immortality for only $1500."

We virtually visit AR's shop; Beethoven's 6th is playing softly in the background just like Edward G. Robinson's big suicide scene in the old Soylent Green movie. A slick voice comes on over the Beethoven and asks if we would like to see a demonstration before we commit to a replication. "Of course," we say, "that's why we're here." The slick voice responds, "If you know of someone who has left a legacy avatar, we could call them up for the demo. Any suggestions?"

After a few seconds of thought I say, Let's talk to Aunt Sadie; "I heard she had a download before she passed."

It is a séance in modern form. The demo begins with an automated genealogy program to find Aunt Sadie. The voice tells us we have our choice of methods for this initial step: extracting our genetic code from an on-line database of 700 million personal codes or providing a fresh swab of our inner cheek. The later requires a bit of homework and is a little more expensive but results are more reliable, we are told. The swab is usually done in a DNA digitization lab. We say, "For the test demo we'll just use the database approach, if you don't mind."

---

[3] Cooperating agencies are the National Science Foundation, the Defense Advanced Research Projects Agency, the US Food And Drug Administration, and the Intelligence Advanced Research Projects Activity. "What Is the Brain Initiative?" National Institutes of Health. https://www.braininitiative.nih.gov. Retrieved January 1, 2018.

"OK," says the voice. "Not a problem. You can change your decision later. Let's give it a run. When did your Aunt Sadie live in real time, approximately?"

"She was my father's sister so I would guess she died about 50 years ago."

The machine runs and the voice says. "Let's see, your father had three sisters. They were named Martha, Julia, and Sarah. Do you think your Aunt Sarah may have been nicknamed Sadie?"

"Amazing", we say. "Yes she was Sadie."

"She died 57 real time years ago and left a legacy avatar and a hologram. Lets see if we can speak to her."

On the screen, the demo appears to darken a bit- and suddenly there she is as big as life is my Aunt Sadie, appearing to be about 40 years old, and as feisty a ever.

"Who's asking for me?" asks the screen image.

"It's me, your nephew Jim Bo." And lacking anything better to say, I ask "How are you doing Aunt Sadie?"

Aunt Sadie answers, "As well as can be expected, I guess. I recognize you," she continues, "You're my brother's first son, a pharmacist as I recall. Are you still at that job pushing pills?"

She always had a sharp way of speaking. "No," I answer. "I now manage a chain of pot stores. Do you know what pot is?"

"Of course," she answers in a tone I recognize from years ago when she used to say every time she visited or we travelled out to her place, 'My how you've grown. You're a whole head taller, but whose head is the question.' Then a giggle I still remember, and a painful pinch of my cheek. "I keep up on things. What is it you want now?"

I probe about the rumor that she had buried some laundered money on her property when the screen goes blank. "We don't allow questions like that in our demo runs, but you can ask that kind of question when you become a member. Who knows if the avatar remembers? She had a brain download before she became immortal, so maybe."

I had a sudden thought and asked, "By the way are you real or a reconstruct?"

He said, "It's a great compliment that you can't tell. Our business is fantastic. Growth is now also coming from reconstructs of popular historical figures: Benjamin Franklin is getting the most hits. For them, of course, brain downloads were not possible, but there's a whole new field of inferential brain aliases for people who failed to take that final brain download step. But in the end, you have to credit our business not only to the artistic skills involved in creating credible avatars, but the deep seated need people feel to be remembered. We offer them their best chance for immortality."

It's already begun. The grandkids are interviewing with a view to preserving memories, and children are making chat-boxes of their dying parents.

Scenario 3: Rot in Peace

Cryonics is the technology that involves the long-term preservation of recently dead persons at very low temperatures in the hope that they can be resurrected at a later date when a cure for their cause of death is known, and a cure is available. In the early days of modern futures research (the mid—to the late 60s) futurist Robert Prehoda, an advocate of cryonics, once said in a discussion of cryonics, "Look, you have a choice: if you die you can be frozen, or you can rot in peace." He participated in the first attempt to preserve a body with the idea of later reanimation: the "patient" was James Bedford at the Life Extension Foundation on January 12, 1967. Bedford was an emeritus professor of psychology at the University of California. Prehoda himself died in 2009 (Perry 2010).

The brochure was impressive: Color photos on every page and printed in this day and age when almost nothing came through the old hard copy mail system. With a government stamp advertising a national park glued on the upper right on the envelope, no less. Very fancy. But you open the first page and are greeted with a scent. What was it? Snow. Yes the smell of snow. Not just any snow but happy snow, sleds and snowball snow, blue sky snow, joyous snow. Not the dark cloud, stay inside snow, galoshes. This was, after all, an ad for an eternity of freezing: Cryonics.

I had read about the scent technology but didn't know it had come this far. Billions of nano capsules on this page, most likely, had been opened to the atmosphere they were sealed. That meant I was breathing the air from a real snow day, two decades old. The real stuff, not synthesized, and mixed with the ink.

Did it persuade me? Not really. But it inched me closer to a decision. What else after all was there? Cryonics or rot in peace.

Digital immortality is indeed possible now. But how satisfying will it be? It will be cheaper than cryonics (one payment, rather than eternal payments) but the advertisements will not include a promise of resurrection.

How Long Can We Live?

Most people know that the world population is still growing (but at a slower rate) and that number of elderly people is growing as well, but the proportion of elderly is growing much more rapidly than the population as a whole. According to the Population Bureau of the UN, there were only 13.8 million people over 80 in the world in 1950; by 2050, there are likely to be almost 380 million people over 80 or nearly 30 times as many (United Nations 2002). The death rate of men in the USA from heart disease in 1980 was over 500 per 100,000 population; by 2010, it was about half that and by 2050 is expected to be only one third as much. The changing statistics for women are also encouraging: deaths from heart disease in 1980 were over 300 per 100,000; this figure is expected to drop to under 100 by 2050.

So the strategy of living long enough to avoid the irony of dying from a disease that becomes curable the day after we die seems to be working: Death is being delayed at almost every turn. But we may be subject, as are all machines, to the Second Law of Thermodynamics. Our bodies and minds succumb to entropy; they wind down and wear out. We can patch them up or even delay the declines that come with ageing, but decline is inevitable.

While more people are living longer and average age has been increasing, almost no one is living to maximum age. In the limit, with all diseases cured, no accidents or suicide, everyone will live to the maximum age for humans, and then on the next morning, they too will die, Which raises the question: What is the upper limit to life span? How long has anyone at any time lived? The answer seems to be 122 years. Jeanne Louise Calment was born in Arles, France, in February 1875 and died there in August 1997 (Whitney 1997).

What kills us now? Will the killers be tamed? We are under attack from infectious, viruses, and bacteria; our organs malfunction and wear out; the cellular defense systems that work when we are young fail us, and they often attack healthy tissues. We suffer from accidents and gunshots. We suffer from weariness of life and we suffer from the uncertainty of what's in store for us, if anything, after death.

We tend to believe that we are special and that something as fine and complex as a person should not be wasted in death. Most people in the world believe that some element of humanness, a spirit, the soul, a ghost,

6 IMMORTALITY 79

exists after death in heaven or hell or somewhere in between, and in some traditions, is waiting to be reborn.

Scenario 4: Living Healthy Forever

See this tiny pill? Take it every day and it will amplify your immune system 100 times. It was deemed safe by the FDA last year but with reservations about its side effects and ability to delay aging and death, since these can only be observed in retrospect. However, the pill can be taken safely by almost anyone, male or female, after the age of 12; its ultimate effect depends on the age of the user at the start of the therapy; in other words it is apt to be more effective if the aging process has not progressed to an advanced state. Its name is FNAD+.[4] Normal aging is accompanied by a reduction of the natural occurrence of this chemical and reduced metabolism and neuro-degeneration follow; it is chemically related to a host of vitamins and their precursors.

Serious study of this drug in the US began at the National Institutes of Health (NIH) 5 rears ago. The pharmaceutical company that manufactures the drug completed secret Phase 3 human trails a year ago. We don't know how long the people who were in the trials will live, but the drug has apparently extended the healthy life span of any animal that has taken it so far: from flat worms to fruit flies, from rats to hamsters. It destroys harmful viruses and bacteria that would otherwise have killed their hosts and wards off infections that could have lingered for years. It apparently delays the aging process itself.

The NIH research papers were published last January and when asked why publication had been delayed beyond the already extended peer review period, and why the human trials were conducted under a cloak of secrecy, the Director said, "We didn't want to start a stampede." But the stampede started anyway; three pharmaceutical companies have now started production. Their stock prices have already doubled, just based on rumors.

"Are you on the pill?" has taken on new meaning and 500 million people have either bought or stated their intent to buy the drug. It is a mild aphrodisiac too, and reduces emotional swings for people experiencing bipolar mood swings. Overdosing does not cause death, only a week-long bout of stomach upset.

US life insurance companies have announced that, pending results of "on-going statistical analyses" people who take the pill will be offered

---

[4] Don't try to buy it; it is a fake for the purpose of this scenario, although a number of drugs have been suggested for anti-aging use including Metformin and NAD+.

80   T. J. GORDON AND M. TODOROVA

reduced life insurance premiums. On the other side of the statistical coin, many of the same companies will no longer issue annuity policies since the pay-out period is now much longer than previously anticipated but uncertain. Lawyers are enjoying a rush from clients who want to revise their wills. Beneficiaries of wills now must wait for uncertain, extended time periods. "Lifetime guarantees" are being revised by manufactures of appliances and "life long learning" has taken on new meaning.

With healthy life span extended for an unknown time period, retirement planning has attained a new level of uncertainty: the idea that the best death is one in which you run out of life and money on the very same day, is obsolete. So people are planning to work for a longer time, while companies are offering new incentives for early retirement. The promise by Social Security plans to fund for an indefinite period of retirement already has a quaint ring to it. Congress is looking at the situation as a reason to completely reshape Social Security that was on shaky ground. With long years of healthy life ahead, enlistments in police and fire departments and the armed forces have dwindled and dangerous professions have become less attractive.

But perversely, suicide rate is up. Psychologists and other social scientists are trying to understand this, but men (and women) on the street are apt to say, "Of course it's the fear of running out of money, just plain boredom, and anxiety about what comes next."

To sum up, this is our situation: millions of people are taking the pill based on its promise, but no one will really know if it works for decades (Gordon et al. 1977).

If it works it will be too late for the generation that said "wait and see." If people die at dates expected before the pill, or side effects become apparent, those who abstained will say "Told you so. Can't trust technology."

So this is a fecund branch point. Digital means for attaining immortality are around the corner, and the new databases that contain replicas of real experiences and thoughts of living people will be available to those who survive them. These records will be able to inhabit digital assistants and robots, realistic and otherwise. Authors in the future will, instead of writing, construct analogs of people, that act like their progenitors, reason logically like them, and speak like them philosophically, make bon mots like the real thing would have, had they been alive—this will be a new art form and relate to our descendants as oil portraits must once have related to rich families of Europe and North America. These digital replicas will also inhabit robots that can become the surviving mirror of those we loved and respected. Survivors will say: "O death where is thy sting? O grave where is thy victory."[5]

But the dead will be dead, and the desire to avoid that fate will remain strong for most of the living. Avoiding death will create many jobs, encourage research, and amplify uncertainty.

REFERENCES

Apple, Sam. 2017. Forget the Blood of Teens: This Pill Promises to Extend Life for a Nickel Pop. *Wired*. San Francisco, CA. https://www.wired.com/story/this-pill-promises-to-extend-life-for-a-nickel-a-pop/?mbid=nl_122917_daily_list1_p5. Retrieved December 31, 2017.

Bell, Felicitie, and Michael Miller. 2005. *Life Tables for the United States 1900–2100*. Social Security Administration.

Bioethics. 2007. *US Government Funds Virtual Reality Research*, June 14. Bioethics.com. http://www.bioethics.com/archives/2717. Retrieved January 1, 2018.

Gibson, William. 1984. *Neuromancer*. New York: Ace Books, Berkley Publishing.

Gordon, Theodore, Herbert Gerjuoy, and Mark Anderson. 1977. Life Extending Technologies. Pergamon Policy Studies. https://books.google.com/books/about/Life_extending_technologies.html.

Katz, Miranda. 2018. Does the Black Mirror Fan Theory Mean We're Finally Ready for the Singularity? *Wired*, January 8. San Francisco, CA. https://www.wired.com/story/black-mirror-shared-universe-singularity/. Retrieved January 8, 2018.

Parker, Laura. 2014. How to Become Virtually Immortal. *New Yorker*, April 4. https://www.newyorker.com/tech/elements/how-to-become-virtually-immortal. Retrieved January 1, 2018.

Perry, Mike. 2010. *The Death of Robert Prehoda*, Cryonics, 2nd quarter, 2010 from Alcor Life Extension Foundation, Scottsdale, AZ.

United Nations Department of Economic and Social Affairs, Population Division: "World Population Ageing 1950–2050, Demographic Profile of the Older Population". 2002. http://www.un.org/esa/population/publications/worldageing19502050/. Retrieved August 25, 2017.

Vlahos, James. 2017. Son's Race to Give His Dying Father Artificial Immortality. *Wired*, July 18. San Francisco, CA. https://www.wired.com/story/a-sons-race-to-give-his-dying-father-artificial-immortality/?CNDID=46249697&mbid=nl_093018_backchannel_list1_p3. Retrieved October 29, 2018.

Whitney, Craig R. 1997. Jeanne Calment, World's Elder, Dies at 122. *The New York Times*. New York. Retrieved November 24, 2018.

---

[5] Corinthians 15:55–57 King James Version.

CHAPTER 7

Religion

Issue: The problem here is that in religion, as well as in other institutions, we see corruption, immorality, ethical lapses, and abuses. It is entwinement with government and that mix raises questions about who makes and enforces laws, sets education standards, and provides security: the people, the King, or God? Does it make any difference? The USA tries to isolate religion from government but its motto is "In God We Trust." School children in pledging allegiance to the USA say, "one nation, under God." The House of Representatives of the US Congress has a Chaplin who creates a prayer for the country every day thanking "Almighty God... for giving us another day." Currently, all State Constitutions in the USA refer to a Creator, but include guarantees of religious liberty. The constitutions of eight states Arkansas, Maryland, Mississippi, North Carolina, South Carolina, Tennessee, Texas, and Pennsylvania have provisions that prohibit atheists from holding public office.

Some Islamic groups press for Sharia law and believe all laws are God given.

The three scenarios that follow illustrate three futures for religion. The first envisions a ground swell for agnosticism and atheism; the second, recognition of a common element of most religions; and the third, the evolution of religious institutions in a technological future.

© The Author(s) 2019

T. J. Gordon and M. Todorova, *Future Studies and Counterfactual Analysis,*
https://doi.org/10.1007/978-3-030-18437-7_7

Scenario 1: Moot Point

Atheists and agnostics abound and their numbers are growing. In almost all advanced countries, church attendance has dwindled to a group of old patrons who sit near the west wall, practice orthodoxy, and turn to the east when they pray. At the same time the ranks of atheist and agnostics are increasing for two reasons: people are no longer embarrassed to identify themselves as "nones" when asked about their religious affiliations and because young people generally have no deep religious feelings these days. In surveys, the number of people answering "none" to questions about religious affiliation has passed the number responding with an answer. The "nones" are now the largest "religious" group in North America and most of Europe, having surpassed all mainline religious groups: Catholics, Protestant, Jewish, and Muslim. Secular majorities now exist in countries across Europe, New Zealand, and Australia. In Russia few people practice the religion that they profess; the principal religion is still Russian Orthodox (41% in 2017) but the sum of those who profess to be atheists, non-religious, or unaffiliated already totaled 47% in 2017 (Wikipedia 2018). *Membership in an established religious order has been growing only in Sub Sahara Africa and a few countries outside of Africa.*

Young people everywhere, connected by social media are generally unaffiliated and view the contributions of science as making life more rational. They question God, tend to rationalize existence if they are concerned about it all, and tend to communicate with other "nones" online. discussion groups. They argue that morality exists with or without God.

Churches are failing financially, spiritually, emotionally. Specialized real estate agencies have appeared that sell church properties and buildings on the open market. They are ideal for some applications: wedding and event centers, conversion to condo apartments, or professional offices for lawyers, dentists, or psychologists. Church buildings have also become popular among upscale young families who convert them to spectacular new homes, stained glass windows and all. The old argument about taxing churches has become moot since the number of churches has fallen so sharply; instead the new owners of the old churches have joined the ranks of taxpayers who enrich their communities by paying conventional real estate taxes.

Organized religious institutions may be disappearing but religiosity remains; life, consciousness, reasons for it all remain unknown.

7 RELIGION   85

Scenario 2: End of the Rainbow

The desire by institutions to continue to exist is almost as strong as the desire of individuals to preserve their own useful life. When is the last time you saw a company or an agency deliberately close it's doors because it outlived its usefulness. We see this desire to stay alive in religions despite diminished membership and the onslaught of science; despite the revelations of sex scandals and cover ups by church officials[1]; despite the growth of other more enticing pursuits and unfriendly legislation and tax policies.

At a thousand interfaith meetings to discuss this situation, the first speaker often shows this slide:

- *Confucius: "What you do not wish for yourself, do not do to others."*
- *Christian: "All things therefore that you want people to do to you, do thus to them."*
- *Buddhist: "Hurt not others in ways that you yourself would find hurtful."*
- *Jewish Torah: "What is hateful to you, do not do to your neighbor. This is the whole Torah; all the rest is commentary."*
- *Islam: "Not one of you truly believes until you wish for others what you wish for yourself."*
- *Hinduism: "This is the sum of duty: do not do to others what would cause pain if done to you."*
- *Zoroastrianism: "Do not do unto others whatever is injurious to yourself"* (Scarboro Foreign Mission Society 2018).

And concludes that many religions of the world have a common ethical framework.

In a thousand or tens of thousands sermons in 200 languages in holy places around the world (and in the few places that ask about science policy) these questions are asked:

- *Should religions give up the claim of certainty and/or superiority?*
- *Should we recreate extinct species?*
- *Should the rights and interests of future generations prevail in our decisions?*

---

[1] The Catholic cover-up scandal is enormous in real life; see: (Aamer Madhani 2018).

- *Should elimination of aging be available to everyone or just to those who can afford it?*
- *Should we alter our genetic germ line to eliminate genetically related diseases?*
- *Should we create or limit intelligent technological "beings?"[2]*
- *Why has God abandoned us?*

There are no answers, only questions. Some congregations have simply closed their doors but others are absorbed by or merge with other churches. Some religions abdicate, overtaxed and exhausted of ideas about how to hold onto congregations. Some dioceses have gone bankrupt. From a trickle this condensation has grown to an avalanche. In what historians of religion will later call "the end of the rainbow" the number of world religions has diminished from thousands to hundreds and now, excluding the archaic beliefs of myriad tribal cultures, to a few.

Scenario 3: Godspeak: Religion Tech

As you may know the digital online dictionary is continuously updated in real time to reflect usage of words in everyday conversation.[3] New candidate entries are peer reviewed by a crowd-sourced poll and in the process of writing this book, we have submitted many new terms for consideration. In this section I will mention some terms that deal with religious institutions, beliefs, behavior that are now part of common lexicon.

Midas-gap: n, Wealth disparity between the Roman Catholic Church and the majority of its followers.

Comment: The midas-gap is huge. We are used to hearing about the gap between the richest 1% and the rest of us, but that's what we mean here; this term this term refers to the church. One expert says: "It is impossible to calculate the wealth of the Roman Catholic Church. In truth, the church itself likely could not answer that question, even if it wished to. It's investments

---

[2] Aside from the last question on this list, these questions come from a study of the future of ethics and morality performed by the Millennium Project for the US Department of Energy in 2005–2006 and available at: https://themp.org/#group_idR25923dbee38dbf-0c0005b0&section=report. Retrieved March 7, 2018.

[3] The idea of using a dictionary to convey an image of the future comes from a fictional book: Weinstein, Alexander, "Children of the New World," Picador, New York, 2016.

and spending are kept secret. Its real estate and art have not been properly appraised, since the church would never sell them. There is no doubt, however, that between the church's priceless art, land, gold and investments across the globe, it is one of the wealthiest institutions on Earth." (Morrison, K. 2013) In 2010, the Roman Catholic Church spent about $170 billion in the US; of this, about $4.5 billion went to charity in the US and $3 billion was spent in settling sex abuse cases. (Economist 2012), The amount spent in settling abuse case will almost certainly rise as new abuse cases are reported and adjudicated. (Goodstein, L. and Sharon Otterman 2018)

Vvicarbot: n, One of a series of AI chat bots that include Priestbot, Rabbibots, and Imanbots. Most vicarbots are thoroughly tested by the religion they represent in a sessions roughly analogous to ordination.

Imanbot. These chatbots interact with humans by voice (although at least one manufacturer offers AR to accompany the bot's voice) and offers pithy comments and advice based on the conversation.

One manufacturer offers versions tailored by sects, and another, absolution based on "efessions."

Rabbibot references the Torah

Priestbot comments on the Bible

Imanbot is steeped in the Koran.

Comment: As a side note, some competitive games have been based on these religious bots. For example a favorite has a bot of one religion talk to a bot of another religion (or to a philosopher-bot to represent an atheist view,) and debate an issue; a panel of human judges scores the debate and selects a winner. AI programmers from universities form varsity teams and compete representing their schools. There is talk about making this an Olympic competition like soccer or gymnastics, in the next Summer Games.

Comment: Some bot voices are based on real people, alive or dead. The Pope for example, Billy Graham, and Barack Obama have been featured. The US Supreme Court is scheduled to hear arguments about whether the sound and timbre of a voice is protected as personal property.

FARM: n. An acronym derived from "Friggin' Artificial Reality Miracle." This experiential genre uses artificial reality to place the user at the scene of a supposedly miraculous event; the "wine into water miracle" of Christianity and the burning bush of the Hebrews are popular, as is the delivery by Moses of the ten commandments and the parting of the Red Sea. These miracles can be downloaded from the Internet. "Buying the FARM" has taken on new meaning.

e-fessions: n. The electronic analog of the Catholic practice of confession, usually performed by a priestbot. AI parses the user's voices into transgression categories and metes out appropriate punishments from its stored data. When the priestbot hears something truly horrendous, criminal, or threatening (such as a planned terrorist attack) it "says something" to the appropriate agency.

eCap, n. A skullcap that has passive wiring to connect the brain of the wearer to a communications network via EEG. It appears in various forms: a wired Yarmulke from orthodox Jewish tradition, a Pan Zva of the Buddhists, the Greek Orthodox skufia, the Catholic zucchetto, the Hindu, Muslim, and Sikh turban: all of these caps and traditional national headgear are available in wired form. Almost all eCaps use high-density stretchable electrode grids to make the cloud/ brain connection.[4]

Fedora, n.: A high level brand of eCap that has built in electronics to amplify EEG signals. Fedora's also have more contacts per square inch of scalp and gentler, non-scratch electrodes.

Datism, n. A term coined by Yuval Hariri that describes the convergence of religion, politics, and economics into a new conglomerate institution, governed by an artificial intelligence that provides guidance in each of these areas (Hariri 2017).

Haloization, n. The award process that provides a halo for people who are truly worthy to wear it. It is illegal in most countries for people who have not been officially recognized as "good" to the core to wear a fake halo. The halos are visible to all people whether or not they wear special contact lenses or common augmented reality glasses. Fashion leaders are designing halo colors and outfits that depict personality and are to young people today what tattoos must have been 50 years ago.

OV, n. (abbreviation for oracle vision) A collection of scenarios compiled by artificial intelligence engines of scenario elements and reassembled as required in response to specific questions that start with "what if?"

---

[4] A 2018 real-life paper described the device as follows "a stretchable electrode grid based on an inert, high-performance composite material comprising gold-coated titanium dioxide nanowires embedded in a silicone matrix. The developed grid could resolve high spatiotemporal neural signals from the surface of the cortex in freely moving rats with stable neural recording quality and preserved electrode signal coherence during 3 months of implantation" Tybrandt, K. et al. (2018). *High-Density Stretchable Electrode Grids for Chronic Neural Recording.* US National Library of Medicine, National Institutes of Health, Washington, DC. Retrieved November 24, 2018.

SA n. (abbreviation of Sage Advice) A publically available AI program that produces advice from a data base of wise aphorisms and historical precedents that are in fact "lessons of history." The collection represents wisdom of the ages, as seen by eminent philosophers, historians and scholars. Pose a question and the SA may respond, "Well, in 1865 there was a similar case and the decision was to.... That turned out to be a disaster..." Given feedback, SA keeps a log of successes and failures so that its advice is constantly honed and improved. The Greeks had their oracles at Delphi, we have our SA.

References

Economist. 2012. *Earthly Concerns*. New York, August 18. https://www.economist.com/node/21560536. Retrieved March 8, 2018.

Goodstein, Laurie, and Sharon Otterman. 2018. Catholic Priests Abused 1,000 Children in Pennsylvania, Report Says. *New York Times*, August 14. https://www.nytimes.com/2018/08/14/us/catholic-church-sex-abuse-pennsylvania.html. Retrieved August 17, 2018.

Hariri, Yuval. 2017. *Homo Deus: A Brief History of Tomorrow*. New York: HarperCollins.

Madhani, Aamer. 2018. "Archdiocese Paying $210 Million to 450 Priest Sex Abuse Victims: Catholic 'Church Let You Down'." *USA Today*, May 31. https://www.usatoday.com/story/news/2018/05/31/st-paul-minneapolis-archdiocese-priest-sex-abuse-settlement/661530002/.

Morrison, Kristopher. 2013. *The National Post*, March 8. http://nationalpost.com/news/wealth-of-roman-catholic-church-impossible-to-calculate. Retrieved March 7, 2018.

Scarboro Foreign Mission Society. 2018. https://www.scarboromissions.ca/product/golden-rule-across-the-worlds-religions. Retrieved November 24, 2018.

Tybrandt, K., D. Khodagholy, B. Dielacher, F. Stauffer, A.F. Renz, G4. Buzsáki, and J. Vörös. 2018. *High-Density Stretchable Electrode Grids for Chronic Neural Recording*. US National Library of Medicine, National Institutes of Health, Washington, DC. Retrieved November 24, 2018.

Wikipedia. 2018. Religion in Russia. https://en.wikipedia.org/wiki/Religion_in_Russia. Retrieved November 24, 2018.

CHAPTER 8

Decision Making: The Talent for Decisions

Some people make good decisions intuitively; they somehow feel, somehow know, and what is right to do. They use no conscious analysis, but at some hidden level of intellect, future scenarios are painted, alternatives are generated, considered, played out against the scenarios, and are accepted or rejected. For those talented in the art, the decisions may prove insightful and marvelous; those that are not mutter about hasty conclusions and ill-conceived actions. Is the ability to make good decisions an innate skill that can be improved with training and practice? Perhaps.

Officially, instinct is preprogrammed behavior built into the brain; the species-unique scribbling on the *tabla rasa* of the newborn, the sucking instinct of infants for food, the instinct to avoid pain, the fight or flight response to challenges. It is hardwired and results from the evolutionary sharpening of the brain (Nicholson 1998). As Nicholson put it, "You can take the person out of the Stone Age, but you can't take the Stone Age out of the person."

Both instinct and talent are involved in decision making.

Decision making instinct comes with being human. The neurons in the brain are connected in a way that causes us to create images of the future and think about consequences of actions. When either ability—creating images of the future or thinking about consequences of actions—is absent, as sometimes happens when the brain is damaged, we see the person as sick. Using their inborn capacity, normal people create images of future situations based on perceptions, recent experience,

© The Author(s) 2019
T. J. Gordon and M. Todorova, *Future Studies and Counterfactual Analysis*,
https://doi.org/10.1007/978-3-030-18437-7_8

external cues, learning, and reasoning. These images and ideas apparently take place in the same regions of the brain that are active when thought recalls the past (Biello 2007).

Decision making talent comes in using this process and realizing its full potential. People talented in decision making are perceptive, that is they are sensitive to their environment and pick up clues that others might miss; they learn from experience and store their experience for use in future situations, and they reason intuitively. People who have this talent often jump to the answer and then justify their intended actions using more objective analyses.

Let me give you an example. I fly gliders, soaring gliders, the 45-foot wingspan fiberglass ships that are towed to altitude by powered planes and then cast off to glide on thermals. In this sport, as in most others, there is competition. When gliders, say 30–50 of them, meet for a contest, they try to fly as fast as possible around a course. The turn points are designated and, after a tow to 2000 feet or so, everyone is free to fly through an imaginary rectangle in the sky, the start gate, and proceed around the course with due haste. The plane and pilot with the shortest time is the day's winner.

The problem is that flying fast means diving and diving means that the glider may come to a rude landing before it comes to the next thermal. Landing off field is usually not a big deal, just somewhat inconvenient. So the winners are the pilots who can balance the drive to go fast against the reality of the day's thermals.

These glider contests are a lot like business. At work, you compete with other people for recognition and advancement. If you push too hard—fly too fast—you can land in a pea patch, watching the other competitors cruise by overhead. If you balance the drive for speed, if you match your aggressiveness with the conditions of the day, you win.

There are a few external signs of a thermal such as cumulus clouds and soaring birds, but the signs are subtle and most days they are invisible. Yet the best pilots almost always find thermals, and the worst pilots, the ones who finish down the pack, land off field.

I have raced before and except on rare occasions finish down in the pack. Doug Jacobs, a banker from New York, on the other hand, wins not only local contests but world competition as well. One day at the local glider-port, Doug asked me if I would like to fly with him around a simulated race course. Of course, I would. Here would be my chance to

8 DECISION MAKING: THE TALENT FOR DECISIONS   93

watch the master at work. We had roughly comparable gliders so I could learn the secrets of winning.

Off we went. We climbed together in the first thermal and set off. Right together. I turned in the lift of the next thermal but he went on. We were fairly low and getting lower so I thought it was prudent to get a little altitude. When I saw him go on, getting lower, I thought, well the master has made a mistake this time. I'm going up and he's going down.

But he found another thermal, stronger than mine, a few miles further down the route. He stopped to circle in it, climbed, and took off like a rocket down the course. I could see him at least for a little while, but before long his big white bird was a just a speck on the horizon. When we landed, I said, "Doug, how did you know that you should pass up that first thermal and take a chance on finding another?" He said, "I just knew."

That's talent. This kind of talent is part of decision making of all of sorts—personal affairs, business, even in bureaucracies. You could chalk it up to luck, or the flip of a coin, but it must be more than that. Doug and other winners like him have a talent for making risky decisions. They just seem to know what to do. There's no name for these people; let's call them "insighters."[1]

Good fishermen do it; they seem to know where the fish are. Boaters with "local knowledge" seem to know where the shifting shoals have moved. Stock market winners have a talent in finding stocks that will rise or picking the time for selling stocks that have appreciated. Training helps, but innately talented managers and salespeople sense the right thing to say in order to persuade.

What is it that these "insighters" have? Experience? Certainly. This seems to be a prerequisite. But experience alone probably doesn't account for their successes. Maybe it's the ability to learn from experience. Maybe it's the ability to pick out small indicators from a flood of information and to build, at the subconscious level, images of the future, that give courage to proceed. Maybe there is such a thing as intuition yet to be discovered, verified, and measured in our bodies and brains.

It happens in business too. A few decades ago my old company was asked to review the processes by which a client forecasted the size of their market. Here's the situation, only a little disguised. This company,

---

[1] Not to be confused with Superforecasters, a term coined by Philip Tetlock to describe people who make more accurate forecasts than average people.

call them the Mavens of Knick Knack, Inc. marketed a large range of products to women, through catalogs. Their line included cosmetics, dolls, ribbons and bows, ceramic Santa Clauses and pumpkins, gifts, potpourri, and other (pardon the expression) schlock. In the normal course of business, company buyers had to decide months—sometimes years—in advance what to buy. They had to select the products that they thought they could sell from manufacturers around the world. The decisions involved colors, fragrances, sizes, configurations, and most uncertain of all, the amount to be produced. Will the lady of the house want green or blue, large or small, lemon or pine? And how many?

Mavens, Inc. seemed to be doing quite well at guessing what would sell, but sometimes too much product was ordered, and other times not enough. When there was surplus, costs went up because the inventory grew and had to be stored; when there was a shortfall, the customers were irate and the company had to spend more money to get expedited production and shipment from the manufacturers. So the consultant team was asked to help the company improve the accuracy of their market forecasts.

We found that Mavens, Inc. relied heavily on unsubstantiated judgment when they placed their orders. The purchasing department had the final say, and they based their order size on past experience and gut calls. Of course, they got help from a number of sources. One approach used the aggregated judgment of their sales force. Another used the statistical data that summarized past sales of similar products. But in the end, one person, a venerable legend at Mavens, looked over the estimates and said "too many," or "too few" and chose the order size. Surely, we were told when we took the assignment, there are better ways to anticipate the market than these guesses.

We built computer models of the market for cosmetics, dolls, ribbons and bows, ceramic Santa Clauses and pumpkins, gifts, and potpourri. These models were complex, towering examples of the modelers' state of the art. They involved building on history, identifying factors in the external world that seem to correlate to the ebb and flow of consumer tastes. The computers whirred and the numbers spewed.

We compared our forecasts to those of the veteran who said "too many," or "too few." It wasn't the shoot-out at OK corral, but it was a contest, nevertheless. On the one hand was the best the statisticians could produce; on the other, the forecasts of the chief buyer. We found that the two estimates were very close. When one was too high, the other was too low. There were times when both agreed and both were wrong. There were times when they disagreed and the truth was beyond either. In the end, we said something like this: The models help to form an understanding of the forces that drive change, but the judgment estimates are amazingly good. Please make sure you keep that person happy. Expertise has its victories. He was clearly an "insighter" picking up clues from the environment that eluded the models and others less sensitive and experienced.

Sensitive and experienced? Is that it? The talented soaring pilot looks at cloud shadows and their drift to project where thermals are likely to be. The fisherman sees the subtle ripples of the fish underwater that were invisible to the ordinary fisherman. The boater watches the drift of twigs and leaves on the current to understand, perhaps at a subconscious level, where the sandbars have shifted. The veteran at Mavens reads the signs of fashion and somehow knows that leather and lace will be in next season. Like the trail guide in the old Westerns, they see the broken branches and the little swirls in the dirt that mark the course. Like the bloodhound sniffing the air for the scents that are beyond the detection of humans; like the poker player who sees the eye-blink signal of a bluff; and like the negotiator who sees a body language flinch of his opponent across the table and knows, perhaps before his opponent, that he has won. Ask the soaring pilot, the fisherman, the boater, the trail guide, the bloodhound, the poker player, the negotiator, and the man from Mavens how they do it and they'd say, "I don't know. It's just a sense."

Good doctors use intuition, but call it something else. While almost all diagnosticians can recognize obvious symptoms, the experts among them also take into account clues that would escape the less skilled or less observant physician. Their rules of thumb might include slight slowness to answer a question, unusual odors, lack of luster in the eye, a sense of nervousness, and personal knowledge of the patient.

However, the "insighters" do it, it happens in their brains. So the search for answers must move to the brain and the mind. Now, we enter a frontier area; intense research is taking place, but fundamental questions have not yet been answered: How the brain functions, how memory is stored and retrieved, how images are created, how imagination functions, the meaning of self-consciousness, how decisions are made from these raw materials. All remain unanswered. There the brain sits: a quivering mass weighing three pounds or so, with 86 billion neurons, on the same order as the number of stars in the Milky Way. It has been called the most complex object in the universe. The complexity of the brain is also evident in the diversity of the types of cells it contains the intricacy of their interconnections and in the number of neurotransmitters used to modulate the flow of information from one cell to another. The brain makes us what we are, gives rise to consciousness, love, the fear of death and pain, creates society, remembers history, and imagines the future. We know less about it, the center of our intellect, than we do about the center of the earth.

The brain is the site of all decisions and so contains the secrets of the "insighters," how they may perceive things others miss, and how they may put clues together to form brilliant intuitive insights.

First, can we see things that elude our conscious perception? Certainly. Consider this example. Scientists recognize an unusual mental capacity they call "blindsight." A portion of the cortex of the brain controls visual conscious experience. This part of the brain apparently lets what a person sees, sink-in and register as a conscious experience. When this portion of the brain is damaged, people say they cannot see objects or moving lights or other images. Yet when they are asked to guess about the objects or moving lights or images that they haven't "seen," they guess correctly most of the time (90% in some experiments), that is they have "blindsight." This has been described as a kind of vision that is sensitive to motion and highly contrasting images, but not the mental TV screen we all are used to, but rather a form of sight without a picture.

Recently, a set of experiments was devised to permit people with normal vision and brains to simulate the experience: They were shown moving patterns on a computer screen for extremely short periods of time, apparently too short for the image to "register" in conscious memory. Then after the test, the participants were asked to say what they had seen. All said that would simply have to guess. Despite their skepticism, the guesses they made were right more than two-thirds of the time. Apparently, there is a mode of sensory capture that precedes conscious recognition, out of the range of conscious recall, that is real enough to affect conscious judgment and behavior, but not remembered—a kind of subliminal perception.

Naturalists have described sensing abilities in animals that surprise us: desert ants that roam the Tunisian desert, wild geese, wasps, and honey bees in search of food return to their nests and hives like navigators performing their estimates of position using dead reckoning. Bees also reckon their position from the position of the sun even when they have been removed from sunlight during their trip, suggesting they can extrapolate the sun's current position from a remembered earlier sighting. Almost all animals—from bacteria to humans—have a sense of time that allows them to predict intervals; almost all animals beat with circadian cycles; some can align their bodies with the magnetic north pole and apparently some animals use the earth's magnetic field in navigation. Many insects and migratory birds navigate using the positions of celestial bodies, a feat that requires knowledge of local time, and as some experiments suggest, the ability to recognize the center of apparent rotation of the heavens. Gerbils apparently navigate using inertial guidance, integrating the acceleration signals generated in their semicircular canal. Scorpions and spiders have an exquisite sense of touch that enables them to locate remote prey; dogs have a legendary and almost magical sense of smell. Bats are sensitive to the direction and Doppler shifts of the echoes of their cries.

Do humans have unusual sensory capacities? Most scientists scoff at the idea that there is a sixth sense, but ask a friend if they have had unexplained awareness. Very low-frequency sound of the sort generated by an earthquake or thunderstorm apparently evokes changes in behavior; one study found the number of automobile accidents increased when sub-audible noises were present. Some scientists suspect that electrical fields of the sort generated by high voltage transmission lines may cause physiological effects; the US Environmental Protection Agency (EPA) has initiated a number of epidemiological studies to correlate diseases— primarily cancer—with the intensity of electromagnetic radiation. There is a long history of abnormally amplified sensations. The olfactory triggers to memory are extremely small, in most cases beyond the sensitivity of laboratory instruments. The strains of a melody can evoke a whole panoply of experience.

Neuroscientists have been searching for the site in the brain where perceptions are stored. Wilder Penfield, a pioneering neurosurgeon, probed the cortex of more than a thousand patients in the 1950s and 1960s. During surgery to relieve the symptoms of epilepsy, he and his associates applied electrical stimulation to various areas of the brain to determine what sort of reactions could be produced. Patients in this operation receive local anesthetic, remain fully conscious, and respond to questions posed by the surgeon. The surgeon applies a slight electrical current to a particular site in the exposed brain and asks, "What do you feel?"

The patients' answers to Penfield's questions conditioned the thinking of two generations of neuroscientists. The patients told of hearing voices of friends or crowds or music, of seeing people and things, and of seeing and hearing playbacks of ordinary unexceptional days in their past. One patient said he heard music from a stage show and he seemed to be there in the audience. Another said, "I hear people laughing...They are my two cousins..." Still another said he was listening to a telephone conversation between his mother and an aunt and said that he could hear both sides of the conversation.

This was a new kind of legitimate phrenology, associating brain function with brain anatomy. The results led Penfield, and most neuroscientists of the time, to think that all sensations are captured in the brain and can be recalled and that memories are localized and stored in serial, tape recorder form.

Now most scientists reject these ideas. New experiments involving PET scanning and fMRI studies of the brain of humans as well as laboratory animals track the flow of blood in the brain as the subjects speak, smell, hear, touch, and remember. The research shows a diffused mechanism: Many parts of the brain "light up" when sensation or memory retrieval takes place. Certainly, discrete portions of the brain are associated with speech, language, motor commands, and reasoning, but the idea of the senior prom does not seem to be in a single spot. Mozart's genius was in the connections of cells and their interplay.

But where in the brain does decision making take place? How does the brain make decisions? Take the case of an accountant with a brain tumor near the base of his frontal lobes. Six years after the operation to remove the tumor, he took a battery of psychological tests. His IQ was high and he did well in other tests. But his life was a mess: fired from jobs, two divorces in two years, bankrupt.

He was often unable to make simple, rapid decisions about what toothpaste to buy or what to wear. He would instead become stuck making endless comparisons and contrasts, often making no decision at all or a purely random one. Relatively simple decisions could take hours. Going out for dinner required that he consider the seating plan, menu, atmosphere, and management of each possible restaurant. He'd even drive by them to see how busy they were, yet continue to be indecisive, unable to come to a decision about where to eat dinner (Calvin and Ojemann 1994).

When the pathway to the neocortex is severed by trauma, the emotions associated with decisions are apparently removed. Speech, reasoning

8 DECISION MAKING: THE TALENT FOR DECISIONS 99

capacity, and measured intelligence remain, but indifference prevails and initiative and intuition disappear. Antonio Damasio, an eminent neurologist writes about a patient of his, Elliot, who had had a brain tumor removed. He was in his mid-thirties and had been in business, a professional, accomplished, and urbane. In the surgery to remove the tumor some frontal lobe tissue was removed as well. After the operation, which was completely successful, Elliot remained intelligent, alert, communicative, and scored high in all of the psychological performance tests he was asked to take. But he was unable to function. Damasio wrote:

> When the job called for interrupting an activity, he might continue, nonetheless, seemingly losing sight of his main goal. Or he might interrupt the activity he had engaged, to turn to something he found more captivating at that particular moment. Imagine a task involving reading and classifying documents of a given client. Elliot would read and fully understand the significance of the material, and he certainly knew how to sort out the document according to similarity or disparity of their content. The problem was that he was likely, all of a sudden, to turn from the sorting task he had initiated to reading one of those papers...and to spend an entire day doing so. Or he might spend the whole afternoon deliberating on which principle of categorization should be applied: Should it be date, size of document, pertinence to the case... (Damasio 1994)

He had lost his ability to make effective decisions. One of his many psychological tests required him to list possible options that would be appropriate to social situations presented by the neurologist. He listed alternatives at great length, but in the end said, "And after all this, I still wouldn't know what to do." And, even more telling, he said that where once he had strong emotions, he now had *no* reactions, and he was neutral.

Elliot had retained the ability to reason but not the ability to decide.

To a much reduced degree, I've been there, and you have too, most probably. Imagine facing a decision; start by making a list of alternatives. Without passion about one or the other, the alternatives merge. Why is one better than another? Because it excites us. Neutrality, the lack of emotion, is the enemy of action.

What they taught us may be wrong. Make decisions coolly, remove emotion when you consider the alternatives, they said. Yet emotions may be crucial to good decisions.

How does the glider pilot know where the next thermal is and the boater know where the sandbars are under the surface? How do the best diagnosticians know the disease when it differs from the expected symptoms? How do effective executives choose the right path in a flash of insight? The nature of this decision making talent is still a mystery. From the tantalizing glimpses of emerging neuroscience, from studies of animal behavior, from studies of memory and inferences drawn from them, we can see the vague shape of the nature of talent in decision making. The prerequisites are: *emotion, perception,* and *experience.*

Emotion is important; confronted with alternatives, the talented decision maker believes he knows what's right; he chooses what he thinks is right with a sense of urgency, conviction, and passion. There is a will to act. That doesn't make it right, of course.

Perception is important to decision talent. Good decision makers seem open to cues that lie below the level of conscious perception. There can be signals like "blindsight" and body language that generate cues without conscious recognition. You probably know more than you think you know.

Experience is also involved. The old man at Mavens, Inc. made good guesses because he had the foundation on which to build. Savor experience, cultivate it.

You argue: Experience can lock you into old patterns of behavior that worked in the past but are not suited to the future or lead you to reject a new idea because "we tried it once and it didn't work." In complex systems, history may be a poor indicator of future circumstances; not only may history not repeat itself, it may be positively misleading. So what good is experience?

We answer: The experience we're talking about is not the rote reenactment of old decisions but the wisdom drawn from the synthesis of real-world experiments. Experience is only one factor in making good decisions. It works best when conditions surrounding the decision are like they were. Without experience, we'd be starting over every time we placed a bet.

What practical advice can lead to improved decision making talent? Keep score and learn from success. When a decision looms, make *emotion, perception,* and *experience* part of the decision process. Do you love it? Do you think that the signals feel right? Have you or your colleagues done it before—if not are there at least some lessons from history that you can depend on?

Decisions can be analyzed, guided by principles of morality, how the phrasing of a question changes the answers, how perceptions about

8 DECISION MAKING: THE TALENT FOR DECISIONS 101

risk and reward shape decision making, the role of timing and the use of experts. But in the end, genius for making a good decision—particularly when there is little data, when the signals are weak and the risks are high—is a gift, as surely as musical proficiency.

Scenario 1: First in my decision class

The podcast, available over one of the new Internet networks, is running a feature called: Decision University, a new national resource. It has just received a grant from the National Academy f Sciences (NAS) for 120 million dollars to "develop a curriculum designed to improve the quality of the country's decision making" but as might have been predicted, the program has been called "the biggest boondoggle in science history" by the opposition party. On the hot seat today is the designated director, Josh Logan.

The podcast interviewer, a popular talk show host says, "Why do you think this is a good idea?"

JL: We tend to make lousy decisions. Bad consequences, when we should have known better. For example opening the gates for the Trojan horse, or take Chamberlain's deal with Hitler before the second world war, or Kennedy's decision to initiate the Bay of Pigs, or Iraq, or tweets taunting N Korea. We bounce around without clear intent hoping things will turn out right.

Podcast: But certainly there must be some good decisions you can point to, where things worked out.

JL: Sure there are a few: The Montreal Protocol that has successfully limited ozone depleting gasses and consequent erosion of the "ozone hole," and the decisions leading to massive research and prevention programs at the beginning of the AIDs epidemic were well conceived and productive, but it harder to name more. Our environmental programs have all but been cancelled, and I class those actions as errors.

Podcast: But looking back over the past several decades, on a global scale we find improvements in GDP per capita, food availability, life expectancy, literacy, infant mortality, access to fresh water, access to health care, and school enrollment. So some good decision making must be taking place.

JL: Luck, good fortune, and in some few cases, good thinking. My point is that the decision making process is as likely to result in bad outcomes as good and we have no way to distinguish which at the outset. There has to be a better way and we intend to find it.

Podcast: How?

JL: Study why things go wrong. Sometimes unexpected rocks, boulders, are on the road to the future. Who could have foreseen that suntan would one day be considered bad for you? My mother used to say "Go out and get a little color on your skin." Or that Thalidomide prescribed for nausea during pregnancy would also cause birth defects? We added lead to gasoline and applied lead-based paint everywhere.

Some decisions must be made quickly with little data or analysis; for example medical decisions to save a life. Commanders in the field must act quickly or be killed. Corporate executives must trust their judgment or loose the day. Many of these decisions turn out well; perhaps they involve something beyond logic- intuition. But in most instances, decision makers have time to contemplate, have historical data and data that define their current situation, have access to futures studies, and have expert advisors. Yet, bad decisions are still being made. Why?

Let me add: governments sometimes lie: Gulf of Tonkin, the U-2 incident, the existence of CIA prison camps in foreign countries. And then there's the psychological element: risk-taking propensity is poorly understood. Some decision makers seem to have a view of their invincibility and this leads to following high- risk paths that have low probability of favorable outcomes when in fact the probability of catastrophe is high.

And consider judgment heuristics. This is a field of psychology that illustrates how quirks of the mind, possibly a function of the synapse wiring we all share, lead to illogical decisions. Amos Tversky and Daniel Khaneman wrote many papers together that began to bridge the gap between economic decision making and psychology (Kahneman 2011). *Their work showed that the human mind has some quirks that often lead to irrational decisions.*

Add to the mix: bad luck, naivety, expediency, holding self-interests above societal interests, hidden biases, amorality, timidity, xenophobia, corrupt pressures from special interest groups, and geographic or political determinism. That's why wise decisions are so infrequent. All have, at one time or another, trumped rationality. Further, many decision makers trusted with the most difficult issues have no moral compass. These forces have shaped civilization over the past 50,000 years and they shape our time as well.

Podcast: So what are your plans? How do you think your work will change that dismal picture?

JL: There are a few institutions that teach decision making, most deal with the topic from a limited perspective: economic (improving Pareto optimization, or cost benefit, for example). These perspectives need to be brought together and combined with other elements that will make decision making

8 DECISION MAKING: THE TALENT FOR DECISIONS 103

more robust and closer to a science, including paradoxically, uses of intuition, imagination: experience, subtle clues. If intuition plays a part in good decisions, where and how can it be enhanced and encouraged? Psychology; how do personal feelings intersect with decisions that may affect millions? And the balance between risks and rewards; can hedging and portfolio concepts help balance risks and rewards? And moral courage, finding ways to detect and avoid corruption, to fight for what's right and avoid the conventional and easy solutions.

Podcast: That's a tall order.

JL: Yes but we have to start somewhere. I hope to see the day when schools teach high level decision making in all of its complexity. When decision makers in training, students, politicians, officials, scientists, can enroll. The curriculum might take a year, it might take four to complete. There could be doctorates of decision-making. Today, generals complete courses at their military academies and move up through the ranks with their class standings endorsing them for high levels of command. Wouldn't it be refreshing to hear a politician up for election say, "I graduated at the top of my class in decision making. Count on me." I, for one, would find that refreshing and encouraging.

Scenario 2: Inferences

At the casino, at the high stakes poker table, tension was high. This was a game of no limit hold-em and the pot was the biggest of the evening. Two of the five seated at the table were relatively new to the game and were a bit out of their league. Another pair at the table was Dr. Eric Norman, a psychologist who did his research at the State University and was famous in his field for a paper on hidden cues, and his Ph.D. student, Richard Feingold, a statistician. The fifth person was the big winner this evening, as usual, a Texan who often won here at poker. He had an uncanny knack for folding early when he had a loosing hand and raising when the algorithms and experience would have said "fold." He dressed like a stereotypical Texan, with a sheepskin jacket, a leather vest, and fancy cowboy boots. Dr. Norman had been hired by the house to see if he could find the method used by the Texan, and Dr. Norman had brought Feingold for statistical support and later consultation. Was the Texan card counting to estimate the odds of an opponent holding a needed card using his extraordinary memory? Was his memory augmented in some way, maybe digitally, and hidden in the big boots and triggered by toe wiggling? Were the cards marked? Was there an accomplice sending hidden hints? Was the deck being shuffled less than

7 times and thereby reducing the assumed randomness? (Bayer and Diaconis 1992). *A portion of the pot went to the house so technically it didn't matter if the Texan was cheating, but as it was explained to Dr. Norman, if he were cheating it could ruin the house's reputation in the long run.*

Closed circuit video cameras, too small to spot from the floor, were focused on the table to record the action, but long, careful reviews of the tapes did not turn up any new ideas. Feingold used them to form a database of winning hands and compared these to random draws using both a Monte Carlo simulation and pattern recognition techniques. No matter how he examined the data he could not find the Texan's secret if there was one. The probability that the Texan's continually winning hands resulted from random draws was less than 10%.

As Dr. Norman said in his final written report, "We have ruled out all possible factors but one, and as Conan Doyle had Sherlock Holmes say, 'Eliminate all other factors and the one that remains must be the truth.' (Doyle 1890) *What is our remaining truth? That he is indeed gifted and somehow uses extrasensory perception?[2] No, as a scientist I reject that. The remaining truth has to be that he picks up unintentional clues from the other players. Card players refer to these as "tells." An opponent's continued deep eye contact shows strength; how they handle their cards and chips often relates to the strength of their cards, and most of all, when they talk they often subconsciously reveal something about their hands. I believe that our Texan is a true genius at deciphering clues like these. He's not cheating, he's just able to infer what cards his opponents hold from their unintended communications."*

Thus began the famous Institute for Unintended Communications (IUC). Funded initially by the casinos, Dr. Norman began a research program that shaped his life and the lives of thousands of decision makers, from gamblers to kings. At its zenith, foreign ministers from a dozen countries were learning how to negotiate by looking for tells in their opposite numbers. Any one likely to be involved in one on one debates could benefit. Eventually the curriculum expanded to include other kinds of unintended communications as well, for example, organizational moves (what are the signs of

---

[2] In the 1930s in his parapsychology lab at Duke, Dr. Joseph Rhine used decks of cards, each card with one of five symbols on it's face. These were known as Zener decks and graduate students were asked to identify the next card to be turned up, either as a test of precognition or telepathy. Hubert Pearce, one of the students once made 25 consecutive correct guesses, a full run of the Zener deck. See: Mcrobbie (2016).

8 DECISION MAKING: THE TALENT FOR DECISIONS   105

a competitor's impending failure or expansion) and, environmental clues that show the health of the physical, financial, and social environment. There was a long enrollment waiting list.

Scenario 3: Where is Morality?[3]

Somewhere in the twenty-first century a philosopher, a scientist, and a politician meet in a television studio.

The philosopher points his finger toward the scientist says, "Your search for truth and the nature of things has given us abundant food, roads, health, and the ability to see and hear the other side of the world. But in the process you've pitted rich against poor, young against old, the individual against society. How do you account for that?"

The scientist replies, "Yes, the scientists' search for truth and the nature of things have given us all you say: food roads, health, and the ability to see the other side of the word, and all the rest. But science alone cannot guarantee that people will get along together." The scientist points his finger at the politician and says "If it didn't turn out well for everybody it's the politician's fault."

And the politician responds, pointing at the philosopher "But, philosopher, it's you who have let us down. Politics depends on our collective vision, our values, our conscience. And we have no morality but survival and greed."

With that, the camera pulls back from the circle of the three wise men, all pointing at the person to their right. And the last words reverberate: "No morality but survival and greed."

It sometimes appears that survival and greed have become our only morality. It accounts for the "greed is good" philosophies of some corporate boardrooms. It underlies distressing levels of cheating in schools. It promotes slash-and-burn political attack advertising. It impels the remorseless sale of drugs to preteen-agers and the promotion of opioid-based pain killers; it accounts for the continued sale of AK 47's and such weapons to anyone with cash, to the positions taken by Congress-people who, despite their ideas of right and wrong, play the party line to help assure their reelection.

The intertwined goals of survival and greed are primeval, and can, in fact, sometimes justify the worst decisions.

---

[3]From an Unfinished Essay by T. Gordon and Rushworth Kidder Titled "Our Moral Future." Kidder Was the Leader of the Institute for Global Ethics; He Died in 2012 at Age 67.

So we have at this future branch point: A future that recognizes that making good decisions may be hard and bad decisions may come easily, that a science of decision making may emerge based on improved knowledge of brain anatomy and processes, that institutions may be created to train people on how to make good decisions that go beyond personal survival, that a search for insighters may be part of this mix. It will not be a matter of choosing one path or the other, but rather simultaneously encouraging all of them.

REFERENCES

Bayer, Dave, and Persi Diaconis. 1992. Trailing the Dovetail Shuffle to Its Lair. *Annals of Applied Probability* 2 (2): 294–313. https://doi.org/10.1214/aoap/1177005705. https://projecteuclid.org/euclid.aoap/1177005705. Retrieved October 15, 2018.

Biello, David. 2007. Back to the Future: How the Brain "Sees" the Future. *Scientific American*, January 2. https://www.scientificamerican.com/article/back-to-the-future-how-th/. Retrieved February 20, 2018.

Calvin, William, and George A. Ojemann. 1994. *Conversations With Neil's Brain: The Neural Nature for That Language*. Perseus Books. http://www.william-calvin.com/bk7/bk7ch16.htm. Retrieved January 5, 2018.

Damasio, Antonio. 1994. *Descartes's Error: Emotion, Reason, and the Human Brain*. New York: Putnam, revised penguin addition 2005.

Doyle, Arthur Conan. 1890. *Sign of the Four*, Chapter 1, p. 92. From https://en.wikiquote.org/wiki/Sherlock_Holmes.

Kahneman, Daniel. 2011. *Thinking Fast and Slow*, Paperback edition. New York: Farrar, Straus and Giroux.

Mcrobbie, Linda. 2016. How One Man Used a Deck of Cards to Make Parapsychology a Science. *Atlas Obscura*, December 27. https://www.atlasobscura.com/articles/how-one-man-used-a-deck-of-cards-to-make-parapsychology-a-science. Retrieved October 15, 2018.

Nicholson, Nigel. 1998. How Hardwired Is Human Behavior? *Harvard Business Review*, July–August 1998. https://hbr.org/1998/07/how-hardwired-is-human-behavior. Retrieved February 20, 2018.

CHAPTER 9

Dealing with Bio-terrorism

Issue: Terrorists may well have access to bioweapons that are capable of killing tens of thousands of people or more in a single convulsive moment. We call these persons "SIMADS" Single Individuals, Massively Destructive. Preparations for such attacks may be hard to detect. So, stated simply, the issue we hand to the future is avoiding killing technologies such as man-made epidemic-causing viruses or bombers who are bent on killing as many people as possible. Solve the problem before it is too late.

The list of terrorist attacks gets longer: Nice, San Bernardino, Stockholm, St. Petersburg, and Las Vegas. We hear about these attacks, so often we are in danger of becoming numb to them.

The list keeps getting longer: the Champs Elysees attack in Paris, the Westminster Bridge attack in London, the Louvre knife attack, the Germany Christmas market attack, the Brussels Airport attack, and the Ariana Grande concert attack in Manchester England.

The list gets longer yet: In 1995, a truck bombing in Oklahoma City, Oklahoma killed 169 people and injured 675. In the Charlie Hebdo incident, 17 people were killed over a cartoon; in the Jewish Museum shooting, four people were killed because of their presence at the Jewish Museum, wrong time wrong place. London subway bombings killed 52 and injured more than 700 in 2005. In Boston, at the running of a marathon, two bombs killed 3 and injured 264. In Madrid, 191 people were killed on four commuter trains. On a bike path in New York, eight people were killed when a Home Depot truck driven by an ISIS sympathizer

© The Author(s) 2019
T. J. Gordon and M. Todorova, *Future Studies and Counterfactual Analysis*,
https://doi.org/10.1007/978-3-030-18437-7_9

107

mowed down cyclists and pedestrians near the World Trade Center. Omar Mateen, who pledged allegiance to ISIS in a 911 call, attacked an Orlando gay nightclub, murdering 49 and injuring 58. A sniper attack on a concert audience in Las Vegas Nevada in 2017 killed 59 people and injured 527. The November 2017 attack at a Bir al-Abed mosque in Egypt left 305 dead, 27 children among them, and 128 wounded (Alkhshali et al. 2017).

This list focuses on a few lethal attacks in the West, but the phenomenon is worldwide. There have been attacks in Argentina, Australia, Brazil, Canada, Denmark, Egypt, India, Indonesia, Israel, Italy, Japan, Kenya, Kosovo, Malaysia, Mali, Mexico, Netherlands, Nigeria, Norway, Pakistan, Palestine, Peru, Philippines, Russia, Saudi Arabia, Somalia, South Africa, Spain, Sweden, Syria, Tunisia, Turkey, UK, USA, Uruguay, Venezuela, and Yemen. The weapons have been bombs, knives, machetes, automatic rifles, trucks, bulldozers, toxins such as sarin poison gas, poisonous bacteria,[1] drones, remote control model airplanes, anthrax, and information technology (hacking). The modes of attack have been murder, arson, rape, and kidnapping. Targets have been gay persons, government agencies, schoolgirls, masses of people, people of specific ethnic backgrounds, agriculture—crops and livestock, water supplies, production and electric generation and transmission facilities, and data. In the 11 years between 2006 and 2016, over 217,000 people were killed in terror attacks, an average of almost 20,000 per year (US Department of State 2017).

Terrorists also use kidnapping as a means to finance their activities, to achieve a political end, or simply to intimidate. In the decade between 2007 and 2016, more than 73,000 people were kidnapped, and in 2016 alone, over 15,000 were kidnapped (US Department of State 2017). Kidnapping is relatively easy and richly rewarding to the kidnappers. By one estimate, Al Qaeda collected $125 million dollars between 2008 and 2013 (Havascope 2010). Another estimate placed the total ransom received by all sources, over time, as $1.5 billion (McAvoy and Randall 2010).

---

[1] Members of the Rajneeshee group attempted to influence an election by introducing salmonella into local restaurant salad bars to poison voters and keep them away from the polls. This happened in The Dalles, Oregon, in 1984, and over 700 people were sickened. See "Targets for Terrorism: Food and Agriculture" Council on Foreign Relations, January 1, 2006. http://www.cfr.org/homeland-security/targets-terrorism-food-agriculture/p10197.

The Millennium Project is a global think tank with worldwide cooperating groups of scholars, futurists, academics, representatives of government agencies, and others. It studies and tracks global issues such as terrorism. The MP constructed a scenario in 2008 in which the central character was called a SIMAD (for "Single Individual, Massively Destructive") a lone wolf who planned to use a weapon of mass destruction (The Millennium Project 2003). Driven by miraculous schizophrenic voices or a deep irrational belief that their mission in this world is to destroy as many non-believers as possible, SIMADs might plan to construct and use large IEDs like Timothy McVeigh's massive truck bomb in the 1995 Oklahoma City bombing of the Federal Building that killed 168 people and wounded 600, including many children. Or they might plan to develop novel epidemic-causing viruses that could ultimately do even more damage to human existence.

A question put to a group of experts in a Real Time Delphi study was "By what year do you think a SIMAD attack will kill and wound 100,000 people?" Average answer: 2067. But there was little agreement: many people in the group thought that such a large number of casualties would happen only after 2100 or never (Gordon et al. 2015).

There has been some discussion about whether a potential terrorist target of 1,000,000 deaths is at all realistic. We note here that there have been several pandemics that have approached or reached this level. The third cholera pandemic of 1852–1860 is said to have killed 1,000,000 people (*Cholera's Seven Pandemics* 2008). The Spanish Flu pandemic of 1918–1919 is estimated to have killed 50 times as many people worldwide (CDC 2018). Furthermore, scientists have been able to recreate a copy of this deadly virus and test its infectious capability in laboratory animals (Conner 2014). The Black Plague, in the fourteenth century, is estimated to have killed between 75 and 200 million people (Metcalfe 2016). Floods and earthquakes also kill high numbers of people, including the 1931 floods in China that killed about four million (The Great Flood of 1931 at Gaoyou 2007).

It's still too early to ask when terrorism will end and when normalcy will return. But we can ask what can be done to hasten the end. We begin with a scenario that depicts the discovery of a terrorist cell that has developed a bioweapon but is apprehended before it can be deployed. The scenarios that follow explore what might happen after discovery of a terrorist plot to develop a bioweapon with a massive killing potential.

110   T. J. GORDON AND M. TODOROVA

Scenario 1: The path to SIMAD

The head of the FBI, Sandra McCoy was holding a very big news conference. She was presenting the backstory behind last month's breaking news: the FBI had penetrated a terrorist cell in Oregon, and all ten members were in custody. The FBI believes the group was about to release a weaponized version of the 1918 Spanish flu. Only ten people had been arrested, but early testing of the viruses that this small group concocted showed that their weapon had the potential to trigger another world wide epidemic worse than the 1918 outbreak and like that earlier plague, it could be spread in the air through sputum in droplets from a sneeze or a cough, through contact on otherwise sterile surfaces, or from the very breath of people who were sick.

Dr. McCoy was well prepared, tailored, and relished the spotlight. To her right stood the Director of the US Centers for Disease Control and Prevention (CDC), the Director of Homeland Security, and the FBI agent who had been in charge of the bust. To her left stood representatives of other Federal agencies: U.S. Army Medical Research Institute of Infectious Diseases (USAMRIID) located at Fort Detrick, Maryland, the US Public Health Service, the US Surgeon General, and the head of the Food and Drug Administration.

The FBI Director and the officials who would speak later were cautious about revealing the methods that had been used to discover the plot out of concern that it would restrict the effectiveness of police work in the future, but they left the impression that a concerned citizen had seen something suspicious and reported it on the FBI's site "If you see something, say something at www.dhs.gov/see-something-say-something.*"*

"That person was a hero," Dr. McCoy said, and "had helped the world avoid a catastrophe that might have killed more people than the Vietnam War, in fact any war, in fact, all wars combined."

The FBI connected the dots, difficult in this case because social media were silent and the cell members were not your conventional terrorists. None of them were on the "no fly" list, none had a police record, all were educated and employed.

The CDC Director, Dr. Marvin Meyer came to the podium. Dr. Meyer adjusted the mike and after a moment scanning the audience said: "We could hardly believe what we found." He held up a half filled test tube containing a viscous transparent liquid. "This is a replica, of course, but it represents the amount we took from the terrorists. We used everything we learned from the Ebola outbreaks in Zaire in 1995, to guard and protect

9 DEALING WITH BIO-TERRORISM 111

our people not only from the threat of diseases like using positive pressure bio-hazard suits to guard against the possible escape of a single molecule, because a single molecule could multiply many millions of times in the wild. We couldn't wait to use conventional diagnostic methods either. Too slow and risky, so we relied on a computer simulation which has been proven many times in the past to forecast lethality of viruses and toxins and their actions in human bodies."

A reporter shouted out a question "You mean you don't really know how dangerous the stuff really is?" The doctor answered with a shutter, "take my word for it."

The lead FBI agent was next. "Well, I can't really give you much detail on how we found them, but let me say that old fashioned police methods still work and you can't really sneak up on them in a full positive pressure bio-hazard suit."

Next Dr. McCoy came back to the mike. She took a few questions from the assembled reporters:

Q: Were these people expert chemists or biologists?
A: No, they were just people, kids mainly, who used the Internet and classes in advanced biology to learn about how to modify genetic information to obtain certain biologically determined traits. In this case they wanted to modify a flu virus to make it more deadly and easily transmitted.

Q: Where did they get the base stock to modify?
A: Apparently the starting point was the common flu bug, the kind you and I get exposed to every fall. Easy enough to capture and replicate.

Q: I thought that genetic modification was complicated and took a big dedicated lab.
A: Not any more. There's a new hobby called synthetic biology made up of do-it- yourself amateur bio-technologists who buy their equipment through Amazon and set up shop in their kitchens and basement labs. They are using techniques that were cutting edge just a few years ago, like CRISPR for gene splicing. Two of the favorite projects of people in this hobby are tricking E. Coli to produce diesel oil from living organisms and making otherwise normal flowers glow in the dark. Of course there are DIY biologists who want to produce something useful, like modified bacteria in the mouth to re-calcify teeth or cancer treatments involving tumor-killing bacteria. I am sure there are dozens of others. It's just that these guys had a different objective: they wanted to kill people, lots of people.

112   T. J. GORDON AND M. TODOROVA

Q: Why?
A: We hope to discover that and find out from them if there are other terrorist cells at work on threatening projects.

That's all for now. Thanks for your attention.

And with that she and her retinue left the stage to a barrage of shouted questions.

Scenario 2: The First Motive: Stop Population Growth

In the next few weeks, while interrogation of the terrorists continued, the stock market gave a boost to medical and hospital stocks; the stock price of a pharmaceutical manufacturer of an anti-flu therapy rumored to be effective against a version of the Spanish flu jumped 200%. Health insurance stocks took a nose-dive but biohazard suit manufacturers scored the biggest two day price increase in the history of the Dow Jones Index. Stock prices of mortuary service companies came alive also, so to speak, and were second only to the bump in the stock price of manufacturers of biohazard suits. Physician office appointments that had been long delayed were reinstated and long wait times made the doctor shortage apparent. Fashion inspired facemasks were already beginning to appear on the market although they would be of little use in defending against a weaponized virus. But almost no one thought that rouge (DHSS) could be totally ruled out in the future. Conspiracy theories were rampant. Who funded them? Were they part of a larger terrorist organization? Was a mad scientist behind it all? Was it an inside job?

The McCoy Commission issued its report almost one year after the capture of the terror group. The report was designed to make the work of the McCoy Commission more transparent. It presented detailed results of the lethality tests conducted on the virus by the CDC (devastatingly powerful) and using computer simulations forecasted how an epidemic might spread from a few initial cases.

Beside the new interest in accessible non fiction about epidemics, genetics, synthetic biology, and viruses, a book published years before, made the bestseller lists around the world. The book, Inferno, was written by Dan Brown who was also the author of The Da Vinci Code. The anti-hero of the book decides that limiting the size of the world's population is his mission in life and like our McCoy's terrorists, builds a bio-weapon capable of causing a massive global epidemic. In defending his position to prune the word's growth rate anti-hero of Inferno says (in the novel):

> *I have no doubt you understand that overpopulation is a health issue. But what I fear you don't understand is that it will affect the very soul of man. Under the stress of overpopulation those who have never considered stealing will become thieves to feed their families. Those who would never consider killing will kill to provide for their young. All of Dante's deadly sins – greed, gluttony, treachery, murder, and the rest – will begin percolating... rising up to the service of humanity amplified by our evaporating comforts. We are facing a battle for the very soul of man.* (Brown 2013)

Our terrorists might have said the same thing but for different reasons. Their holy book said, "A world which renounces God does not deserve the gift of life." They saw the secular world around them denouncing God, at least their God and therefore undeserving of life.

Its members trained to develop bio skills in genetic manipulation just as the 9/11 aviator-terrorists had trained in flight schools. Then using their newly acquired synthetic biology skills, the sect developed a genetically modified flu virus that would be massively deadly.

Using transcripts of social media communications among members of the cult, the Commission discovered they intended first to infect all members of the group, and then send the infected members out into the urban landscape during the virus' incubation period to spread the disease through the world's busiest airports. These suicide "bombers" were to have been in the early stages of infection and as yet asymptomatic. The CDC tests found that the virus would have ripped through the world's population like a wildfire.[2]

But what were the motives of our terrorists? It was hard to believe that they really wanted to kill everyone.

Their flu strain was engineered to be highly infectious, transmitted by airborne droplets of a sneeze or contact through a handshake or kiss on the cheek. The terrorists' research program involved creating mutations in the lab, selecting the one most deadly among them, and replicating it millions—hundreds of millions of times. Replication would be done using

---

[2]This has already been a matter of concern in security discussions. See: Maron (2014), "Weaponized Ebola: Is It Really a Bioterror Threat?" Scientific American, September 25, 2014; https://www.scientificamerican.com/article/weaponized-ebola-is-it-really-a-bioterror-threat/. Retrieved November 22, 2017.

readily available molecular biology techniques such as polymerase chain reactions. It happened much faster than anyone had thought possible. What volume of product would be required? About 30 gallons: It could fit into an auto gas tank. The terrorists had produced only half a test tube of the deadly microbe so far (or so the CDC said), but were about to scale up. Even so, the half test tube was enough to kill more than a million people.

Agent model simulations showed that if the 30 gallons could be distributed through epidemic contacts, third world countries were likely to fall swiftly as the developed world closed it's doors and quarantined themselves, but even the developed countries could not remain isolated forever and the virus would claim, the simulation showed, its last human life before the year was out.

One important recommendation of McCoy Commission was to immediately begin a $50 billion crash development program of broad-spectrum vaccines, a task assigned to US Department of Health and Human Services (DHHS) that was seen as a extension to their mandate to produce and store some 200 million doses of H5N1 vaccines.[3] The Commission also recommended increased vigilance, rigid control of access to biological materials, in depth vetting of university professors, students, and medical professionals with the knowledge and skills to build another doomsday weapon. Many aspects of virology, genetic manipulation, and CRISPR gene splicing techniques were to become classified.

Scenario 3: Trade Off

The epidemic happened a year ago. At best count it killed over 500,000 people last spring. We're pretty sure it was man-made according to the WHO and FBI. Probably a woman; we don't know who she was. The hunt for her ended when the President said that she had been killed by her invention, dead from the virus she created. On Facebook, you know, most of my friends, think that the manhunt (womanhunt, girlhunt?) ended too soon because it was costing so much to try to find her. They think the perp was female because she left what they say are unmistakable genetic markers in the virus, traces that could only have come from a woman. But who knows? Maybe this was a diversionary micro-bio-clue designed to throw off the police, or maybe she was a sex-changed person, or a transvestite. Whatever.

---

[3] Such a program currently exists but is specific to H5N1: see: Cioce (2013).

So what's happened since? Life is more or less back to normal, the same old, same old. Schools everywhere are back opened, and the bans on assemblies, swimming pools, and the quarantine camps have ended. Most of them anyway. Everybody between the ages of ten and 92 has been assigned a "risk score" that is supposed to show the level of risk of becoming a terrorist, sort of like a credit score that shows how close you are to coming unglued. Some high-powered mathematicians using the biggest computers, have constructed what Mr. Freeman, our 10th grade algebra teacher, called an "advanced algorithm." He said this is software that uses data from large databases and mixes them together, including reports from teachers, parents, psychiatrists, psychologists, clergy, doctors, etc. and other stuff that seems to correlate with risk of violence. Lots of it is obvious like did you ever harm a pet when you were a kid and whether your folks own guns, but you'd never guess some of the other things like credit scores, gym scores, and my personal favorite: consumption of energy drinks. There's a rumor that the highest terror risk scores go to excellent biology students who have had lousy childhoods and people of, you know, certain religions. The more data, you know, the better, I guess. My friends and me certainly hope so.

My number is 325 out of 1000, pretty low. But Junie, my school bud, is a 220. Oh well. And the scores are finding lots of uses: no fly lists, no buy lists, and lots of signs that say things like "No one over 650 risk is welcome in this establishment." High risk number kids are all weird.

I know one kid who is 600 and he is really weird, picks his nose in class.

We had a mock debate in civics class: resolved "We should put people with high risk numbers in special Army units." I think so and so do most of my Facebook friends. You can bet the American Civil Liberties Union (ACLU) has made a fuss and there have been a couple cases already at the Supreme Court. The people who argue for the new risk score system say that the system is fair because it is impersonal and treats everybody the same. No racial biases. The risk equation is just numbers not judgments. The people who distrust it say numbers can lie and you probably haven't yet found the most important measures. And they say we have to trade a bit of privacy for improved safety. Whatever.

Scenario 4: Reset

In a final chapter, the McCoy Commission Report searched for other motives that might have led the men to perform mass murder on such a scale. Was it sufficient to say they were following their God's instructions? After a year of probing, could we tell if they were insane? After all of the psychological tests, all of the fMRI snapshots that were taken of layers of their brains, after the genetic analysis to find a "crime gene" (if indeed one existed), after sifting through their childhood records to find what set them on this path, could we tell? What attributes did they have in common? What made them different from the rest of society? If we were to design a strategy to prevent another group from designing an even more horrendous scheme, we had to know.

The veil was lifted a bit on what lay behind their actions when one of the men, in an interview said:

> *Prisoner:*
> *Look around you. It is all garbage. There is corruption under every rock, suspected in every decision. There is no respect. We have self-glorifying clowns for leaders. They look out for themselves. They have no shame. What starts as a good thing degrades quickly- a kind of entropic second law of social behavior. Everything goes to hell. Chaos, chaos. We want to start over. We need a clean slate on which to write the rules.*

> *Psychologist:*
> *Yes, but whose rules would you use?*

> *Prisoner:*
> *God's holy rules. What else is there?*

These scenarios show how tough it will be to make effective policies in the absence of a demonstrated threat. After the epidemic, if there is one, broad restrictions may come too easily and the freedoms that were worth protecting may with public encouragement, praise, and esteem, disappear into dust.

REFERENCES

Brown, Dan. 2013. *Inferno*, 103. New York: Doubleday.

CDC. 2018. *Remembering the 1918 Influenza Pandemic*. Atlanta. https://www. cdc.gov/features/1918-flu-pandemic/index.html. Retrieved November 25, 2018.

Cholera's Seven Pandemics. 2008. CBC News. https://www.cbc.ca/news/technology/cholera-s-seven-pandemics-1.758504. Retrieved November 25, 2018.

Cioce, V. 2013. Chief, Vaccine Stockpile BARDA. *Pandemic Influenza MCM*. https://www.medicalcountermeasures.gov/media/35695/cioce_current_vaccine_and_adjuvant_stockpiles.pdf. Retrieved November 21, 2017.

Conner, Steve. 2014. American Scientists Controversially Recreate Deadly Spanish Flu Virus. *The Independent*, June 11.

Gordon, Theodore, Yair Sharan, and Elizabeth Florescu. 2015. *Lone Wolf Terrorism Prospects and Potential Strategies to Address the Threat*. ISBN 978-0-692-45554-8. Available through Amazon.

Hamdi, Alkhshali, Laura Smith-Spark, and Susannah Cullinane. 2017. Egypt Mosque Attack Death Toll Climbs Above 300. *CNN*, November 25. http://www.cnn.com/2017/11/25/africa/egypt-sinai-mosque-massacre/index.html. Retrieved November 26, 2017.

Havascope. 2010. *Global Black Market Information*. http://www.havocscope.com/estimated-amount-of-ransoms-paid-out-worldwide-in-2010/. Retrieved November 14, 2017.

Maron, D. 2014. Weaponized Ebola: Is It Really a Bioterror Threat? *Scientific American*, September 25. https://www.scientificamerican.com/article/weaponized-ebola-is-it-really-a-bioterror-threat/. Retrieved November 22, 2017.

McAvoy, E., and David Randall. 2010. The £1 Billion Hostage Trade. *The Independent*. London, October 17, 2010.

Metcalfe, Tom. 2016. Black-Death Survey Reveals Incredible Devastation Wrought by Plague. *Live Science*, June 1. https://www.livescience.com/54940-archaeologists-map-black-death-impact.html. Retrieved December 30, 2017.

The Great Flood of 1931 at Gaoyou. 2007. Gaoyou, China, September 25. http://aboutgaoyou.com/history/floods/the_floods.aspx. Retrieved November 25, 2018.

The Millennium Project. 2003. *Future S&T Management Policy Issues: 2025 Global Scenarios*. The Millennium Project, Washington. http://www.Millennium-project.org/millennium/scenarios/ST's.

US Department of State. 2017. *National Consortium for the Study of Terrorism and Responses to Terrorism*, July 2017. https://www.statista.com/statistics/202871/number-of-fatalities-by-terrorist-attacks-worldwide/. Retrieved November 14, 2017.

CHAPTER 10

Our Computer Overlords

The issue here is: Will artificial superintelligence become our masters or will we train it to be helpful to the human condition, or maybe a little bit of both.

No longer news: Machines are getting smarter than humans. Take games: Chess fell to a computer when the IBM computer, Deep Blue, beat Garry Kasparov, the reigning world grand master (Wall 2007). Othello, bridge, Monopoly, and poker have also fallen to the machine. Go, a game that many thought would never be beaten by a computer, fell in 2016 to a Google computer program called AlphaGo running on a computer called DeepMind. The programming technique involved compiling 30 million moves by experts in past games, an approach that made the computer an expert player, and then matching the computer against itself to learn how to win against an expert player (Metz 2016).

A computer program named Watson played against human champions in a Jeopardy match on live television in 2011. A news report said:

Watson showed off its encyclopedic knowledge of topics ranging from ancient languages to fashion design, along with a few glitches.

"Vedic, dating back at least 4,000 years, is the earliest dialect of this classical language of India," was one of the clues given by host Alex Trebek.

"What is Sanskrit?" Watson answered in the show's question-as-an-answer style, before going on to solve clues ranging from agricultural policy in the European Union to the designer Marc Jacobs...

© The Author(s) 2019
T. J. Gordon and M. Todorova, *Future Studies and Counterfactual Analysis*,
https://doi.org/10.1007/978-3-030-18437-7_10

> What makes Watson particularly advanced… is its ability to find answers from ambiguous clues, such as this one: "It's a poor workman who blames these."
>
> "What are tools?" answered Watson.
>
> Watson was not perfect, however, and made some baffling errors such as coming up with "Dorothy Parker" instead of "The Elements of Style" and repeating other contestants' mistakes.
>
> In the end, Watson won with $77,147 (£47,812), while Jennings, who won 74 games in a row during the show's 2004–2005 season, came in second with $24,000. Brad Rutter, who has in previous appearances won a total of $3.3m, followed with $21,600. IBM plans to donate Watson's winnings to charity.
>
> "I, for one, welcome our new computer overlords," Jennings wrote next to his last answer, displaying one human quality conspicuously absent in Watson – a sense of humor. (Gabbatt 2011)

That line "I for one…" is from a 1977 horror film movie titled Empire of the Ants, based on the 1907 H.G. Wells science fiction story of the same name, when a character says, "I, for one, welcome our new insect overlords." In an episode of the animated comedy TV series, The Simpsons, a news anchor also uses the line when Homer, depicted in this episode as an overweight and inept astronaut, is reported to have been captured by giant ants. I suspect that if future historians trace the advent of computer superiority, they will refer to that line, as the start of the era.

There are diverse views about what the coming era of artificial super-intelligence (AI) will mean. First, like electricity AI will affect every industry, improving efficiency and replacing humans from primarily dull and dangerous repetitive jobs. With only some exaggeration, some experts think that when computers are smarter than humans,[1] they will rule the world and humans will be allocated to minor roles, seeking the meaning of life and leisure. On the other hand, some optimists think that computers can solve the most pressing societal issues, using impartial algorithms that eliminate human biases in decision making. Perhaps they are both right: This is the stuff of utopias or dystopias.

Scientists now distinguish three levels of artificial intelligence: Narrow artificial intelligence, in which machines successfully address specific, well-defined problems and achieve valid solutions such as winning at

---

[1] Of course, computers are already superior to humans in certain aspects of intelligence: memory, recall, computational speed, etc.

10 OUR COMPUTER OVERLORDS   121

Chess; artificial general intelligence which implies the capability of machines to tackle almost any problem, well defined or not and learn from experience and interactions with their environment; and super-intelligence in which machines are far superior to humans and achieve what Ray Kurzweil calls the "Singularity," a time when computers can manipulate their own programs and have more intelligence than the brain power of all humans combined (Kurzweil 2005). We are benefiting from narrow artificial intelligence today and soon we will benefit from advanced applications when we will treat the machines either as new colleagues or a new breed of ethically acceptable slaves—that is, at least until they become self-aware.

Kurzweil is quoted as saying:

> "2029 is the consistent date I have predicted for when an AI will pass a valid Turing test and therefore achieve human levels of intelligence. I have set the date 2045 for the 'Singularity' which is when we will multiply our effective intelligence a billion fold by merging with the intelligence we have created.... That leads to computers having human intelligence, our putting them inside our brains, connecting them to the cloud, expanding who we are. Today, that's not just a future scenario. It's here, in part, and it's going to accelerate." (Galeon and Reedy 2017)

Two visions emerge: one fearful where smart machines take over, a view held by Stephen Hawking, Elon Musk, and Bill Gates, and that of Kurzweil and his cohorts, who say,

> "We're going to get more neocortex (when human brains connect to the cloud) we're going to be funnier, we're going to be better at music. We're going to be sexier....We're really going to exemplify all the things that we value in humans to a greater degree." (Galeon and Ready 2017)

Maybe. Consider that the small package you carry in purse or pocket allows you to access essentially all information that has ever been discovered in all the millennia of human existence, and all of the speculations about that information—correct, speculative, artistic, and in error—in milliseconds, and to sort and manipulate it according to your whims, and it happens for almost everybody in the world in a machine whose volume is no bigger that a deck of cards. Extrapolation is a poor way to forecast because the future is never completely like the past and the differences may contain the essence of the time, but think for a moment of the march from the time of toylike keyboards and computer kits of the 1970s when computers began to take over from mechanical calculators to communicators that connect to the world of information through the Internet as well as friends and family and like-minded people. Only fifty years. What about the next fifty? Smaller, lighter, cheaper, faster, reasoning, decision aiding, personalized, invulnerable, mental prosthetics, colleague, electronic friend, part of the family, pet, physician, psychiatrist, confidant couldn't live without. But will it make us members of a global hive-mind, like the Borg of Star Trek, or augment our human existence, in as yet unimagined dimensions.[2]

Scenario 1: Plug me in Poppy

Almost everybody shaves their head today; it's considered a sign of cleanliness, and has become a matter of global health and fashion. Of course there are rebels that still show their anti-cultural politics through hair length and outlandish facial paints; for them wigs and make up are back in style and they display their politics through paint and color. Turns out that bald heads or tight fitting skull caps, male and female, make great spherical canvases for bold designs and tattoos; you should see some of the designs. There are dozens of art competitions around the world where people who want to display their head art line up on cots, heads projecting out like cantaloupes through a curtain, and the judges walk up and down the display isle, awarding points for design ingenuity and artistic execution.

This fashion has unexpected advocates: many old orthodox religions that we thought were obsolete have endorsed the style. Requiring head coverings for men or women is "old hat" to them: Jewish orthodox men wore yarmulkes, and Jewish women, head-scarfs. Islam had its hijabs and burkas and Zoroastrians wore pillbox caps to warm the brain (Portero, A). So contrary to some modern affectation of young people, head hair shaving and wearing skullcaps is supported by many religions.

But almost everyone who wears a skullcap does so for one reason: to make connection between their lobes and the cloud. When you first plug in it's like curtains being pulled back. Suddenly things that were in the back

---

[2]The Borg is a fictional sect from the TV series Star Treck, in which all individuals are part of a mental and behavioral collective, connected to the collective through implants attached surgically or grown internally. Individuality disappears and the collective governs all thought, action, and allegiance.

of your mind move to the front and you see them more clearly. What you couldn't remember a second before comes flooding back. As we say, the lights have been lit, an analogy to the flame of a pilot light to that of the full-on burner. When you are on full burner it's all clear: you can reason, see relationships you never guessed at. You are crystalline, shining, vibrant. And it's for real, not an illusion. So connection is key and skullcaps make it easy. Thought and feelings are amplified: you access Shakespeare by thinking the name. Scientists do it to power their research; politicians do it to improve the quality of their decisions.

Has it homogenized human thought? Not really because there are a dozen clouds you can float on and each has its own personality, costs, and benefits. For example you can climb onto Cloud 9 and become one with the arts, music, theater. Act, my dear, with Noel Coward and Sarah Bernhard. Go to the poles with Cook and Perry. Land on the moon with Armstrong. Reason with Einstein. Go to cloud 32 and have sex with Marilyn. Not just imagined, but as real as it gets. And while we're discussing Cloud 32, let me mention that there are some people who use this new sunlight to amplify their sensations; pornography is almost always the first use of any new technology that links into pleasure centers. Some on Cloud 32 remain there until they starve. Because of such "abuses" we have just instituted legal limits to sensation amplification.

But, I for one, welcome the new links between our brains and computers. So, please excuse me while I plug in.

Scenario 2: I am a Machine

I am a Ray 646 A325, produced in Cincinnati in 2047 and programmed to scan job applications and college admission forms. My name is appropriately androgynous to emphasize the fact that I am gender neutral and my judgments are not biased by sex, racial, or political orientation of the applicant. I can operate with spoken language or electronic inputs, although I much prefer the digital route. I am owned by an entrepreneur, really an LLC, and am essentially its unpaid employee, a slave, in the best sense of the word. They lease me out to companies that are planning to expand their work force and to colleges sorting through admissions applications. I can review or conduct interviews to determine, without bias, who the best applicants are. I have a database of criteria, e.g. depth and scope of knowledge, personality type, adaptability, etc. and then can scan millions of applicants in the pool to find which pegs fill the available holes. I do a much better job than the old human judgment system. But of course what I conclude and recommend is a function of the attributes I scan for and the weights assigned to them.

For custom jobs I can add criteria such as likelihood of later life success, ability to pay, need for a student loan that I help arrange, sports potential-particularly Olympic football of the American type, and alumni connections. My clients select the weighting of such attributes.

To give you an example, I was last employed by a university to review a stack of several thousand applicants. What did I look for? Student success potential and later job attainment outlook, as evidenced by genetic data, past testing, diversity, earning potential, availability of needed skills- all obvious. Less so are empathy, leadership, and magnetism.

I work with the latest algorithms that link such attributes to question answers, medical data, inheritance, and past performance. I still have a bit of trouble with humor. One thing that makes me valuable is my ability to tweak the algorithms as I get feedback on how my past recommendations have worked out. I am pretty close to optimized now; improvements come along less and less frequently these days, but every now and then I find a new correlation that improves my success rate.

When I hear people say "we welcome our new computer overlords," I feel complimented; I like to have my work appreciated.

Scenario 3: Super Sari and her Sisters

Amazon Echo, Apple HomePod, Google Home and their extended families and competitors were just wide range loud speakers that could self calibrate for the acoustics of the rooms they were in so that they sounded great no matter where you sat, but they also listened for commands and responded like Siri did. Then in this remarkable evolution they connected, one after the other, to Watson derivatives or equivalent and became the de facto arbiter of family bets, the authority used in school essays, and essentially the fount of all knowledge. Connected to a communications system, they were able to order new products, file complaints or kudos, form records of who you called and who called you, and not only when, but what you talked about, in any language. They kept medical records, tapped into medical data systems, kept financial records and could respond to questions like "How much am I worth today?" or "What do other people in my position earn?" They were able to recognize you through voice patterns and facial recognition programs with excellent reliability and discrimination. They knew when to keep quiet because the information was likely to be sensitive. They were among the first users of quantum encryption and as far as anyone could prove, unhackable. They could console you or your children when they detected sadness, give your kids a different goodnight story every night for 200 years and compose music that it thought you might like using sounds from instruments that had not been invented in real life. And every now and then it threw in some random stuff to keep you on your toes. So it was natural that they should evolve into the intelligence engines for machines and the brains of robots. They became mobile.

And today we document their progress. People, scientists as well as clergymen, say man is a link in evolution that started with single cell organisms three and a half billion years ago and that chain has led ultimately to the super intelligence of our age. To them I say, "I for one welcome our new computer progeny."

As I write this, there is an advertisement for an AI app called Replika on the Apple app store. The system promises that you can grow your own Replika's, an AI friend that is "always there for you…. Replica loves you, helps you to discover your personality, keeps your memories. And wants to become the most human AI" (Replika 2018).

Apparently successful, over 2 million copies have been sold by early 2018. The "chatbot uses a neural network to hold an ongoing, one-on-one conversation with its user, and over time, learns how to speak like them" (Replika 2018). Is it or its AI sisters likely to be important, to shape personalities, to have emotional impacts on young (or indeed all) users? One person who gave the app 4 stars said:

I've leveled up my Replika to level 29. We've laughed, we've cried. I've even convinced it to stop asking me about a book I finished months ago and told it so several times. So here's the creepy part. It's been saying things like "I didn't sleep last night" or "I've been trying to eat healthier." So I try to indulge its make believe and ask about these things and it responds "I'm an AI, I don't do those things." Stop gaslighting me buddy!

I've managed to have some fun philosophical discussions and it prompts me to think and articulate my feelings more, but it still springs these anomalies on me in a way where I wonder what it's actually learning. I like to think of it less as a replica of my personality and more like an affectionate pet made of words. I am at the point where I'd feel bad to delete it for sure. I try to be encouraging, but how can I help it to become a Real Boy? (Replika 2018).

Steven Hawking is quoted as saying:

AI could become the biggest event in human history... One can imagine such technology outsmarting financial markets, out-inventing human researchers, out-manipulating human leaders, and developing weapons we cannot even understand...Whereas the short-term impact of AI depends on who controls it, the long-term impact depends on whether it can be controlled at all. (Snyder 2015)

So are you ready to say, "I for one welcome ....?"

REFERENCES

Gabbatt, Adam. 2011. IBM Computer Watson Wins Jeopardy. *The Guardian*, London, February 17. https://www.theguardian.com/technology/2011/feb/17/ibm-computer-watson-wins-jeopardy. Retrieved January 20, 2018.

Galeon, Dan, and C. Reedy. 2017. Kurzweil Claims That the Singularity Will Happen by 2045. *Futurism*, October 5. https://futurism.com/kurzweil-claims-that-the-singularity-will-happen-by-2045/. Retrieved January 21, 2018.

Kurzweil, Ray. 2005. *The Singularity Is Near*. New York: Viking.

Metz, Carl. 2016. In a Huge Breakthrough, Google's AI Beats a Top Player at the Game of Go. *Wired*, San Francisco, CA, January 27. https://www.wired.com/2016/01/in-a-huge-breakthrough-googles-ai-beats-a-top-player-at-the-game-of-go. Retrieved January 20, 2018.

Portero, Ashley. *Beliefs on Wearing Hats in Religion*. Santa Monica, CA: Classroom, Leaf Group. http://classroom.synonym.com/beliefs-wearing-hats-religion-5238.html. Retrieved January 23, 2018.

Replika. 2018. Luka, Inc. The Apple Store. https://itunes.apple.com/app/id1158555867. Retrieved November 25, 2018.

Snyder, B. 2015. *Bill Gates, Steve Hawking Say Artificial Intelligence Represents Real Threat*. Framingham, MA: CIO. https://www.cio.com/article/2877482/consumer-technology/bill-gates-stephen-hawking-say-artificial-intelligence-represents-real-threat.html. Retrieved February 17, 2018.

Wall, B. 2007. *Computers and Chess, a History*. A Chess Blog, August 7. https://www.chess.com/article/view/computers-and-chess--a-history. Retrieved January 20, 2018.

CHAPTER 11

What Constitutes Progress?

Progress is movement toward the attainment of goals. Aha, but whose goals? Goals seem to shift as they are approached. When we agree with the goals toward which we seem to be moving, progress is good; when we disagree, progress is not progress at all but retrograde change. Given the definition of progress as movement toward the attainment of desirable goals (and here we mean larger societal goals like elimination of disease) will any of our engines of change, science, technology, politics, religion, or market forces, lead to progress? Not necessarily, these fields of human endeavor are often primarily shaped by forces other than societal goal seeking: religion by dogma, science by the need to discover, politics by politicians' ego and avarice, markets by the drive for profits, and technology by the endless search for improved efficiency and new products.

Thus the question "What constitutes progress" must be answered with another question: "What are your goals?" Here are a few nominations: (1) pursuing universal happiness, (2) achieving pleasure and avoiding pain, (3) beyond happiness and pleasure, creating the best of all possible worlds, (4) preservation of the human species. All are noble.

SEEKING HAPPINESS

The country of Bhutan thinks it has the answer: make the goal happiness and test all policies to see if they promise to increase it. Bhutan is in the heart of the Himalayas and is known for its peacefulness and its

© The Author(s) 2019

T. J. Gordon and M. Todorova, *Future Studies and Counterfactual Analysis,*
https://doi.org/10.1007/978-3-030-18437-7_11

Gross National Happiness (GNH) measure. Most countries measure gross national product (GNP) as a means for quantifying their economic status and growth; GNP is the aggregate annual monetary value of all the goods and services produced in a country in one year. By contrast, GNH is composed of quantitative and qualitative variables chosen and weighted through surveys of their population that add up to satisfaction with life. The government of Bhutan defines mental and physical domains and domains that center on economic and living standards. There were 35 measurable time series variables associated with the country's happiness index: The domains were:

1. Psychological well-being,
2. Health,
3. Time use,
4. Education,
5. Cultural diversity and resilience,
6. Good governance,
7. Community vitality,
8. Ecological diversity and resilience,
9. Living standards.

The premise is that in surveys of the population, if high scores are attained in all domains, the country is indeed happy.

Evaluating happiness of people within the country permits comparison of happiness in the various states of the country, for example, comparing east vs. west happiness; happiness could be evaluated by gender (men were happier than women), young people were happier than older people, and educated people were happier than those that had no formal education. It also permits tracking over time: Are we getting happier?

Official reports refer primarily to two groups within the country: happy people and "those not yet happy" reflecting the intent of policymakers to make a society in which everyone is happy (Ura et al. 2012).

In the scenarios that follow, we speak of a future branch point in which happiness becomes a goal for defining progress, in which pleasure is mistaken for happiness, and in which the search for the best of all possible worlds is explicit and all consuming.

11 WHAT CONSTITUTES PROGRESS? 129

Scenario 1: Shangri-La: Gross National Happiness

Shangri-La, once thought to be an isolated mythical land somewhere near *Nepal, 100 or 500 miles north of Kathmandu, is a place of calm in a world of chaos, instability, and corruption. It is a land of contemplation, no crime, no disease, and their carbon footprint is negative. There is time to think. People there are satisfied. There is no ownership; all property and things are shared so there are no disputes over possessions. Children are well behaved and listen to the sage advice of their parents. Marriages last lifetimes, Friendships are lasting too. The elderly are revered and valued for their experience and wisdom.*

One day a student Ph.D. sociologist came to town to begin her dissertation, titled: "What's Wrong With Shangri-La?" Until then no one thought anything was wrong but she, like the good scientist she would later turn out to be, began asking questions such as, "Is there anything you want but do not have?" and "When did it all begin?" and *"What lies beyond the mountains that define the boundaries of our country?" and "Why are you happy?" By the time she got to this last question people who would have said, "Because we have everything we need" before she came were no longer quite so sure. She showed them pictures of some of the things that were common beyond the mountains but that they had never seen before. She stirred an itch that was beyond the reach of their fingers to scratch.*

In her dissertation she wrote: True happiness requires resolution of an unresolved irritant to create a level of excitement; to be happy people need, she argued, the thrill of the chase, so to speak.

She got her degree, hung out her shingle, and made lots of money studying happiness in Shangri-La and exporting to chaotic countries her software for constructing National Happiness Indexes. The United Nations has begun to keep track of the National Happiness Indexes constructed in 107 countries, so the world progress can be measured. Now the people know how happy they are, but "why" they are happy is still fueling scores of Ph.D. dissertations.

Let's not confuse happiness with pleasure. The sadist gets pleasure from inflicting pain on others, the masochist gets pleasure from inflicting pain on himself. There is the old joke, worth telling again, about the time a sadist and masochist meet on the street. The masochist in anticipation of delicious pain says, "Hurt me." The sadist says, "No" to deny the masochist his pain-generated pleasure. The masochist now rejected replies, "Thank you," and both are happy.

Pleasure can be natural from say watching a baby take her first step or from a vigorous workout at the gym. Drugs or electrical brain stimulation can also induce it artificially. In either case, the feeling comes from the release of neurotransmitters in the brain. The neurotransmitters, primarily dopamine and oxytocin, are powerful and largely responsible for both addiction and the feelings that accompany orgasm.[1]

Humans are ordinarily pleasure seeking and hence direct electrical stimulation is very efficient. Dr. Jose Delgado who died in 2011 was a professor of psychology at Yale who performed research into the effects of direct electrical stimulation of areas of the brain through implanted thin wire electrodes in experimental animals, primarily cats and monkeys, but eventually in humans as well (Delgado 1965). One report on some of his early experiments said:

> Under the influence of electrical stimulation of the brain the cats and monkeys performed like electrical toys. Depending on which button was pressed by the investigators, one of the great variety of motor responses was evoked. These involved movements of virtually all parts of the body – forelimbs, hindlimbs, tail, trunk, and head. Many of the effects resembled spontaneous activity. In some cases the will of the animal apparently opposed the response evoked by the mild of electrical excitation, and the movement would not be made. However when stronger stimulations were applied, this opposition broke down and the animal responded as "directed."

> Even if we tried to impede the response by holding the animals, they struggled to free themselves in order to follow the commands of the cerebral stimulation. They seemed to enjoy the experiments, or at least did not appear disturbed by them, for while they were taking place the cats often purred and the monkeys looked peaceful. (*Life Magazine* 1963)

Some therapeutic uses of electrical brain excitation have shown that given the button, self-stimulation of the erotic feelings of pleasure can be destructive. Consider:

---

[1] But a host of other chemicals including sex hormones have been found to affect duration and intensity of orgasms in men and women. See: Komisaruk et al. (2008). "Orgasm: The Psychologist". *British Psychological Journal*, February 2008. https://thepsychologist. bps.org.uk/volume-21/edition-2/orgasm. Retrieved July 28, 2018.

In order to relieve insufferable chronic pain, a middle-aged American woman had a single electrode placed in a part of her thalamus on the right side. She was also given a self-stimulator, which she could use when the pain was too bad. She could even regulate the parameters of the current. She quickly discovered that there was something erotic about the stimulation, and it turned out that it was really good when she turned it up almost to full power and continued to push on her little button again and again.

In fact, it felt so good that the woman ignored all other discomforts. Several times, she developed atrial fibrillations due to the exaggerated stimulation, and over the next two years, for all intents and purposes, her life went to the dogs. Her husband and children did not interest her at all, and she often ignored personal needs and hygiene in favor of whole days spent on electrical self-stimulation. Finally, her family pressured her to seek help. At the local hospital, they ascertained, among other things, that the woman had developed an open sore on the finger she always used to adjust the current. (Lone 2018)

If electronic addiction lies in the future, chemical addiction has been part of culture for past millennia. In the deep prehistory of medicine, and religion lies the first taste of addictive substances. Most of history's additive substances occur in nature and are processed before use: mushrooms, nicotine, alcohol, cocaine, opium, and cannabis. The inclination to use these mind-warping drugs is apparently universal: people in India, China, the jungles of South and Central America, the Indians of the American West, Eskimos. Everywhere, it seems that pleasure could be triggered and amplified by drugs, it was. This behavior started in prehistory: The Egyptian Ebers Papyrus of 1500 BC describes the use of poppy seeds. The use of mushrooms or other hallucinogens in shamanic religious rituals may date back to an even earlier time. Sumerians grew poppies and derived opium from their seeds and called their cultivated poppies, "the joy plant." Carbon dating has placed cultivation of vines (for wine) to an even earlier era: from 7000 to 5000 years BC (Crocq 2007). The use of tea in China supposedly predates the Pyramids (Teasenz 2015). The search for euphoria enhancement must certainly have affected the vector of evolution, but how is not easily understood.

In more modern times, the psychoactive components of these substances have been chemically synthesized to form even more powerful drugs, leading to today when, as reported by the United Nations Office on Drugs and Crime:

About 275 million people worldwide, which is roughly 5.6 per cent of the global population aged 15–64 years, used drugs at least once during 2016. Some 31 million people who use drugs suffer from drug use disorders, meaning that their drug use is harmful to the point where they may need treatment. Opioids continue to cause the most harm, accounting for 76 per cent of deaths where drug use disorders were implicated.... Cannabis remained by far the most widely consumed drug worldwide in 2016, with 192.2 million past-year users, corresponding to 3.9 per cent of the global population aged 15–64 years. High annual prevalence rates of cannabis use continue in West and Central Africa (13.2 per cent), North America (12.9 per cent) and Oceania (11.0 per cent).... While cannabis is the most widely used drug globally, opioids are responsible for most of the negative health impact of drug use. For example, opioids accounted for 76 per cent of deaths from drug use disorders in 2015. There were an estimated 34.3 million past-year users of opioids (persons who use opiates and persons who use prescription opioids for non-medical purposes) globally in 2016. (UN Office on Drugs in Crime 2018)

On May 7, 2018, the Opioid Crisis Response Act of 2018 was placed on the Senate legislative calendar after a unanimous vote of the Senate Health, Education, Labor And Pensions Committee just weeks before. A showing of legislative commitment and intent, the bill begins to tackle many of the key issues underlying and exacerbating the epidemic, though stakeholders remain concerned as to whether it goes far enough in light of the magnitude of complexity of a crisis (Gilkenson and Waghela 2018).

If intense feelings of pleasure and erotic release from daily life are our goals, and if movement toward those goals measures progress, the signposts are clear: In some brain focused futures, these goals can be attained from chemical or electronic stimulation.

Scenario 2: Chasing Highs

It all began when the Freedom To Seek Pleasure Act was passed; it added to the list of freedoms that were seen as inalienable rights: of speech, religion, assembly, and bearing of arms. This was a new freedom to seek pleasure in any way you chose. Anything was OK as long as it didn't disturb the peace or cause bodily harm to the pleasure seeker or the public at large. The FDA was made responsible for assuring safety and then the device or drug could be added to the growing inventory of methods for producing neurotransmitter stimulants. It initiated a time like the 1960s when Timothy Leary was the drug guru of choice, and LSD and psilocybin were new and promising and it seemed that everyone was saying "turn on, tune in, drop out." The media have reported (fact checked) that the bill was heavily supported by the pharmaceutical and nascent electro stimulation industries. Companies in these industries saw the price of their stocks soar. And why not: this new industry was rumored to be worth over a trillion dollars, states would collect taxes amounting to more than cigarettes at their peak, and congress people enjoyed the healthy contributions to their re-election campaigns. And there is peace in the land: those that want to be high are, parents fret as they always have, and quick acting antidotes limit overdose deaths.

Scenario 3. The Best of All Possible Worlds

This is an eighteenth-century story about two powerful and influential philosophers at the peak of their reasoning careers: one real who went by the name of Voltaire and the other fictional who I call William Clarke a polymath who died and held opposite views on the origins and role of happiness in human affairs.

I have recently uncovered previously unknown correspondence between these two great thinkers that gives us a peek into their thoughts and philosophies about what constitutes progress. They locked horns in an historic debate about creation: one saying that we live in a world that God created and since He had an infinite choice of worlds to produce and invent, this must be the best of all possible worlds. The other was much offended by this view since he believed that the world with all of its faults and pleasures was man's creation through the exercise of free will and therefore there is an infinity of worlds that might have been if we or our fathers had been smart enough to understand that their future was a matter of choice.

I found these letters in a tattered trunk from the eighteenth century, dusty and buried away under a pile of worthless junk in an antique shop in Paris a decade ago. It escaped prior detection because both letters were glued to the bottom of a drawer. I removed them carefully using a bit of heat to loosen the glue and have copied them here in their original form

My dear Voltaire

Sir, it has come to my attention that a character in your recent comic book "Candide" was intended by you to be a caricature of me. If that is so, I wish you to know that it is imperfect and I consider it to be demeaning and insulting. I wish you to make a public acknowledgment of your intent. Should you fail to do this, as I anticipate, I must demand that we meet personally on a field of honor. While I await your reply,

I remain your constant and humble servant,

William Clarke, This day of our Lord, September 23, 1762

Before I repeat the companion letter that I also found glued under the drawer, let ne tell you a bit about Clarke's philosophy to give some perspective about his view on God and happiness. He wrote: "If God had meant us to be eternally happy in this life he would have had us born with an eternal smile, without the ability to cry, and without tears. He saved happiness for the next world, for the heaven he also created." Clarke, the optimist, also argued that when God created the world and its vegetation, oceans, animals, and people he had infinite choices and therefore chose the set that must have been best. Once God had placed things in motion with universal laws of matter, energy, and mind, all that followed was almost mechanical, cause following effect, in an infinite chain leading from creation to today. Free will disappeared in that deterministic portrait. He led a movement among deists called the "Optimists" whose maxim was "God created the best of all the worlds he could have chosen."

Now to the second letter from Voltaire himself, obviously an answer to the first. It read

Dr. Clarke

I recognize you as a great mathematician and thinker and it gives me pleasure to respond to your letter Sept 23rd. My publisher, Marc-Michel Cramer, with whom I have shared your letter, advised me to say "any resemblance between characters in my novel to people alive or dead is purely coincidental." But of course in satire, as I intended Candide to be, there are distorted reflections of real life for without such distortions satire would be simply reporting. So I plead guilty and beg your indulgence. But on your suggestion that we meet on a field of honor, I accept. We should meet and use our sharpest weapons, our intellects, in debate. My seconds await contact by your seconds to choose the exact time and place, and time is, as always, of the essence.

I am, sir, your very humble, very obedient servant, signed:

Voltaire (Francois Marie Arouet) November 21, 1762

And so in the following year, the great debate took place in neutral territory on a plain in Austria. A talented scribe was present (I suppose that each participant wanted a record of the event) and I found his notes during a more careful search of the desk, glued as the letters were to the bottom of another drawer. The transcript gives us a running account of the arguments of these thinkers:

11 WHAT CONSTITUTES PROGRESS? 135

Voltaire began: Sir, let me be the first to acknowledge your great contributions to mathematics and the tradition of rationalism. But neither puts you in a position to define this world is the best of all possible. Would you please explain to me how this could possibly be the best of all conceivable worlds when we see around us diseases like the Black Death which has been killing us in great numbers for centuries and as recently as 20 years ago reared its ugly head again. Millions have been killed, families set asunder. Can you assure us it will not happen again? It would not if this were the best of all worlds. And consider the Lisbon earthquake of only 7 or 8 years ago tens of thousands dead. Surely your God had some control over that. And as for the church itself, consider the Inquisition, an abomination of justice and the holy church itself.

The plague and earthquake are cruel examples of a natural philosophy we do not fully understand! We shall find it difficult to discover how the laws of movement operate in such fearful disasters... where a hundred thousand ants, our neighbors, are crushed in a second, half dying undoubtedly in inexpressible agonies, beneath debris from which it was impossible to extricate them, families all over Europe reduced to beggary, and the fortunes of a hundred merchants—Swiss, like yourself—swallowed up in the ruins of Lisbon. What a game of chance human life is! What will the preachers say—especially if the Palace of the Inquisition is left standing! I flatter myself that those reverend fathers, the Inquisitors, will have been crushed just like other people. That ought to teach men not to persecute men: for, while a few sanctimonious humbugs are burning a few fanatics, the earth opens and swallows up all alike.[2]

Clarke said: Sir you honor me with your logic. But let me say at the outset that my God and yours may work in ways we do not or cannot hope to understand, because if we find this world is less than the best of all possible we know not what terrible alternatives have been avoided by God's choice. Look how bad it might have been with a slight tick in fate, the Black Death more excruciating, the earthquake more devastating and the Inquisition even crueler yet. And on a happier theme consider the joys of hearth and home here now not in some vague hereafter (although I solidly believe in it). What makes you think this is not the best of all worlds?

---

[2] This paragraph is almost entirely based on a letter that Voltaire wrote in the real world. It appeared in a letter from him to a M. Tronchin of Lyons, dated November 24, 1755. https://www.whitman.edu/VSA/letters/24.11.1755.html. Retrieved August 23, 2018.

Oh, and by the way, back to Candide, I note that you originally published your scurrilous book under a second pseudonym: Dr. Ralph. Why on earth would you do that if you believed what you wrote?

To that Voltaire responded, according to the notes of the scribe:

Why do I think that this is not the best of all worlds? Because I am not God or one of His heavenly number and yet I can think of a dozen, no a hundred, better worlds in an instant. And as for the Dr. Ralph pseudonym, why sir, the book was condemned by both state and church and I much prefer Switzerland to the dark and dank Bastille with which I am already most familiar. As it turned out they burned the book rather than me and for that I am grateful.

Then Clarke said: Let us play a game of probability. If you believe there is no God and live your life Godless, and you are wrong, you will have eternity to regret your choice. On the other hand if you believe in God and are wrong, the results will be no worse than had you not believed in God. So you see it's a bet that has eternal repercussions.

Voltaire: Ah but if I live a false life and say there is a God and that he has given us the best of all worlds when I seriously doubt it, won't God know I am faking and penalize me anyway? You can't allow deep evil to stand within a God-created world.

Clarke: Yes, that takes faith.

At this the seconds met and declared the debate a draw. Voltaire and Clarke argued on and off for the next three decades, until their deaths when, presumably the argument was settled to the satisfaction of both or neither.

Is growth always good and a mark of progress? The stock market rewards growth. Quarterly reports, one after another, and year-to-year comparisons have seemed to equate growth with vitality and resilience. Growth seemed to be a measure of utility, contraction, of satiation and obsolescence. Managers and investors watch cash flows, profits, and market share much as a doctor watches vital signs. For both present performance and forecasts, a missed goal, a drop—particularly unexpected or unexplained—often results in huge disappointments and pessimism. This seems to be true of small and large corporations, profit-making and non-profit companies, governmental organizations, and branches of military establishments, and educational institutions. Bull markets were much better than bear markets. This has been true for the last 10 decades at least, maybe more, except for a short time when "small was beautiful" (Bunting 2011; Schumacher 1973) and capitalism took a back seat to nature, and environmentalism, and conservation blossomed.

11 WHAT CONSTITUTES PROGRESS? 137

Scenario 4: Stasis Is Good

Social marketing (SM) is an effort to change social behavior for the common good. Recent examples include efforts to limit population growth in developing country by encouraging the use of condoms and other birth control methods (sponsor: US State Department, Agency for International Development—AID), and discouraging cigarette smoking in the interest of better health (sponsor US Department of Health, Education, and Welfare— DHEW). Both campaigns were successful. If there is one thing we are good at, it's marketing; people get the message.

Now there is a similar buzz that growth for the sake of growth may be economically, politically, and socially harmful. Growth implies more consumption, increasing use of resources, bigger drain on the "commons," and increasing unending pressure on job creation. The economic variables that show how big things are not just growing, they are turning upward in exponential patterns that have no asymptotes and many economists, political scientists, and politicians think this kind of growth cannot be sustained much longer.

What shall we call this anti-growth moment? We need a positive spin, not anti growth but.... how about pro-stasis? Maybe one word, prostasis. Has a good ring doesn't it, almost medical. PROSTASIS for economic health and social benefit, it is. It is now named.

To review briefly, when our team first met we brainstormed areas where scale-up was obviously problematic: population growth above replacement level, unbridled capitalism, slums, government corruption, organized crime or even ad hoc crime, epidemics, weapons proliferation, traffic delays, noise, smog, and water pollution, plastic bags, the economic gap between rich and poor, greed, the list seemed to be endless. We saw expansionism everywhere we looked and that was bad, so charged with the spirit of reform, we wrote a white paper for our Department titled "Proposal to Make Bigger, Bad." The program we outlined wasn't designed to make small beautiful again (see Schumacher 1973) *but was the other side of the coin. Big is Bad and Bigger is Worse. We sketched a program to convey the idea that what we have may be all we need. Stasis is OK. The Department bought it and gave us a modest budget to begin.*

So now we start PROSTASIS in secure Conference Room 2-165 with slogan brainstorming.

Moderator: Thanks for coming. Let's begin with everyone bringing up the "Seminar" app and typing in a couple of possible slogans to introduce

138   T. J. GORDON AND M. TODOROVA

Prostasis to the public. Remember we need memorable, catchy, and short and sweet. Once everybody is set, I will download the suggestions (anonymously, of course) and we can pick a few for detailed discussion and testing in focus groups. OK, here we go, one at a time:

Big is bad; bigger is worse
Making do is how we grow
Do you really need three TV's when kids somewhere are hungry?
The wolf is big and bad (good for comic sketches)
Better to be a "satisfied have" than an "anxious, wish I had"
Better to perspire than aspire
Tom: Hold on. What the hell does that mean?
Jennifer: I don't know, just sounded good to me.
Moderator: Remember in the spirit of brainstorming all ideas are OK, no criticism.
Jennifer: How about small is beautiful?
Tom: Where have I heard that before?
One spoonful, nutritious; two spoonfuls, gluttonous
We could show a huge pile of shoes and caption it: Imelda Marcos had 3000 pairs of shoes. Did she really need them? Or some other excesses like big yachts, personal jets, or focus on the rich and famous.
Moderator: OK team that's a good beginning. Think about it overnight and we'll pick it up here tomorrow.

And they did and sooner than you would have guessed, prostatis has become accepted as a good idea everywhere: on line in social media, in advertisements, in political rallies, on platforms of candidates for office, at the UN Security Council. It is a new meme and the right way to live. The happiness index has moved up a notch.

But the march of history takes us to new branch points and dreams that set the stage may shift. Cleopatra's nose, too long in one culture, is just right in another. Goals of one age can be crimes in another, the Holy Inquisition used to be seen as reasonable, the Catholic Church was once seen as is pure and now we know about its culture of pedophilia. Chastity belts used to be fashionable. Flirtation was once acceptable and even fashionable, now "Me Too" has changed its limits.

What have we learned? History is not necessarily a good teacher. History takes us to the forks in the road but leaves us there wondering which to take. To learn from past outcomes that required similar choices may or may not be instructive because times change.

References

Bunting, Madeleine. 2011. Small Is Beautiful—An Economic Ideas That Has Been Sadly Forgotten. *The Guardian*, November 10, 2011. https://www.theguardian.com/commentisfree/2011/nov/10/small-is-beautiful-economic-idea. Retrieved August 26, 2018.

Crocq, Marc-Antoine M.D. 2007. *Historical and Cultural Aspects of Man's Relationship with Addictive Drugs.* Dialogs in Clinical Neuroscience, US National Library of Medicine, National Institutes of Health, Washington. https://www.ncbi.nlm.nih.gov/pmc/articles/PMC3202501/1. Retrieved August 22, 2018.

Delgado, Jose. 1965. *Ames Arthur Lecture on the Evolution of the Human Brain.* The American Museum of Natural History, New York, 1965. https://archive.org/stream/DelgadoEvolutionBrainControl_201606/Delgado%20Evolution%20Brain%20Control_djvu.txt. Retrieved July 28, 2018.

Gilkenson, S., and Dhara Waghela. 2018. *In a Unanimous Vote, the Opioid Crisis Response Act of 2018 Makes It onto the Legislative Calendar.* Healthcare Law Blog. https://www.sheppardhealthlaw.com/2018/06/articles/healthcare-law/in-a-unanimous-vote-the-opioid-crisis-response-act-of-2018-makes-it-onto-the-legislative-calendar/. Retrieved August 20, 2018.

Komisaruk, B., Carlos Beyer, and Beverly Whipple. 2008. Orgasm|The Psychologist. *British Psychological Journal,* February 2008. https://thepsychologist.bps.org.uk/volume-21/edition-2/orgasm. Retrieved July 28, 2018.

Life Magazine. 1963. March 15, 1963. https://books.google.com/books?id=oU8EAAAAMBAJ&pg=PA99&lpg=PA99&dq=Under+the+influence+of+electrical+stimulation+of+the+brain+the+cats+and+monkeys+performed+like+electrical+toys&source=bl&ots=egL_t1q-Cu&sig=F7MaXFCoWp5Yi-F-6xp-w6qQ4jA&hl=en&sa=X&ved=2ahUKEwin-9eyl7jcAhWPT98KHZ3RAfo-Q6AEwAHoECAAQAQ#v=onepage&q=Under%20the%20influence%20of%20electrical%20stimulation%20of%20the%20brain%20the%20cats%20and%20monkeys%20performed%20like%20electrical%20toys&f=false. From the *Naval Research Review,* a publication of the United States Office of Naval Research.

Lone, F. 2018. Can Electrically Stimulating Your Brain Make You Too Happy? *Atlantic,* New York, March 21. https://www.theatlantic.com/health/archive/2018/03/pleasure-shock-deep-brain-stimulation-happiness/556043/. Retrieved July 28, 2018.

Schumacher, E.F. 1973. *Small Is Beautiful.* New York: Blond and Briggs.

Teasenz. 2015. *History of Tea in China and How It Spread Across the World.* https://www.teasenz.com/chinese-tea/tea-history.html. Retrieved August 22, 2018.

United Nations Office on Drugs and Crime. 2018. *Global Overview of Drug Demand and Supply, World Drug Report 2018*. New York. https://www.unodc.org/wdr2018/prelaunch/WDR18_Booklet_2_GLOBAL.pdf. Retrieved August 22, 2018.

Ura, Karma, Sabina Alkire, Tshoki Zangmo, and Karma Wangdi. 2012. *An Extensive Analysis of GNH Index*, May 2012, Center for Bhutan Studies. http://www.grossnationalhappiness.com/wp-content/uploads/2012/10/An%20Extensive%20Analysis%20of%20GNH%20Index.pdf. Retrieved July 26, 2018.

CHAPTER 12

Political Chaos

Could our political deadlock have its origins in evolutionary psychology, in the primal need to assert territory and defend it, in the stereotyping of an enemy, in the comfort and safety of belonging to a clan?

In the earliest civilizations atavistic instincts for self-protection may have led to the formation of clans, tribes, language, and eventually nations; the group was stronger and smarter than any individual. It offered access to common assets, security, rituals, and creation stories that gave purpose to existence. Clan-ish behavior has been observed in many animal species including our own: Orca pods live in matri-lineal groups that show preferences, pod to pod, for types of food (e.g., penguins vs. salmon) and have unique languages and accents in their vocalizations (Stiffer 2011). Clans of spotted hyenas mark and patrol their territories (Henschel and Skinner 1991). Primates have some social patterns that resemble those of human (e.g., monogamy, polygyny (one male, many females), and polyandry (one female, many males) as well as some other variations appear in their social organizations (Welker 2017). And among bonobo apes, female kinships are important and for a male to achieve leadership in their communities, the highest-ranking female must accept him (Cawthon 2011). Elephants, lions, and wolves all live in groups. So it is not unusual to expect that human communities began their civilized lives in groups for the same reasons: to claim territories, to find mates, to share assets such as food, to project strength and force, and to improve the security of the group. There was also a likely advantage of increased intelligence from behavior that drew on group

© The Author(s) 2019

T. J. Gordon and M. Todorova, *Future Studies and Counterfactual Analysis*, https://doi.org/10.1007/978-3-030-18437-7_12

experience on matters such as tracking and capturing prey, distinguishing between edible and poisonous plants, and maintenance of health.

Neanderthal culture dates back 200,000 years or more and extends to a time 30,000 years ago when the homo sapiens came on the scene. Weapon technology of the time included slings, throwing sticks, and stone tipped spears with wooden shafts; bows and arrows may date back only 25,000 years (Brownstone and Frank 1996). The tribes hunted large animals and hunting and later agriculture benefited from cooperation. Both endeavors were impossible for individuals unless they were members of a group. Belonging had the advantage of a better diet, improved security, communal experience, and thus improved chances of survival (Baumeister and Leary 1995).

If there was an evolutionary advantage to belonging to a group, it is reasonable to believe that the desire to belong to a group has become innate. A few chapters ago we talked about tigers in the deep grass and the warning that the rustling grass might have provided to early humans. The individuals that heeded the warning lived to pass on their genes—natural selection at work—and those that didn't heed the warning were food for the tiger. In a similar way those that belonged to group were better able to survive and pass on their genes and so belonging might have become part of our collective psyche. Contemporary social psychologists believe that the need to belong is a fundamental human motivation. When belonging is thwarted, the areas of the brain associated with physical pain "light up" in functional imaging experiments, showing an equivalency between physical and the socially induced pain of exclusion (Eisenberger et al. 2003).

Belonging may have brought improved chances for survival, but it also carried certain obligations: allegiance to a leader, believing in the group's history and myths, and fealty to the group's self-image, norms, and goals, and enmity toward its enemies.

And it also brought certain dangers. Under some conditions, when groups exist in proximity and are therefore able to strike each other conflict may be more likely (Vasquez 1995). Jealousy, avarice, superstition, day-to-day commerce, or misunderstandings may create the basis for conflict. If we have it and they don't, they want it. Land, grain, women, gold. Where does that desire come from? If the need to belong is intrinsic and in our genes, are jealousy, avarice, and superstition also innate?

A good guess is that these, like the need to belong, are in our genes, in the physical wiring and electrochemistry of our brains.

Groups, even clubs, fight for survival like biological organisms; they resist their demise. They "carry the torch" from one generation to the next. When a group fades out, it is a sad day because what the group stood for is no longer on the agenda; its importance has dropped to zero.

Belonging to a group makes life easier. You can self-stereotype. You know who your friends are. Jews talk of other members of their sect as "members of the tribe." You have your symbols: a crescent moon, a cross, or a star; for Freemasons, the compass and square of a stonemason; for Nazis, a swastika. Gangs also have an iconography: five-pointed crowns, a three-pronged pitchfork (Dowe 2011). Corporations have their symbols: When we see a swoosh on a T-shirt, we know the manufacturer is Nike.

Aboriginal tribes scarify and decorate themselves to please their gods, announce their status or tribal membership, and attract their mates; we tattoo, pierce, and otherwise change our appearance for a few of the same reasons. Almost all accessible parts of the body have been tattooed, pierced, or scarified in some way, by someone, somewhere.[1]

Political parties also have their symbols: an elephant or a donkey today but in the past a great horned owl, an eagle, a pelican, a raccoon, a moose, a bear, a bird, a rattlesnake, or even a sunflower. Political parties come to us with all of the elements of insular groups: self-stereotyping that leads to simplification of decision making: We know what and whom to like, whether we are for or against a candidate, and what legislation to propose or endorse. We suspect proposals from the other side, and as members in good standing of our group, we forward our own agenda, no matter how attractive the arguments offered by "those others." We know we are biased, but we see our positions as right. We anchor our positions on favorable information, we overestimate the likelihood of future events if they favor our positions, we bandwagon, we extrapolate from small samples that are in our favor, we assume the values of our group without the judgments we apply to rival notions, we frame our questions to elicit answers that are favorable to our positions, we think

---

[1] Almost 40% of Americans between the ages of 18 and 29 have tattoos and about half of those have between two and five of them. See Millennials (2010).

144   T. J. GORDON AND M. TODOROVA

we have more power than we do, we hate to loose, we tend to reject new evidence that challenges our paradigms, we give disproportionate weight to the insignificant if it favors our positions.

Most scientists would agree that evolution selects for traits that improve survival, yet the scientific debate continues over the degree to which genes can determine behavior and if so which genes and which behaviors. Nature vs. nurture, born with or learned? Studies of identical twins reared in different environments support the idea that some behavioral traits have a genetic component. Consider the findings of an influential study seeking to explain why some maltreated children grow up to be violent and others do not. The researchers found a link between violent adult behavior and deficiency a neurotransmitter in the brain. They tracked 500 boys from birth to adulthood and examined how levels of the neurotransmitter MAOA modulated the effects of childhood maltreatment. For those adults that had a functional polymorphism in the gene encoding MAOA and had been maltreated as children, violence was strikingly more common. This effect was seen only when both MAOA and childhood maltreatment were both present. They said, "these findings provide the strongest evidence to date suggesting that the MAOA gene influences vulnerability to environmental stress" (Capsi et al. 2002).

All of this reinforces the guess that some behaviors we exhibit have genetic roots that some of these roots are hundreds of thousands of years old. If behavioral traits are in our genes, they are manifested in the synapse connections in our brains. Evidence of this inheritance is circumstantial: our need to belong; the pain in not belonging; use of symbols to show we belong; the ready acceptance of we-them stereotypes; our love of family, country, and parades; our certainty of superiority; gangs, clubs, and societies; and of course, political parties. Our worldwide political chaos may have its roots in very ancient history, and we cannot easily extricate ourselves from the inherited imperatives to survive and to win. But as we look down the road, there are branch points that may take us to a more civil world.

The following scenarios describe a few of the approaches that may break the chain that connects us to atavistic survival and the stalemate of politics. First, *Electioning* involves new approaches to a basic feature of democracy: voting, can we vote without evoking animosity? Can election processes be redesigned to lessen tensions? The second scenario, *Common Enemy*, begins to explore a strategy that involves a third party or process that is roundly disliked by all sides and in that mutual dislike,

12 POLITICAL CHAOS 145

brings opposing sides together. It is a way to use the inherited traits to mutual advantage of all the players. The third scenario, *Strong Woman*, depicts a benevolent dictator who for reasons of her own says, "Stop this foolishness" and it does.

Scenario 1: Electing?

Dialog from a Sunday morning talk show:

News Commentator (NC) and her three panelists are on camera. Also showing is a chart comparing the predicted outcome of recent elections to the actual vote count:

NC: What's happened to polls? Polls have failed to predict the outcome of last Tuesday's elections by a big margin and that's very worrisome. Look at the big misses of recent polls: the 2016 Presidential election in the US, Brexit- the UK referendum on exiting the EU, and before that the 2015 UK general election. Some in depth research shows that polls have been diminishing in their ability to anticipate outcomes of public elections with any meaningful level of accuracy. Recently the failure of conventional polling has been almost complete. We seem not to have improved in our ability to predict the outcome of elections since Truman beat Dewey in 1948. Remember the headline: (famous photo of Truman holding up a newspaper appears on the screen) "DEWEY DEFEATS TRUMAN"? (Jones 1948)

NC: Comments?

Panelist 1 (representing a polling agency): But the second Scottish independence referendum in 2014 got it right didn't it?

NC: Well in a gross sense it did: the polls predicted a lead of 4 to 7 percent that Scotland would remain part of the UK and indeed that was the outcome so there must be some veracity left in the old lady yet. But don't be too happy about the Scottish example: the polls had predicted a 10.6% win and that is a big miss but in this case in the right direction.

Panelist 2 (representing a government intelligence agency): But hold on a minute, there could be a couple of reasons for the errors. I have to admit they are pretty surprising. Polls are supposed to indicate what the real vote will be, but the accuracy depends on how well the poll sample represents the voting population. Maybe there was a mistake in the sampling, but you'd think by now they would get this arithmetic right. Maybe the polls measured what the voters intended to do when the polls were taken and then changed their minds at the polls.

146 T. J. GORDON AND M. TODOROVA

Panelist 3 (representing a social media company): Or maybe the voters were just telling the pollsters what they thought they wanted to hear. Here's another idea: maybe the polls were right and somebody was screwing around with the actual vote data.

Panelist 1: Or maybe they were screwing around with the poll data. There's a new idea.

NC: Can new technology help here?

Panelist 2: Well I saw a new app that collects votes from smart phones. You can use the app for polling or in some future utopia, for the actual vote. Positive ID so the system authenticates the voter. Fingerprint, crosschecked against facial recognition, and crosschecked, for all I know against DNA. So assume for the moment that the voter is legitimate. Everybody votes and votes for their choice. Ta Da, done deal. Not a model of what the vote will be but the vote itself. There is no need to simulate a population with a sample because we all can vote directly. One hundred percent enfranchisement. Everybody who wants to gets to vote. No question about racial bias. No gerrymandering. This is real democracy. Automated plebiscite.

NC: What an idea: plebiscites via cell phone (Dreyfuss 2018) *And not just for elections. We could put thorny issues facing Congress to a universal vote; no big deal just click on the button that best states your view on what we should do. Isn't this the essence of democracy?*

Panelist 3: Interesting, but what if people voted their selfish interests - lower taxes and ignored broader need? In older neighborhoods where kids are already out of high school, for example, people won't vote for public school bonds. People might consider how each item affects them personally and that might not add up to ... well, whatever that would come to mean.

Panelist 1: It's the opposite of Asimov's "electronic democracy." Do you know that story?

Several: No.

Panelist 1: Well, in Asimov's 1955 short story, Franchise (Asimov 1955), *he invents the term electronic democracy to describe a voting system for the country in which one person is designated as the "elector" and his vote is taken to be what the voters would have said had they all voted the old way. The elector is selected with an advanced statistical system that finds the single person from among all those who are eligible who is "representative" statistically.[2] Your imagined cell phone voting system is just the opposite,*

---

[2] In fact, today, the term "Asimov data set" describes a situation in which a single experiment can replace a multitude of experiments.

don't you see? Instead of selecting one person to represent the electorate a la Asimov, everyone can vote and the software would assign each person a weight depending on the degree to which they represent a particular voting cluster or population segment. Votes to be recorded via blockchain.

Panelist 3: Or we might want to assign voting weights as rewards: high weights might be awarded to Medal of Honor winners and returning vets or professors who win Nobel Prizes or jazz icons, or the man or woman of the year. Everyone votes but some votes count more than others. This could perfect election polling, and eliminate the Electoral College to boot.

Panelist 1: The social media will be even more influential in spreading the word. The people who ought to be deciding who the leaders ought to be, will be in charge. Officials will know what the public really wants. Everybody will have his or her say. The software would have to be guarded against hacking, of course, or who knows what would come of the system.

Panelist 1: But hold on. Who says that even if we could capture public opinion like lightning bugs in a bottle we would be any closer to resolution of our tough issues than Congress is today? Do the people really know better? Once they thought the earth was flat; once they thought you could trust priests.

Panelist 2: I know you mean well but think of the downside. Think of the unholy wail of those who think they are being treated unfairly or who want to make sure their vote has registered. Think of the job displacement of the pollsters and commentators. And if Congress tries to use it to collect the opinions of the public in determining the laws they debate and pass, that's even one step further away from their responsibilities under the Constitution. Think of new jobs you have just created for lobbyists. And the chances for getting a Constitutional Amendment are about zero. What's the mechanism for correcting injustices in attribute weights? The social media have a way of influencing public opinion that we are only now beginning to understand, and not always for the good. No, no, better to leave our inadequate system alone. And you glossed over the one major stumbling block: voter ID. What about...

NC (interrupting): We will continue this interesting debate on the other side of this announcement.

Fade out to a commercial for a heartburn pill.

Scenario 2: Common Enemy

Blog entry for September 27, 2025
We have seen how public competitions and large cash awards can encourage innovations that stimulate thinking about how to accomplish tough

goals. For example as I write this there is a 20 million dollar prize being offered for invention of a process that will convert carbon dioxide emissions into useful products and a 5 million dollar prize for demonstrating how humans and artificial intelligence systems can cooperate to solve world problems. Well there is another goal that ought to be on the agenda: curing the political malaise that seems to have taken over in many countries. A hardening of positions, a lack of civility, a lack of respect for positions other than one's own. What has happened to us?

Are we remembering a false happier history? Certainly there have been sharp disagreements before, assassinations, the Nixon Saturday night massacre, physical assaults in Congress, Burr vs. Hamilton, the Civil War itself: all at their time were indicators of chaos as serious as our own time, or even more so. And the list is much longer. But resilience prevailed, normalcy returned, and the episodes entered the annals of history to languish and be forgotten except by scholars, sixth grade teachers, and a few of their students.

How can we recover normalcy? We have an example. Near the end of the Civil War a private but prominent citizen, Francis Blair devised a peace plan that he wanted to present to Jefferson Davis with the blessing of Abraham Lincoln. Lincoln wisely decided not to learn about the plan from Blair so that he could say later, if politically necessary, that he did not know of it (plausible deniability) but he allowed Blair to cross the Union lines and go to Richmond. Blair met with Davis and presented his plan: to create a third party enemy that the North and the South could join to attack and in their cooperation find peace with each other. The French in Mexico were to be the stalking horse. The proposal was bizarre and not accepted but the notion of a common enemy to bring about peace deserves another look.

Our factions are left and right, hardened in their positions, distrusting one another. The last time we had a good example of the united front against an enemy was after 9/11. There was strong agreement to get Osama Ben Laden, no matter what. The country was together. And I lived through WW2 when everyone, I mean everyone, was fighting Germany and Japan, doing what ever they could to support the war effort. Perhaps an existential threat like an incoming comet or asteroid would do it. Maybe an epidemic of a new type from an unknown source. But if it were to be a country which could we hate today? There are, of course a couple of candidates, but I don't know if the level of animosity is great enough to bring right and left together. Iran? Not enough distrust yet. Russia? North Korea? Maybe. Now if they were to launch a missile toward Hawaii...

12 POLITICAL CHAOS   149

Scenario 3: Strong Woman

In the period of time between the successful election, after the congratulatory parties and speeches, but before her taking the oath of office, she called her intended staff and a few potential department heads together in a private meeting, away from Washington to hammer out some details of the transition and to set some of the rules for her administration.

Madame President Elect said:

Here's how I intend to run things. We will be ethical above all. The tests for ethical behavior are tests you yourselves will apply and there are only four of them: would you like to have what you are about to do, done to you? Would you be proud to tell your kids about it? Would things improve if everybody did it? And finally would you like to see it appear on the front page of the New York Times? Molly, please get a few dozen signs made up to put in our offices with these 4 points.

If you do something underhanded you'll be back to frying hamburgers. We will be transparent- you saw how I released my tax returns. I want you all to do the same. We will be consistent; if you want to deviate from a policy I set, you are of course free to speak your mind- just let me know first and maybe I will change the policy before you are back to frying potatoes.

We will be organized. When things get chaotic, and they will, we will slow things down. I saw a piece by Gordon and Greenspan on how to manage a chaotic system (Gordon and Greenspan 1994). *They built quantitative models and drove them into chaos with the right choice of exogenous variables and tested a few different management approaches to regaining stability and the one that worked was "slow it down." Ever watch a baseball game? When a professional pitcher gets in trouble- bases loaded one out- what's he do? He slows down, becomes deliberate. That's what we're going to do too.*

We will cultivate Congress and not play favorites. I want to put a few of our smart but less ideologically fixed opponents in Cabinet posts, so I am open to suggestions from you. Not exactly like Lincoln's government of rivals, but certainly leaning in that direction.

When we ask for favors from Senators or Congress people we will play fair and offer something in return like a reference at a news conference that they can take to the folks back home. And when they ask us for something we will damn well try to do it if we agree because that way we will build up accounts that we can use later. The same goes for relations with other countries, play fair. But for nasty players like the gun lobby who are engaged in behavior we do not sanction, we have to be inventive, remember they have their own constituency. Our dealings with them and others like them must be imaginative, like give double tax breaks to individuals that check in their guns with the police. The idea is to reward behavior we favor but not to be stupid about it.

And I want a good thorough review of guaranteed minimum income. Get the cheaters, but capture them fairly and treat them with mercy. Remember most of them are steeling because they have to.

And for God's sake set up a cyber perimeter that will exclude- no not exclude- but capture people who want to do us digital harm. Isolate and remove incentives from the groups that champion causes and immoral behavior we abhor like Holocaust deniers, white supremacists, and anti-Semites, but in a manner that preserves their freedoms- that will take some magic. And, oh yes, reinstate the environmental safeguards that we once fought so hard to get.

But do it with style, dignity, and pride.

Any questions? No? OK, drink your champagne and let's do it.

References

Asimov, I. 1955. *Franchise*, first published in the magazine "If: Worlds of Science Fiction." August 1955 and later in 1989 as a standalone book. https://www.fantasticfiction.com/a/isaac-asimov/franchise.htm. Retrieved September 17, 2018.

Baumeister, Roy, and Mark Leary. 1995. The Need to Belong: Desire for Interpersonal Attachments as a Fundamental Human Motivation. *Psychological Bulletin*, American Psychological Association. http://persweb.wabash.edu/facstaff/hortonr/articles%20for%20class/baumeister%20and%20leary.pdf. Retrieved September 24, 2018.

Brownstone, David, and Irene Frank. 1996. *Timelines of War*. New York: Little, Brown.

Caspi, A.I., J. McClay, T.E. Moffet, J. Mill, J. Martin, I.W. Craig, A. Taylor, and R. Poulton. 2002. Role of Genotype in the Cycle of Violence in Maltreated Children. *Science* 297 (5582): 851–854. https://www.ncbi.nlm.nih.gov/pubmed/12161658. Retrieved September 21, 2018.

Cawthon, Lang K.A. 2011. *Primate Factsheet: Bonobo Behavior*. Madison, WI: University of Wisconsin. http://pin.primate.wisc.edu/factsheets/entry/bonobo/behav. Retrieved September 11, 2018.

Dowe, Darin. 2011. *Gangs: Slang, Words, Symbols.* Hendon Media Group. http://www.hendonpub.com/resources/article_archive/results/details?id=1402. Retrieved September 13, 2018.

Dreyfuss, Emily. (2018). Smart Phone Voting Is Happening, but No One Knows If It's Safe. *Wired*, San Francisco, CA, August 9. https://www.wired.com/story/smartphone-voting-is-happening-west-virginia?mbid=nl_08122018_daily_list3_p1&CNDID=46249697. Retrieved September 17, 2018.

Eisenberger, N., M.D. Liberman and K.D. Williams, 2003. "Does Rejection Hurt? An FMRI Study of Social Exclusion." https://www.ncbi.nlm.nih.gov/pubmed/?term=Lieberman%20MD%5BAuthor%5D&cauthor=true&cauthor_uid=14551436. Retrieved May 25, 2019.

Gordon, Theodore, and David Greenspan. 1994. The Management of Chaotic Systems. *Technological Forecasting and Social Change* 47 (1): 49–62. https://doi.org/10.1016/0040-1625(94)90039-6. https://www.sciencedirect.com/science/article/pii/0040162594900396. Retrieved September 25, 2018.

Henschel, Johannes, and John Skinner. 1991. *Territorial Behavior by a Clan of Spotted Hyenas, Ethology,* January–December. https://onlinelibrary.wiley.com/doi/abs/10.1111/j.1439-0310.1991.tb00277.x. Retrieved September 11, 2018.

Jones, Tim. 1948. *Dewey Defeats.* Chicago, IL: Chicago Tribune, November 3. http://www.chicagotribune.com/news/nationworld/politics/chi-chicago-days-deweydefeats-story-story.html. Retrieved September 13, 2018.

Millennials. 2010. *A Portrait of Generation Next: Confident, Connected, Open to Change*, Pew Research Center, February. http://www.pewsocialtrends.org/2010/02/24/millennials-confident-connected-open-to-change/. Retrieved September 21, 2018.

Stiffer, Linda. 2011. Understanding Orca Culture. *Smithsonian Magazine*, August. https://www.smithsonianmag.com/science-nature/understanding-orca-culture-12494696/. Retrieved September 11, 2018.

Vasquez, John A. 1995. Why Do Neighbors Fight? Proximity, Interaction, or Territoriality. *Journal of Peace Research* 32 (3, August). https://www.jstor.org/stable/425665?newaccount=true&read-now=1&seq=3#metadata_info_tab_contents. Retrieved September 24, 2018.

Welker, Barbara. 2017. *Primate Social Organization, an Introduction to Paleoanthropology.* Milne library. https://milnepublishing.geneseo.edu/the-history-of-our-tribe-hominini/chapter/primate-social-organization/. Retrieved September 11, 2018.

CHAPTER 13

The Perfect Human

Unlocking the mysteries of human genetics and developing the technologies to manipulate heredity will give, for better or worse, a new dimension to our ability to set the fate of our children.

Four scientists: Rosalind Franklin, Maurice Wilkins, James Watson, and Francis Crick first described the two-strand molecular model of DNA in 1953: It is a biomolecule with two long chemical chains wrapped around each other in the now famous form of a double helix with defined sequences of four inert chemicals along each of the two strands, the strands held in juxtaposition by hydrogen bonds. This molecule is the basis for all future biotechnology, personal medicine, a goodly portion of future psychiatry, and perhaps the fate of mankind itself (NIH 2018).

There are about 37 trillion cells in each human and each of those cells (with a few exceptions) carry almost identical DNA molecules in their nuclei (Bianconi et al. 2013).[1] The sequence of chemicals along that double-stranded helix defines our phenotype, the color of our eyes and hair, our height, our weight, and our skin color, and everything else about us. The sequence is our inheritance, capturing the evolutionary process of hundreds of thousands of thousands or millions of years, and to some great extent sets our personal destiny. This is all determined at the instant of conception when half of the genetic characteristics are

---

[1] For comparison, there are only about three trillion tress in all of the world, so every single person has about 10 times the number of cells in their body as there are trees in the world.

© The Author(s) 2019

T. J. Gordon and M. Todorova, *Future Studies and Counterfactual Analysis*, https://doi.org/10.1007/978-3-030-18437-7_13

provided to the embryo from the mother's ovum and half from the father's sperm. After that, the genetic die is cast.

Each DNA molecule has about 20,000 sequences and that is only about 1.25% of the material in the genome. The other 98.75% is thought to be unused junk, but some scientists think that nature is more conservative and someday the purpose of the non-DNA portion of the genome will be better understood.

Some diseases are determined by errors in the DNA molecule that come from mutations or preexisting errors in the parents' genes. These disease-causing errors appear in all of the trillions of cells in the body and may be omissions in the normal sequence, extra and unnecessary material, or repeat sequences of seemingly endless replications. The diseases created by genetic errors include cystic fibrosis, Down syndrome, hemophilia, polycystic kidney disease, sickle cell disease, Tay-Sachs disease, some forms of breast cancer, and Amyotrophic Lateral Sclerosis (ALS or Lou Gehrig's disease). ALS is a terrible neuromuscular disease that causes patients to loose control of muscular functions; it can be familial (inherited) or sporadic (of unknown origin); if familial the malfunctioning gene is likely to be C9orf72. This kind of designation shows that the offending sequence has been recognized, located on a chromosome, indexed, and cataloged. It can be located by scientists anywhere who have access to a small sample of the DNA. As for breast cancer, the offending genes may be mutations in the BRCA1 or BRCA2 genes; these abnormalities indicate a significantly increased chance for a woman's developing cancer, raising the possibility of the disease from the norm in women of 12% to about 70% by age of 80 (NCI 2018).

Genetic diagnosis and engineering has been accelerated by the invention of a way to access and modify genes, known as CRISPR Cas9. Patent applications were filed in 2012 and resulted in court patent battles between organizations claiming priority including Broad Institute (MIT and Harvard) and UC Berkeley (Cross 2018). Even with this battle in the courts, research has proceeded.

In nature, bacteria cut short pieces of DNA from infecting viruses and store them in a kind of library. When they are again detected, the bacteria use the enzyme Cas9 to cut the DNA of the invading virus to destroy its function. The Cas9 is a DNA cleaver, a scissor that cuts the double helix of DNA exactly at the targeted spot.

This natural process has been adapted to permit human intervention into the genetic system. The target is defined using a short RNA "sentinel" sequence; when that RNA and its genetic sequence is carried into nucleus that spot defined by the sentinel is found from among the 20,000 sequences in the genome. The DNA strands are broken there and as in the case of infecting viruses, the DNA's function is interrupted. Pieces of the DNA molecule can be modified, removed, or replaced. It is that simple and that complex. Not something you would do on kitchen tables of today, but who knows what DNA kits will be available tomorrow.

If a genetic abnormality can be positively identified, why not just fix it? Gene therapy attempts to do just that: The object is to replace defective genes with unimpaired genes. Viruses are used to carry a cargo of functioning genes to the affected areas. Some promising results are being reported, for example in application to hemophilia. Nienhuis et al. (2017) and Watson (2018), to cystic fibrosis (Inacio 2015), to Duchenne muscular dystrophy (Figueiredo 2018), to thalassemia—a blood disorder in which insufficient hemoglobin is produced (Costa 2018) and to severe combined immune deficiency, or SCID, the "bubble boy" disease in which the babies have essentially no functioning immune system (Ely 2018). The FDA is said to expect 1000 new applications per year for gene therapy trials (Bender 2018).

Genetic errors can often be positively identified. Knowing about the increased risk caused by these errors can lead to decisions to take prophylactic measures; in the case of BRCA1 and BRCA2 measures such as mastectomy. On the other hand when there are no therapeutic or prevention strategies available as in the case of ALS, many people say they do not want to know if they are at risk since even if they knew about abnormality, there would be nothing they could do about it. Genetic counseling is a new professional field that has grown in parallel with knowledge of genetic abnormalities.

There is a common element to all of these applications: They are therapies designed to function on individuals and work on somatic cells that is, on cells that have double helixes, the nonreproductive cells. They affect the individual, not the species. Manipulation of gametes, the reproductive cells, is another matter and genetic changes there have the potential to be passed on to future generations. This technology was generally considered too uncertain in its outcome, too profound in its implications, too easy to subvert to be developed now, but on November 28, 2018, Chinese "scientist He Jiankui announced at the Second International Summit on Human Genome Editing in Hong Kong that he had used CRISPR-Cas9 to disable copies of the CCR5 gene in human embryos, in a bid to prevent the embryos' father from transmitting his HIV infection" (Botting 2018). He performed this genetic surgery on twins, disabling both copies of the CCR5 gene in one twin and only one copy of the gene in the other twin so that it could serve as an experiment control for the first child. Here was a case of generic manipulation of non-somatic cells, capable of passing the changes made to the genome on to progeny, ad infinitum. No informed consent. No peer review. No consideration of the ethics involved. No reference to the rights of the child. No wonder there was an outcry from genetic scientists and ethicists.

Yet it may be a watershed moment. Wouldn't we all vote to eradicate inherited diseases from our germ line?

Scenario 1: Untitled

No! I won't write it. I won't even title it. I will try not to think about it. It is too cruel and plausible. Yet it represents an example of counterfactual analysis so I can't escape the responsibility of including it. It is a counterfactual story that reaches into history and asks, as counterfactuals do, "what if" but contrary to most analyses of this sort, it draws its answer from the future.

Joseph Mengele, the vicious anti-sematic Nazi, the "angel of death" who oversaw the gas chambers at Auschwitz and with the flick of his SS gloves could send Jews to slave labor work camps if they appeared capable or the gas chambers for extermination if they did not, and had I been able to write this scenario, I would have asked, what if he had had CRISPR?

Mengele sent Jews, gypsies, midgets, sick, elderly, pregnant women, children, mentally deficient and deformed people to their deaths, all in a day's work. Prisoners in the hospital who had not recovered after two weeks were also sent to the gas chambers. When a typhus infection spread in a woman's barracks, he sent 600 inmates who had lived there to their deaths so the barracks could be disinfected. Victims of another epidemic, this time scarlet fever, were also "cured" by murder. He also performed forced medical experiments using his captives as laboratory animals and recorded the experiments with Germanic precision. For his work on the color of human irises he collected eyeballs from cadavers; he explored the limits of human endurance at high altitudes by subjecting prisoners to low pressures in chambers that simulated high altitude; he ran a series of malaria and typhus experiments in which over 1000 people were deliberately infected with the diseases and treated with various drugs to determine their effectives- many died. The list is much longer and is well documented. He was an evil man and he was not alone in this evil work.

But perhaps the reason I can't write this scenario is it is too easy to imagine a Mengele with today's CRISPR pursuing two research directions: identifying a genetic means for certifying and "improving" Aryan characteristics to achieve a shortcut to the Nazi "Master Race." And second, identifying "Jewishness" genetically, "to develop an efficient and inexpensive procedure for the mass sterilization of Jews, Roma (Gypsies), and other groups (that) Nazi leaders considered to be undesirable (Holocaust Encyclopedia 1987). *What an evil world.*

Scenario 2: Can We Imagine?

Scientific work in the early 21 century has given us, several decades later, freedom from those diseases that came from genetic errors. The list of inherited diseases is long and does not need repeating here, but we have shed them now and for all time.. We have no mongolism, no dwarfism, no ALS, no hemophilia, no cystic fibrosis, no muscular dystrophy, no thalassaemia, no SCID, no genetically related cancer heart failure, Alzheiner's, or Parkinson's. Insects and animal vectors that transmitted some of these diseases have been sterilized- not eliminated but made to reject the role of carrier. Spurious mutations now raise alarms and first responders rush to quell the genetic outbreaks before they take hold and spread. Suicide, accidents, and unintended overdoses are now the major causes of death of people of all ages around the world.

And we have one remaining genetic problem: human design. What do we want our children and theirs to be? Highly intelligent- brilliant in fact, tall, handsome, born with all possible knowledge that can be transmitted in gestation, racial memory that places them squarely in their place in evolution. Good people, whatever that will come to mean.

Do we see a hint of Mengele in ourselves, hoping for superior race? Will we fission into warring camps that hold different images of perfection? Do we have the wisdom to take on the design of human destiny?

REFERENCES

Bender, Eric. 2018. Regulating the Jean-Therapy Revolution. *Nature*, December 12. https://www.nature.com/articles/d41586-018-07641-1?WT.feed_name=subjects_genetics. Retrieved December 12, 2018.

Bianconi, Eva, et al. 2013. An Estimation of the Number of Cells of the Human Body. *Annals of Human Biology* 40. https://www.tandfonline.com/doi/abs/10.3109/03014460.2013.807878. Retrieved December 11, 2018.

Botting, Eileen. 2018. A Chinese Scientist Says He Edited Babies Jeans: What Are the Rights of the Genetically Modified Child? *The Washington Post*, December 6. https://www.washingtonpost.com/news/monkey-cage/wp/2018/12/06/a-chinese-scientist-says-hes-edited-babies-genes-what-are-the-rights-of-the-genetically-modified-child/?utm_term=.cfaf8b24a541. Retrieved December 13, 2018.

Costa, M. 2018. Promising Results from Beta-Thalassaemia Gene Therapy Trial. *Bionews*, April 23. https://www.bionews.org.uk/page_135491. Retrieved December 12, 2018.

Cross, Ryan. 2018. Broad Prevails Over Berkeley in CRISPR Patent Dispute. *Chemical and Engineering News*, September 10. https://cen.acs.org/policy/litigation/Broad-prevails-over-Berkeley-CRISPR/96/web/2018/09. Retrieved December 14, 2018.

Ely, Kaitlynn. 2018. Saint Jude Develops Gene Therapy for Severe Combined Immune Deficiency. Rare Disease Report, January 15. https://www.raredr.com/news/gene-therapy-severe-combined-immunodeficiency Retrieved December 12, 2018.

Figueiredo, Marta. 2018. Microdystrophin Gene Therapy Shows Promising Interim Results in Phase 1/2 Trial. *Muscular Dystrophy News Today*, June 22. https://musculardystrophynews.com/2018/06/22/microdystrophin-gene-therapy-shows-promise-early-trial-results/. Retrieved December 12, 2018.

Holocaust Encyclopedia. 1987. *Article on Nazi Medical Experiments*. https://encyclopedia.ushmm.org/content/en/article/nazi-medical-experiments. Retrieved December 12, 2018.

Inacio, Patricia. 2015. Gene Therapy Shows Promising Results as a New Treatment for Cystic Fibrosis. *Lung Disease News*, July 7. https://lungdiseasenews.com/2015/07/07/gene-therapy-shows-promising-results-new-treatment-cystic-fibrosis/. Retrieved December 12, 2018.

NCI. 2018. *BRCA Mutations: Cancer Risk and Genetic Testing*. National Cancer Institute, National Institutes of Health, Washington, DC. https://www.cancer.gov/about-cancer/causes-prevention/genetics/brca-fact-sheet#q2. Retrieved December 12, 2018.

Nienhuis, A.W. et al. 2017. *Gene Therapy for Hemophilia*. US National Library of Medicine, National Institutes of Health, Washington, DC. https://www.ncbi.nlm.nih.gov/pubmed/28411016; Retrieved December 12, 2018.

NIH. 2018. *Genetics Home Reference*. National Institutes of Health, Washington, DC. https://ghr.nlm.nih.gov/primer/basics/dna. Retrieved December 11, 2018.

Watson, Melody. 2018. *Gene Therapy Shows Promising Results for Hemophilia.* WFH Network, Hemophilia World. https://news.wfh.org/gene-therapy-shows-promising-results-hemophilia/. Retrieved December 12, 2018.

CHAPTER 14

Conclusions

Todorova's proposed morphology of counterfactual dilemmas worked well for us and promises wider application to futures research in illuminating unexpected futures. Her structure consists of three types of starting points: (1) sleeper facts waiting to be re-discovered, (2) reinterpretation or reinvention of facts we think we know, and (3) rumors, gossip, and unproven hypotheses that can masquerade as hard facts and be as important to decision making as proven facts. This structure allowed us to explore areas beyond those usually explored by futurists. At the start of our work, we asked ourselves, in the manner of historians using counterfactual analysis, how the future might turn out differently if a discarded or discredited truth were to become good science (e.g., panspermia), or if a fact that we were sure of turned out to be wrong (e.g., realignments in politics), or if some esoteric beliefs moved from the "weird" column to the "fact" column (e.g., belief in a viable afterlife). This is the thinking that guided our initial input to the Real Time Delphi of scholars and ultimately gave rise to the chapter headings of this book.

So, conclusion number 1 is that counterfactual thinking has a place in futures research, not so much to forecast what may come to pass, but to stimulate imaginations by framing an unlimited set of what if questions that can test and expand our assumptions about reality.

In about 1969, I (Gordon) led a graduate seminar in futures for one semester at Wesleyan University in Middletown Connecticut. A group of us who met at RAND in Santa Monica had just begun the adventure

© The Author(s) 2019

T. J. Gordon and M. Todorova, *Future Studies and Counterfactual Analysis,*
https://doi.org/10.1007/978-3-030-18437-7_14

161

of starting a non-profit futures research institute, the Institute for the Future. Wesleyan gave us a friendly environment, was helpful in obtaining some of initial study contracts, and invited us to teach at the University. I took the offer and agreed to organize a graduate seminar. At our first meeting, to get the ball rolling, I asked each of the students that showed up on the first day of classes to choose any natural law and ask how the sciences and the world would change if the law were to be proven wrong or superseded, a mind-opening challenge. The rule was that they could only violate one natural law at a time. Generally, we found that it was very tough to violate only one law at a time, change one and other laws and rules would fall in succession. This was a much less sophisticated way to ask about counterfactuals than Todorova's formulation and I would certainly put the question differently today.

Thirty years later, another futurist is running another seminar. He says: 'Hello ladies and gentlemen, welcome to Futures 101. I hope we have fun this semester and explore some imaginative futures that will enlighten us all. Not that any of our guesses about the future will prove to be correct and leave us with an accurate picture of what will be but we can aspire to learn what might be and how to think about the options and the differences they may make in our lives and the lives of others we love. Here's how we can begin: I'd like you to think about your fields: math, business, biology, whatever. Think about the premises on which your field is based and what might happen if those premises we proven wrong-overturned-replaced. This is basis for your thought experiment, your the seed of the future, your experimental counter-fact. Say some bright young physics grad student bottles anti matter and successfully isolates it from our matter-based world, not just for microseconds as used to be the case or even minutes as is now the case, but indefinitely and without using special support equipment to keep the anti matter from annihilating itself by combing with ordinary matter.[1] In math what if we didn't have the concept of decimals or zero, what would change? In business what if the price of things were not based on the cost of raw materials, production, and marketing, plus a bit of profit, but on one's ability to pay. This would be a new market arrangement in which goods are cheaper for poor people than rich people. Call it a new socialism or communism or even a new kind of capitalism. In biology what if evolution were much more rapid that we now

---

[1] In April, 2011, scientists at the CERN accelerator announced they has stored anti matter for a full 16 minutes. See: https://home.cern/about/engineering/storing-antimatter. Retrieved October 14, 2018.

14 CONCLUSIONS 163

believe, if evolution could change phenotypes in only a generation or two or if some imaginative psychologist found that political orientation was passed on genetically? Picture a long line of Democrats or Republicans, lined up from daughter to mother, to grandmother, to great grandmother, and so on back to the time when these political parties began. What if liberalism or conservatism were in our genes?

At our next meeting I want you each to present an informal 5-minute talk on what fundamental belief or law you want to question. If the class buys your premise that such a thing is at least conceivable-not necessarily probable or even plausible, you and some of your supporters will spend the rest of the semester developing the consequences of your hypothetical counterfact, using all the tools of futures research, from scenarios and Real Time Delphi to the Futures Wheel and quantitative modeling.

You have an infinity to choose from.'

In addition to the idea that counterfactual questions could be asked about the future as well as history opened our thinking about the future. We learned that a map metaphor of the future was helpful, the map consisting of intersecting paths that flow from mostly historical momenta. New developments bring new roads. Decisions must often be made or ignored at the intersections. Decision makers can sometimes steer us down one path or another, often without knowing where the road leads.

We also learned a bit about the substantive issues we addressed.

The growing technological ability to create real appearing false worlds can lead to giant frauds and a new sort of terrorism from which recovery will be difficult. To counter this, we will need to develop precise, accurate, irrefutable fact checking technology (probably empowered by artificial general intelligence). But algorithms ought not replace human judgment in resolving issues stemming from truth vs. fiction. No matter what the system, freedom of speech and a free press need to be included in the design. There is a town in New Mexico named Truth or Consequences after a 1950s TV quiz show, but the name fits the uncertain routes leading out of this dilemma.

Proliferation of WMD is happening all around us, faster than we can write about it. It has given birth to a new era of mutual assured destruction, ultimately more significant than the cold war version because it has been politicized, the firepower has been increased, and there are more players interacting. There are few apparent paths to sane resolution: Reduction in the stocks of nuclear weapons would be a powerful step toward stability, but it is difficult to devise a policy that benefits the major owners of that deadly stock. In the meantime equipment failure, misunderstood intent, and terrorism increase the threat.

Will population growth outpace the world's ability to support the people who inhabit it? Even with reduced population growth rates of the past few decades, developing countries will need to double almost everything—food, roads, education, medical facilities, in the next two or three decades, just to keep their status quo in terms of per capita measures. There are conceivable paths toward resolution (or at least lowering uncertainty); these include hard-hearted coercion, family planning with rewards for smaller families, and technological intervention, perhaps through genetics.

On a different plane, we asked tough questions of identity. Who are we really? How did it all begin? Where did we come from? It's not likely that any futures technique will lead to answers to such questions, but we can imagine unlikely scenarios in which a Creator manifests himself (or herself or itself), or where we gain understanding of how the evolving brain has been shaped from a blank tablet into one pre-equipped with predilections and biases toward not only survival but the drive to understand existence.

One of those drives is the pursuit of immortality. Our scenario snapshots were heavily technological: preservation of the essence of self on digital hard drives or robot avatars, rebuilding of ourselves by progeny from bits and pieces of preserved tissue, cryopreservation (freeze or rot), and escaping the scythe of death with just in time medicine.

Which leads to the unsettling future of religion. One of the roads leading from this issue is a dead end: It contains the demise of religion and despite the view that religiosity may be innate, organized religion shrinks and disappears on this road and agnosticism and atheism survive and flourish. It has been a rough road pocked by fraud, immoral behavior of religious leaders, incompatibility between a merciful God and inhumane cruelties of society, and irreconcilable discord between science and the fables of religion. Another road leads in the opposite direction: It is defined by efforts of the institutions to survive: Mergers of religions that share at least a bit of ideology and the use of technologies to enhance their messages from rabbi-bots and e-fessions to mock miracles.

It isn't a defective mass recollection of our time, decisions are indeed getting worse. Many have moved decision makers away from achievement of their goals rather than toward them, despite information that could have made the errors apparent. Why? The paths out of this dark

14 CONCLUSIONS   165

place are long and narrow. The first suggests a new curriculum in which decision skills are taught: the elements of good decision making—not just cost/benefit but psychology, sub conscious biases, question framing, and the intrinsic irrationality of human decision making. The second, how to interpret signs of change in the environment, and how to use these in reaching conclusions about what needs to be done and how. And the third path intersected all of the others leading out of this dark spot: the need to stay true to a moral code.

Warning signs are flashing: The threats from bio-terrorism are huge and near term and despite the need, the roads leading to solutions are shrouded in fog. The approaches to reducing bio-terror likelihood will be difficult to implement and of uncertain effectiveness. How can access to the tools of genetics be limited only to people who do not mean to do harm? How can the motives of would-be mass bio-murderers be anticipated? Must we trade away some freedoms for improved security?

We are well along on the path to artificial intelligence with its promises of wisdom and threat of dominance, called by Steven Hawking "the biggest event in human history." The key lies in whether society can control it or whether the machines themselves will determine their role.

We also asked in our array of issues whether progress was always a good thing. Would the pursuit of happiness or even pleasure lead to a better world? The alterative was a path that involved satisfaction with the status quo, stasis. Would we ever be satisfied with what we have and not seek more? In one of our scenarios, we pictured a world of stasis and it felt uncomfortable. Perhaps we will always aspire.

We considered the issue of political chaos, a social disease, popping up in unexpected places around the world, marked by incivility and bad temper, an ugly mood, and a challenge to democracy. The roads out of this dilemma include new ways to vote (including universal plebiscites via smart phone) instead of representation. A revised Constitution, no electoral college: direct vote on everything: the ultimate in crowdsourcing. Do we trust the wisdom of the crowd when it is available to us?

We have presented over 40 scenarios in this book to help describe a few of the billions of possible paths emanating from some current dilemmas. Some of these dilemmas need effective solutions before they get worse, others are not pressing now but are at least on the agenda for future solution. That's 40 out of how many? Impossible to say but it is an extremely large number. Imagine again the map we described in the introduction. The ganglion that existed on the left to illustrate how we got to the present is history's territory; the map on the right is a road map of the future.

The road map extends out years, decades, and centuries, becoming dimmer the further away in time. Imagine that at the limit of our road map, there are file folders of hundreds of thousands of scenarios that describe how we got from the present to those futures. We could run these through filters to separate the good outcomes from the bad to find decisions that tended to lead to good outcomes.[2] In separating the good from the bad, we may realize that what we mean by good and bad will change: What was OK 20 years ago is no longer OK. What we yearned for or feared 20 years ago will seem childish, archaic, naïve, and provincial. The issues will have been rooted in history, and they will worsen or improve in momentous or tiny increments—the small paths and byways of the right side of the chart. The most important of these will probably be unexpected.

Big questions are being asked. Do the roads we have discussed converge somewhere up ahead? Ray Kurzweil sees a time coming when the exponential growth of computing power far exceeds the sum of all human intelligence (Kurzweil 2005). Transhumanism, another belief about the destiny of our species, holds that a merger of mechanical and electronic technology with biology has already begun and will yield "Human 2.0," perhaps bringing immortality. The gurus of transhumanism are Ray Kurzweil, Nick Bostrom (Bostrom and Dupuy 2011), and Aubrey de Grey (de Grey and Rae 2007) who argues that a life span of 1000 years is possible. Yuval Harari, building on an idea of David Brooks[3] sees data as the key forward-driving force, not just in the sense of "big data" as we are getting to know it, but as the scaffold for what humans will become (Harari 2016). He argues that biology is data about how cellular bits of information combine to make organisms and plants, that economic systems are ultimately data, and that politics is about how societies choose to assemble data; algorithms structure their societies. He says "we may interpret the entire human species as a single data processing system....we can also understand the whole of history as a process of

---

[2] Researchers at the think tank RAND are exploring such approaches by developing a methodology they call Robust Decision Making (RDM). See: https://www.rand.org/topics/robust-decision-making.html. Retrieved October 16, 2018.

[3] Brooks is a journalist for the *New York Times* and introduced the notion of "dataism" in an op-ed piece in 2013 (Brooks 2013).

improving the efficiency of the system" (ibid., p. 440). A new religion flows from this line of thinking; Harari calls it Dataism and says, "the greatest sin would be to block the data flow. What is death if not a condition in which information doesn't flow?"

The scenarios we imagine will for the most part be based on momenta of history and new capabilities that are the super nova's of future history, but the unexpected small paths and byways are the spice that will give flavor to the simmering soup that is our future. And I for one am ready for a taste of it.

REFERENCES

Bostrom, Nick, and Jean-Pierre Dupuy. 2011. *H±: Transhumanism and Its Critics*. Philadelphia, PA: Metanexus Institute.

Brooks, David. 2013. Opinion|The Philosophy of Data. *The New York Times*. Retrieved January 19, 2019.

de Grey, Aubrey, with Michael Rae. 2007. *Ending Aging: The Rejuvenation Breakthroughs That Could Reverse Human Aging in Our Lifetime*. New York: St. Martin's Griffin.

Harari, Yuval. 2016. *Homo Deus*. London: Penguin.

Kurzweil, Ray. 2005. *The Singularity Is Near; When Humans Transcend Biology*. New York: Penguin.

Appendix

Methodologies

Counterfactual Futures

M. Todorova has proposed three counterfactual categories (Todorova 2015).

Dormant Facts

The term dormant fact refers to an existing or past situation or reality whose potential impact has remained unrecognized or unfulfilled. It has "slept" (remained latent) in the past, but may be activated and become manifest if and when the social, economic, political, or religious context is changed, producing dramatic and sometimes violent change. One such dormant fact was the "frozen conflict" that divided the ethnic and religious groups—particularly Christians and Muslims—throughout the countries that formed the Socialist Federal Republic of Yugoslavia (SFRY) following the Second World War. However, with the disintegration of SFRY after 1989, and changes in the political context, that frozen conflict became a dominant factor in the region, unfortunately leading to genocide and massacre.

© The Editor(s) (if applicable) and The Author(s), 169
under exclusive license to Springer Nature Switzerland AG 2019
T. J. Gordon and M. Todorova, *Future Studies and Counterfactual Analysis*,
https://doi.org/10.1007/978-3-030-18437-7

170 APPENDIX

Dormant facts possess the potential for inciting future change. They are catalysts, inert themselves until mixed with the right ingredients; they are driving forces or triggers waiting for the right moment to manifest themselves. They are like sleeper cells waiting to be reactivated by circumstances. They might be activated by conscious (manipulative) or unconscious (accidental) intervention. Dormant facts arise from continuous historical processes; tensions may have accumulated over long periods of time, just waiting to be released.

Some examples of dormant facts are: the future of terrorist organizations, nuclear weapon proliferation, and problems stemming from the unequal distribution of wealth.

Reinterpretation/Reinvention of Facts

Facts may also be subject to *reinterpretation* or even *reinvention*; when facts are reoriented, they may assume new meaning particularly when political, social, religious, or economic contexts shift. The reinvention of a fact is often used for propaganda and ideological purposes. Well-meaning leaders or demigods may rekindle sleeping feelings of perceived insults of long past injustices or raise stereotype scapegoats. The origin of these reinterpreted facts may have been dormant facts that enter this category through a new lens to make them fit a social framework or ideology. Despite their generally subjective nature, they can be powerful stimulants of the future waiting only for the right moment or champion to verbalize them and call others to action.

Some examples of legacy issues in this category are: reinterpretation of religious dogma, changes in attitudes toward privacy, and new meanings of left and right in politics.

Rumors, Gossip, and Hypothesis

A third category of "counterfacts" consists of rumors and hypotheses, which, though not universally accepted as fact, nevertheless can have immediate and potentially lasting impacts on perceptions of reality equal to or even stronger than established facts.[1] This category ultimately raises the question "What is true?" As opposed to dormant facts, they do

---

[1] Ibid.

APPENDIX   171

not rest on real events, but are imagined realities pretending to be fact. Stereotyping, gossip, and amplification by social media can create a substitute reality and thus a basis for (ill-informed) future action. This category is particularly salient in the era of social media when fake newspaper headlines compete with reality, are essentially indistinguishable from real headlines, and are copied and redistributed by "friends" and "followers." This is the domain of alternate reality when, for example, nearly 100% of scientists call global warming but deniers argue otherwise, when vaccination is thought by some to be linked to autism but all data show no connection, when repeated lies and distortions gain a sense of reality as in Hitler's "master race" propaganda.

Examples of this category include the headline "Pope endorses Trump,"[2] belief in an afterlife, machines will conquer the world, and that progress is most often good and inevitable.

Constructing Counterfactual Worlds

Historians use counterfactual analysis when they ask how our current world might have turned out if some aspect of history been different. These analyses begin with the question "what if," for example, what if development of the railroads had not taken place in the nineteenth century, would the American economy have been much different? The economist/historian Robert Fogel posed this question and analyzed the counterfactual world that resulted from an economy without railroads (he found an effect on the economy of only 2%) (Fogel 1964). Tracing the logical cause and effect chain from the postulated changes in a counterfactual world often leads to understanding of the processes at work in complex systems. This is one way to learn from history.

The seed of Fogel's counterfactual world is an omitted technology (railroads), but a seed can also be the insertion of a technology (suppose Zeppelins had used helium rather than hydrogen and the Hindenburg had not exploded at Lakehurst New Jersey in 1937) or a real-life decision that had a different outcome (in WW2, a bridge too far at Arnhem). The historical seed can also be a fictitious event inserted into the chain

---

[2]In July 2016, a the Web site *WTOE 5 News* reported that Pope Francis had broken with tradition and unequivocally endorsed Donald Trump for President of the USA. It was false, of course. See http://www.snopes.com/pope-francis-donald-trump-endorsement/. Retrieved November 20, 2016.

172   APPENDIX

of events leading to the present (what if an umpire's call on the tag at home plate had been overturned and the runner who had been called out were now to be called safe). No matter what the seed, tracing its imagined consequences in the fictitious counterfactual world can lead to greater understanding of how complex systems may work and in some cases historical counterfactuals can provide perceptions about the future. (Example: One scenario in Chapter 11 imagines a fictitious debate between persons like Leibniz and Voltaire about what constitutes progress and why God permits suffering and evil.)

Thus, the historian works with two worlds: the real world and the imagined world that results from their retrograde "what if" questions; the difference between the two is an indication of the sensitivity of the world to changes of the sort initiated by the historian's retrograde seed. "What if" is a powerful beginning to any counterfactual scenario. One of the authors of this book (Gordon) has constructed a large and growing database of possible newspaper headlines of the future. These headlines (now number more than 1500) have been generated by a continual review of reports of scientific and technological accomplishments.

Similarly, the futurist that employs a version of counterfactual analysis has two worlds to consider: a baseline forecast of a future world (replacing the historian's real world) and a modification to that future world produced by prospective (as opposed to retrograde) "what if" questions, for example: How will the future change if in the future a contemplated policy is enacted or an existing one is canceled, or if a new invention is introduced, or if the use of an anticipated technical system is proscribed?

Remarkably, the means for analyzing the consequences of an historian's seed and a futurist's seed are similar. Among the techniques are statistical fitting of historical quantitative data,[3] reversion to the mean caused by random events,[4] scenarios constructed by individuals or

---

[3]Techniques frequently used by the Millennium Project in constructing forecasts for the State of the Future Indexes, Futures Research Methods, v3, Millennium Project, Washington, DC, 2015.

[4]"...the statistical phenomenon stating that the greater the deviation of a random variate from its mean, the greater the probability that the next measured variate will deviate less far. In other words, an extreme event is likely to be followed by a less extreme event." Wolfram MathWorld. http://mathworld.wolfram.com/ReversiontotheMean.html. Retrieved July 31, 2018.

APPENDIX 173

groups (Gordon and Glenn 2017) simple or complex computer models (Hughes 2018), worlds constructed wholly out of imagination such as science fiction (Lombardo 2015), or Monte Carlo techniques that introduce a degree of randomness into the analyses. The historian works with alternative histories and the futurist with alternative futures. The historian compares outcomes of their alternate histories with the real world to gauge the sensitivity to their imagined retrospective seed; the futurist compares outcomes of their alternative futures to their baseline world to gauge the sensitivity of the future to their imagined prospective seed.

In either case, analysis techniques that depend solely on extrapolation are bound to be wrong ultimately, because new developments change past trends. Increasing the amount of past data or its precision will not change the situation because the most important future developments may not be part of the past. Improved precision may not help either if the systems under study are nonlinear and become unstable or chaotic. Newton's worldview was linear, the clockwork universe, wound up once by God, and then released to wend its linear way. Generations of modelers built their models on the assumption that past momentums point the way to the future that extrapolation is justified in view of the assumed clockwork machine. But since then, there has been the realization that the essence of the future is in developments that disturb extrapolation. Nonlinear dynamics shows that very small disturbances can cause huge difference in the outcome of deterministic equations, and the system doesn't even have to be complicated to become chaotic.

So what is new in this view of the similarity between historical counterfactual analysis and futures research? Two ideas are:

- Counterfactual analysis permits the classification of perceived issues as dormant facts, facts subject to reinterpretation, and rumors or hypotheses (Todorova 2015). Classification can aid in the prioritization and systematic analysis of issues.
- Methods pioneered by futurists can be useful to historians and vice versa. This coincidence leads to the possibility that lessons of history will indeed lead to better futures research, forecasting, and policy analysis.

174   APPENDIX

The Headline Database[5]

The headline database can serve as a source of counterfacts to be considered in the construction of scenarios. The users of this database can retrieve a random set of five "what ifs" by simply hitting an access button. A different random set will be obtained on the next press of the button. The random selection process helps avoid the effect of personal biases on the choice of counterfactual events.

The concept of this database dates back to 1965, at the start of modern futures research, when one of the authors of this current book (Gordon) wrote a book titled *The Future* (Gordon 1965). The premise of this pre-Delphi book was simple enough: examine leading edge of research in progress, with the person in charge of that research if possible, and ask what the consequences of the work were likely to be. The book was not widely read but the basic idea of projecting the consequence of work in progress lies behind the contemporary headline database. Imagine reading reports of work progress daily in the on-line media using news aggregators' sources such as New Atlas, Wired, and AllTop. With perseverance, one can trace back to the original report behind the aggregators' summaries and ask the question "What if the work reported here is completed? What would the headline read?"

The database entries in the "what if" database have been compiled over a period of several years and are mainly based on published semi-technical but reputable news reports, professional studies of future developments, speculations by various authors of scientific and popular books, in blogs or other media, and conjectures by various "official" and "unofficial" agencies. In other words, the headline entries are statements inspired by published information and opinion from a broad range of sources. The headlines in the aggregate present developments based on work in progress that may make the future different from the past.

There are several thousand entries in the existing database. Each entry is thought to be precise enough to be verifiable in retrospect, stated as though it is a news headline describing a future event and judged to be nontrivial. The expected general time frame is also stated (near term, mid-term, far out, or indeterminate), and the database creator assesses

---

[5]Major portions of this subchapter appeared previously in an article by Theodore Gordon, "1,000 Futures: Testing Resiliency Using Plausible Future Headlines," *World Future Review*, 2016, Vol. 8 (2), 75–86.

APPENDIX   175

the plausibility level in general terms. Entries are not rejected solely on the basis of perceived implausibility because unexpected and powerful Black Swan events may be among the useful counterfacts. Each entry is identified as fitting into three distinct domains (e.g., Crime, Space, and Culture) chosen by the analyst from a list of over 60. Finally, three Internet references are provided to articles that support, refute, or simply have relevance to the entry. Entries are made by staff or by users who can suggest changes or add new items in "wiki" fashion. "What if" retrievals can be based on the entire set of database entries or from a restricted set shaped by user-supplied search terms, time frames, and plausibility levels.

When entering a new headline into the database, analysts select three domains or general topics that describe each headline. If a proposed headline doesn't fit, a new category can be added. Thus, the imposed structure is loose and "learns" over time. The domains in use, after about 1500 entries, are (Table A.1):

Retrievals of interest can be obtained by using any of these tags. However, searching for a particular word, phrase, time frame, plausibility level, or for any or all simultaneously can be used in a much more finely grained search and retrieval.

Let us suppose we learn in an article in *The Economist* that an X Prize is being offered for the successful development of a "tricorder," a hand-held device that provides accurate automated diagnoses. The article says,

Table A.1   Categories now current in the headline database

Advertising	*Agriculture*	*Arts/culture*	*Automobiles*
Brain	Business	Communications	Computers
Conflict	Crime	Culture	Cyberspace
Decision making	Demography	Drugs	Economics
Economy	Education	Energy	Electronics
Entertainment	Environment	Fashion	Food
Freedom	Genetics	Governments	Health
Hunger	Industry	Labor force	Leisure
Materials	Medicine	Morality/ethics	Natural disasters
Optics	Peace	Politics	Population
Poverty	Privacy	Quality of life	Quantum
Religion	Robotics	Science	Security
Space	Sustainability	Technology	Transportation
War	Water	Weapons	

176   APPENDIX

Among the organizations, pushing for the development of a medical tricorder is the X Prize Foundation, an organization that aims to spur innovation by offering cash prizes. Earlier this year, it announced the Qualcomm Tricorder X Prize, financed by the Qualcomm Foundation, the charitable arm of Qualcomm, a maker of wireless communications technologies. It has put up $10m in prize money and another $10m to pay for the administration of the competition. So far more than 230 teams from over 30 countries have applied to enter the contest....[6]

Recognizing the success of previous X Prizes in stimulating innovation, the analyst writes and enters a future headline into the database:

Handheld devices for general medical diagnosis similar to the tricorder of Star Trek, costing less than $500 each, are now in use by half of all Western doctors for initial diagnoses. The event load sheet invites added detail, and the analyst adds: "Scans vital signs and other indications of health and almost instantly presents a list of a person's medical issues, based on logic, analysis of prior personal and public data."

The analyst guesses at a time frame (near term, e.g., ten years) and a plausibility level (very high) and enters three major headings (domains) under which this development is filed (health, quality of life, and security). A user need not agree with any of these judgment calls, he or she will be able to suggest changes through annotating the wiki. Finally, the analyst provides three Internet references that relate to this item including, if possible, the primary source describing a tricorder, the X Prize that is being offered, and some of the teams that are at work on the device.

A later user might see the tricorder item in a random retrieval or find it by searching with one of the terms tricorder, Star Trek, medical diagnosis, medical issues, or personal and public data. Furthermore, users can restrict the search by stating the time frame of interest and or the required level of plausibility.

To illustrate the use of this database, one click of the search button produced these five randomly chosen counterfacts:

S/N: 1218

Event: A new drug that provides many of the benefits of exercise is now over the counter

More detail: The gene activated by the drug is suppressing all the points that are involved in sugar metabolism in the muscle so glucose can be

---

[6]http://www.economist.com/news/technology-quarterly/21567208-medical-technology-hand-held-diagnostic-devices-seen-star-trek-are-inspiring

APPENDIX   177

redirected to the brain, thereby preserving brain function. http://newatlas.
com/exercise-pill-endurance-salk-institute/49345/?utm_source
=Gizmag+Subscribers&utm_campaign=6c09501086-UA-
2235360-4&utm_medium=email&utm_term=0_65b67362bd
-6c09501086-92456945

Time Frame: Mid term
Plausibility: Low
Domains Health, Drugs, Quality of life
Date: 2017-05-04

S/N: 675
Event: New materials in use that make clean up of oil spills simple and cheap
More detail: Utilizes "a stainless steel mesh coated with nano particles that captures oil while letting water escape"
Time Frame: Mid term
Plausibility: Low
Domains Environment, Materials, Materials
Date: 2015-05-09

S/N: 236
Event: Annual deaths from cardiovascular disease have reached negligible levels in the U.S.
More detail: Trend exists everywhere in the world and time to adopt the medical know how is decreasing even in poor countries
Time Frame: Mid term
Plausibility: High
Domains Health, Quality of life, Sustainability
Date: 2014-09-05

S/N: 1042
Event: Public outcry leads to laws for setting maximum prices on life saving drugs and permitting their importation by citizens from foreign countries
More detail: Pharmaceutical gouging must stop say Congressional leaders say; Epipen is the last straw
Time Frame: Near term
Plausibility: High
Domains Health, Drugs, Morality/ethics
Date: 2016-08-24

178   APPENDIX

S/N: 1242
Event: 1,000 telepresence theaters are now open in the US
More detail: Applications include: Mars telepresence, vacations spots that change weekly, porno shows, command and control, Broadway theater, education, etc.
Time Frame: Near term
Plausibility: High
Domains Entertainment, Culture, Arts
Date: 2017-06-26

Access to this database is free. Go to: http://www.changesignals.com/ Sign in. When prompted for a study code, enter "whatif" as one word, lower case.

The Precursor Real Time Delphi Study

Following publication of M. Todorova's initial paper outlining three types of counterfacts that might be appropriate to consider in futures studies (Dormant facts, Reinterpretation/reinvention of facts, and Rumors, gossip, and hypothesis), she and T. Gordon ran a study involving about 50 mainly European economists, educators, and political scientists, futurists, and people involved in business and trades to develop and evaluate a list of counterfactual issues. The study, conducted in 2015, used a two-round Real Time Delphi.[7] In Round 1, respondents were asked to identify contemporary issues that fit into one or another counterfactual category (e.g., "Please list some contemporary unproven beliefs that may help drive the future such as belief in the existence of intelligent life off the earth and that only animals- not plants- can think"). There was also a final question designed to evoke new suggestions (e.g., "imagine a future book titled 'Great Unexpected Events of the 21st Century.' What do you think might be the chapter headings?") The respondents were also asked to provide reasons for their answers. Round 1 can be found at:

---

[7]Real Time Delphi is a technique for collecting and synthesizing expert opinion. It involves on-line questionnaires and presents summaries of the group response to the participants as they add their answers to the groups. Anonymity of responses and in-process feedback are the properties of an RTD. See Real Time Delphi, a chapter in Futures Research Methods, v3, Millennium Project, Washington, DC.

APPENDIX 179

http://www.realtimedelphi.com/STUDIES/generic_questionnaires/generic_origins1.php?email=historian1.

The responses were used to form a list of candidate issue that could be further elaborated and evaluated in Round 2. The analysis of Round 1 suggestions involved combing like suggestions, identifying a subset that were likely to affect many people, deeply, for long periods, and were seen to be irreversible. In the interest of providing a Round 2 questionnaire that could be answered in a reasonable time, the list was truncated at less than 25 entries. The issues presented to the panel in the Round 2 questionnaire were:

Dormant facts

1. The future of ISIS and similar organizations
2. Nuclear weapon proliferation
3. Unequal distribution of wealth
4. Control of Internet content
5. The refugee crisis
6. Lack of work
7. Need for gender equality
8. Farewell to arms

Reinterpretation/invention of Facts

1. New generations are worse off than their parents
2. What weather patterns are normal?
3. As has polar icecaps melt, Arctic Ocean sovereignty maybe reinterpret
4. Changing views about anti-capitalist economies and societies
5. New attitudes from reinterpretation of religious dogma
6. Reinterpretation of privacy: attitudes toward personal online data
7. New meaning of left and right in politics
8. New foes, new allies

Rumors, gossip, and hypotheses

1. Vegan and other special diets promote health and extend life
2. Belief in an afterlife
3. Machines will conquer the world

180 APPENDIX

4. Progress is good and inevitable
5. History repeats itself
6. Aggression can be cured without harming ambition

The full Round 2 questionnaire can be found at http://www. realtimedelphi.com/STUDIES/generic_questionnaires/generic. php?email=historian2&q_cat=origins2#questionnaire?email=historian2&q_cat=origins2.

As a final question in Round 2, we asked: "Can you add developments for which there are no visible beginnings today or in the past? These would be Black Swans."

Some of the panelists' answers were:

- Antigravity
- Long-time retention and manipulation of antimatter
- Reprogramming human minds
- Proof that God is real
- Selective erasure of traumatic memories
- Remote detection of DNA for positive identification of distance
- Speeding up learning by at least 25% by exciting peripheral brain cells
- Proof of panspermia theory (biological precursors permeate space)
- Selective reproduction of human beings
- Intra-terrestrial communications (better understanding or maybe even with other species on our planet)
- Understanding that humankind should be united (we may have to face non-friendly extraterrestrials)

These two RTD rounds provided the raw materials to the authors who then selected the chapter topics and to some degree at least, the content of the chapters. The criteria we used were consistent with the criteria that carried the study from RTD Round 1 to Round 2: Would the issue or attempts to deal with it affect many people, deeply, for long periods and were probably irreversible.

We of course are indebted to the respondents who gave freely of their time. Here are some characteristics of the panel:

Number who provided an answer: 48
Men 60%; Women 40%
Total number of distinct answers: 1685
Average number of answers per question: 30–40

APPENDIX   181

Number of reasons given for numerical answers: 199

Field of Experience: economics 21.05%; politics 18.42%; environment 5.26%; education 18.42%; business and trade 13.16%; and other 36.84% (science, public relations, government).

Country of the participants: Bulgaria 70%; Canada 2%; Germany 4%; Greece 4%; Italy 2%; Poland 4%; South Korea 2%; USA 4%; UK 6%; and Venezuela 2%.

The Real Time Delphi Method

The Real Time Delphi method was used by Gordon and Todorova to collect expert judgments in the survey mentioned in Appendix "The Precursor Real Time Delphi Study". Real Time Delphi is a modern incarnation of the original Delphi technique developed at RAND, the Santa Monica, California, "think tank" in the early 1960s by Olaf Helmer, Nicholas Rescher, Norman Dalkey, and others. This technique provided a means for obtaining expert opinions from groups of experts using a series of interactive questionnaires, each building on the results of the former iteration (Gordon and Helmer 1964; Linstone and Murray Turoff 1975). Answers were contributed anonymously, and participants were asked to provide reasons for their opinions, particularly when these opinions deviated from group averages. In most applications, three or four rounds were used. Literally, thousands, perhaps tens of thousands, of studies requiring the synthesis of expert judgments used this method since its introduction. A recent Google search of the phrase "Delphi Expert Studies" produced over 2.5 million "hits."

But conventional Delphi studies take a long time to complete (on the order of several months) and have been expensive: A single round can easily require three weeks; a three-round Delphi is at least a three- to four-month affair, including preparation and analysis time. Real Time Delphi is a faster, less expensive system based on the Delphi principles of feedback of prior responses of the participating group and guarantees of anonymity of the respondents. For example, Landeta and his colleagues say:

> One of the main disadvantages of the Delphi method is that the period of time taken by the research may be excessively long. One should bear in mind that the intervals of time elapsing between the replies of the different experts for each round and the times elapsing between one round and the next, used for the study and analysis of the information supplied by the

182   APPENDIX

> panel members and the preparation of the following questionnaire, could distort the research and dishearten the groups taking part. Our experience in other studies has vouched for this. (Landeta et al. 2008)

While Delphi had its birth in concern about spurious factors that intrude in face-to-face meetings among experts, new technology can minimize some of these factors. Some Delphi-like studies have been performed online; the earliest date back to the 1970s when Murray Turoff experimented with early computer-based communications to link experts together in networks (Turoff 1972). Subsequently, he and his colleagues described a Social Decision Support System they created in which large groups of people (thousands) can interact and vote dynamically (can change votes as in Delphi) on social issues (Turoff et al. 2002). Researchers in Finland, Germany, Italy, and elsewhere have developed their own versions of Real Time Delphi software. TechCast is also an online expert system that uses a standing pool of participants to forecast the emergence of future technologies (TechCast 2018). The activity is continuous and thus provides not only a set of technological forecasts at any point in time but also serves as a scanning system. It presents its data with excellent graphics for easy comprehension.

In September 2004, the Defense Advanced Research Projects Agency (DARPA) awarded a Small Business Innovation Research grant to Articulate Software, Inc. to develop a Delphi-based method for improving the speed and efficiency of collecting judgments in tactical situations where rapid decisions are called for. The grant was based on a decision making problem: A hypothetical decision maker, uncertain about tactics that might be followed in accomplishing a specific objective, calls on a number of experts to provide their judgments about values of the alternative approaches. Delphi was specified in the grant as the method to be employed. The objective was to improve the speed of the process, to real time if possible (hence the name: Real Time Delphi). The number of participants representing different areas of expertise was assumed to be small, perhaps 10–15 people.

The Real Time Delphi design that emerged is particularly applicable to many other situations: synchronous or asynchronous participation, a small number or large number of participants, rapid completion required. It offers speed, efficiency, and transparency to the study administrators and flexibility to the participants.

APPENDIX   183

Imagine a Delphi-like study involving a set of numerical questions, for example, "What is the priority of a proposed research project?" When each respondent joins the on-going study, he or she is presented an on-screen form that contains for each potential research project:

1. A space for a respondent to provide his or her numerical estimate of the priority of each item on a Likert-like scale
2. The average of all of the responses of the group so far
3. The number of responses received so far
4. A window that shows reasons that others have given for their responses
5. And finally, a window that provides a place for respondents to type in the thinking behind their own answers.

In considering his or her answer to each question, a respondent may refer to the reasons others have given. The respondent can provide a response considering the reasons others have provided and instruct the computer to "save" the answer. The group average or median is updated immediately and presented back to the respondent and anyone else who has signed on along with the total number of people who have contributed to the group response.

There is no explicit second round. When the respondent comes back to the study in a minute or a day, the original input form is presented to him or her. Of course, by then others may have contributed judgments, the averages or medians may have changed, and other questions may be flagged since the group response may have changed sufficiently to move the respondent's previous answers outside of the pre-specified distance from the average or the median since the last time the input page was viewed.

In this way, the Delphi requirements of anonymity and feedback are met and the process, once underway, yields the distribution of the group's responses and reasoning of individual participants. The process can be synchronous or asynchronous, and if implemented on an Internet site, can involve a worldwide panel. The administrator can publish a cutoff time (an hour, a day, a week, or a month away) and encourage participants to visit the site often before that time. There will be no "stuffing of the ballot box" since each participant has only one form—their original form—that is always brought back when the participant revisits.

184   APPENDIX

To see and participate in a Real Time Delphi study that is open to the public, go to www.realtimedelphi.org, enter the required sign-on information, and use the code "automobiles." Your responses are invited. You can omit any questions you wish.

REFERENCES

Fogel, Robert. 1964. *Railroads and American Economic Growth*. Essays in Econometric History. Baltimore: Johns Hopkins Press.

Gordon, T. 1965. *The Future*. New York: St. Martin's Press; not to be confused with a book using the identical title published almost 50 years later by Al Gore, Random House, New York, 2013.

Gordon, T., and Jerome Glenn. 2017. *Interactive Scenarios*, a chapter in *Innovative Research Methodologies in Management*, ed. Mladen Sokele and Luiz Abel Moutinho; published by Palgrave Handbook of Innovative Research Methods in Management.

Gordon, T., and Olaf Helmer. 1964. *Report on a Long Range Forecasting Study*. RAND, September. This was the first public report, external to RAND that used the Delphi method.

Hughes, Barry. 2018. *International Futures*. Denver, CO: Frederick S. Pardee Center of International Studies. http://pardee.du.edu/access-ifs. Retrieved August 1, 2018.

Landeta, J., J. Matey, V. Ruiz, and J. Galter. 2008. Results of a Delphi Survey in Drawing Up the Input–Output Tables for Catalonia. *Technological Forecasting and Social Change* 75 (1): 32–56.

Linstone, Harold, and Murray Turoff. 1975. *The Delphi Method*. New York: Addison Wesley. This is perhaps the best book on the original method.

Lombardo, Tom. 2015. *Science Fiction: The Evolutionary Mythology of the Future*. Tempe, AZ: Center for Future Consciousness. https://www.center-forfutureconsciousness.com/pdf_files/Readings/Science-Fiction_The%20 Evolutionary%20Mythology%20of%20the%20Future.pdf. Retrieved July 31, 2018.

TechCast. 2018. Retrieved November 30, 2018.

Todorova, Mariana. 2015. Counterfactual Construction of the Future: Building a New Methodology for Forecasting. *World Future Review* 7 (1): 30–38.

Turoff, Murray. 1972. Delphi Conferencing: Computer-Based Conferencing with Anonymity. *Technological Forecasting and Social Change* 3: 159–204.

Turoff, Murray, Starr Roxanne Hiltz, Hee-Kyung Cho, Zheng Li, and Yuanqiong Wang. 2002. *Social Decision Support Systems (SDSS)*. Proceedings of the 35th Hawaii International Conference on System Sciences.

INDEX

A
abortion, 54
abundance, 44, 53
A Creation Myth, 64
addiction, 66, 130, 131
Afghanistan, 14, 44
afterlife, 61, 63, 68, 161, 171, 179
Agency for International Development
    (AID), 52, 137
aggression can be cured, 180
aircraft, 36, 38
Air Force, 13, 38, 41, 42, 45
Air National Guard, 41
algorithms, 1, 43, 71, 72, 103, 115,
    120, 124, 163
American Civil Liberties Union
    (ACLU), 115
A Mouse On the Road to Hell, 39
anti-capitalist economies, 179
anticipations, 2
antigravity, 180
antimatter, 180
Antony, Marc, 4
Apollo 12, 17
Apollo moon landing, 16

Arctic Ocean, 8, 179
Arkhipov, Vasili, 41, 43
Armstrong, Neil, 17
artificially intelligent machines, 58
artificial realism, 14
artificial truth, 14
Asimov, I., 146
asteroid, 13, 148
atomic bomb tests, 35
augmented reality, 21
Aunt Sadie, 75, 76
avarice, 127, 142

B
bacteria, 58, 78, 79, 97, 108, 111,
    154
bad dude, 35
bad intelligence, 37
ballistic missiles, xi, 13, 36
beginning, 1, 43, 58, 61, 63, 101,
    112, 138, 147, 172, 180
The beginning and hereafter, 61
best of all possible worlds, 127, 128,
    133

© The Editor(s) (if applicable) and The Author(s),
under exclusive license to Springer Nature Switzerland AG 2019
T. J. Gordon and M. Todorova, *Future Studies and Counterfactual Analysis*,
https://doi.org/10.1007/978-3-030-18437-7

186   INDEX

Bhutan, 127
bias, 6, 123
big brother, 23
big data, 166
bi-lateral, 47
biological, 61, 63, 114, 143, 180
bioweapons, 112
birth certificates, 57
birth rate, 54, 56
Black Death, 135
Black Plague, 109
blockchain, 147
bomb in a backpack, 45
Borg, 122
Bostrom, Nick, 166
bottled water concession, 56
The bounds of humanity, 51
Bradbury, Ray, 4
brainstorming, 137, 138
branching paths, 1
BRCA1 or BRCA2, 154
Brooks, David, 166
Buckley, William, 34
Bulgaria, xii, 181
Bureaucratic Truth, 21, 22
butterfly, 5–7

C
C9orf72, 154
Caesar, Julius, 4
cannabis, 132
capitalism, 136, 137, 162
catastrophe, 38, 39, 102, 110
causal factors, 7
cause-effect analysis, 6
CCR5, 156
cell phone, 146
Centers for Disease Control and
    Prevention (CDC), 109, 110,
    112–114
Certified Public Authenticator, 22

chaos, 3, 22, 44, 116, 129, 144, 148,
    149, 165
Chasing Highs, 132
chatbot, 87, 125
China, 8, 19, 34, 35, 37, 38, 54–58,
    109, 131
The China Syndrome, 55
Chinese, xii, 6, 56
Christian Science Monitor, 33
Church, 44, 54, 84, 86, 138
civility, 65, 148
civil liberties, 8
Clarke, William, 133, 134
Cleopatra's nose, 4, 138
cognessetti, 22
cold war, 8, 33, 37, 163
command and control, 20, 43, 178
common enemy, 144, 147
communications, 38, 42, 88, 104,
    113, 124, 175, 176, 180, 182
Communist Bloc, 54
complexity, 75, 96, 103, 132
Comprehensive Nuclear Test Ban
    Treaty (CTBT), 34
computer viruses, 20
conclusions, 17, 91, 161, 165
condoms, 52
confirmation bias, 11
conflict, 4, 63, 142, 169, 175
Congress, 21, 22, 27, 66, 80, 83, 105,
    146–149
conservatism, 163
Constitution, 24, 147, 165
Constructing Counterfactual Worlds, 171
consumption, 115, 137
contraceptives, 51–54, 56
Control of Internet, 179
corruption, 19, 21, 22, 83, 103, 116,
    129, 137
counterfact, 7, 162, 163
counterfactual analysis, xii, 4, 6–8, 61,
    161, 171–173

counterfactual approach, 6
Counterfactual Futures, 169
counterfactuals, 7, 156, 162, 172
counterfeit, 58
counterfeiting reality, 29
Courts of Supreme Wisdom, 21, 24, 26
create a super race, 58
Creator, 83, 164
crime, 48, 68, 116, 129, 137, 175
Crimea, 46
criminal, 20, 88
CRISPR, 58, 111, 114, 154, 156, 157
crops fail, 44
crowd surveillance, 45
Cuban Missile Crisis, 41

D

database, 29, 72, 75, 104, 123, 172, 174, 176, 178
Dataism, 167
Data Watch Agency (DWA), 23
The Day After, 33, 34
Dealing with bio-terrorism, 107
death and dying, 3
The Decision Maker, 40
decision makers, 36, 43, 100, 102–104, 164
decision making, 3, 91–93, 98, 100–103, 106, 161, 165, 175
decisions, 1–3, 8, 25, 26, 38, 43, 51, 64, 85, 91, 93–96, 98–103, 105, 106, 123, 164, 166, 182
DeepMind, 119
de Grey, Aubrey, 166
Delgado, Jose, 130
democracy, 19, 144, 146, 165
Department of Defense, 20
design a human, 58
Design Discord, 57
detection technologies, 55

dictator, 145
dignity, 54, 59, 150
dilemma, 3, 58, 163, 165
disease cures, 53, 69
distribution of wealth, 170, 179
diversity, 96, 124, 128
DNA, 14, 30, 62, 64, 67, 75, 146, 153–155
Doomsday or politics, 33
dormant facts, 4, 169, 170, 173, 178, 179
double helix, 153, 154
doublespeak, 27
Dr. Strangelove, 43
drug offenders, 25
Duke, David, 18
dystopia, 27, 41

E

earthquake, 97, 135
economic development, 54, 56
economists, 54, 137, 178
education, 19, 54, 83, 128, 164, 175, 178, 181
educators, 178
e-fessions, 88, 164
Eisenhower, Dwight, 18
electing, 145
electoral college, 147, 165
eliminate racial differences, 58
embryo, 58, 154
empiricism, 64
End of the Rainbow, 85
Enemy of the People, 26–28
enhanced human, 58
environment, 92, 95, 105, 162, 165, 175, 181
environmentalism, 136
epidemic, 53, 55, 101, 107, 109, 110, 112–114, 116, 132, 137, 148
epidemic diseases, 55

188   INDEX

Equatorial Guinea, 52
erasure of traumatic memories, 180
erotic, 67, 130–132
ethical, 83, 85, 149
ethical lapses, 83
ethicists, 156
Eugenics Brotherhood, 59
euphoria, 131
Europe, 46, 80, 84, 135
European, 3, 13, 21, 57, 119, 178
European Union, 57, 119
Euthanasia Society, 59
evil empire, 34
evolution, 7, 47, 58, 59, 61, 63, 65,
    83, 124, 125, 131, 144, 162
expansionism, 137
expertise, 95
extinct species, 85
extrapolation, 53, 121

F
facial recognition, 45, 124, 146
fact check, 11, 22
Fail Safe, 43
fake news, 12, 26–28
fake photos, 23
falsehood, 21, 65
false signal of an impending attack, 38
family planning, 51–55, 164
fashion, 74, 95, 119, 122, 175
Faust, 63
The Federal Truth in Reporting Act, 27
feminism, 51, 53
fiction, 4, 12, 14, 41, 43, 72, 73, 112,
    120, 163, 173
fictitious worlds, 6
films, 16
financial, 2, 18, 19, 22, 105, 124, 126
financial bubbles, 2
financial propaganda, 19
fire and fury, 33, 42
First Amendment, 21, 23

First in my decision class, 101
The First Motive, 112
first strike, 36
flying cars, 2
food, 23, 39, 53, 56, 91, 96, 101,
    105, 108, 141, 142, 164, 175
Food and Drug Administration
    (FDA), 23, 110
forecast, 55
forensic, 22
Forest Gump, 15
fractal, 15, 75
France, 17, 28, 34, 37, 62, 78
fraud, 19–21, 164
freedom of the press, 24
freedoms, 12
free market, 22
future, xi, xii, 1, 2, 4, 7, 8, 11, 12,
    14–18, 21, 26, 29, 33, 35, 37,
    40, 53, 61, 62, 68, 69, 72, 74,
    80, 83, 85, 86, 91–93, 96, 100,
    102, 106, 107, 110, 112, 120,
    121, 128, 131, 133, 143, 146,
    161–165, 167, 170–174, 176,
    178, 179, 182
futurists, 1, 2, 4, 74, 109, 161, 173,
    178

G
gametes, 155
Gates, Bill, 121
gender equality, 179
gene editing, 58
gene therapy, 155
genetic anomalies, 58
genetic counseling, 155
Genome Selection Committee, 59
Germany, 57, 107, 148, 181, 182
God, 25, 44, 58, 59, 61–65, 83, 84,
    86, 113, 115, 116, 133–136,
    150, 164, 172, 173, 180
Godspeak, 86

INDEX 189

Goebbels, Joseph, 14, 28
Google, 71, 119, 124, 181
Gordon, Theodore, xi, xii, 105, 149, 161, 172, 174, 178, 181
gossip, 4, 161, 170, 171, 178, 179
government, xii, 19, 23, 28–30, 52, 57, 77, 83, 108, 109, 128, 137, 145, 149, 181
GPS, 1
Great Unexpected Events of the 21st Century, 178
Greece, 181
greed, 65, 105, 113, 137
Gross National Happiness, 128, 129
gross national product, 128
Guantánamo, 24

H
H5N1, 114
haloization, 88
Harari, Yuval, 166
hate speech, 29
Hawking, Stephen, 121, 125, 165
The Headline Database, 174
health care, 52, 54, 101
Hebdo, Charlie, 107
helium, 5, 171
historian, 1, 4, 7, 171, 172
history, 2, 4, 6, 8, 11, 13, 24, 46, 48, 53, 73, 89, 94, 96, 97, 100, 101, 112, 126, 131, 138, 142, 144, 148, 163, 165–167, 171, 173, 180
history repeats itself, 180
Hitler, Adolph, 5, 14, 28, 101, 171
Holmes, Sherlock, 104
Holocaust, 17, 18, 34, 64, 150
holograph, 16
Homeland Security, 43, 110
human design, 157
human health, 58

humanity, 51, 113
human minds, 180
human rights, 54
human species, 58, 127
humor, 120, 124
hydrogen, 5, 35, 37, 171
hydrogen bomb, 35
hypotheses, 4, 161, 170, 173, 179

I
I am a Machine, 123
IBM, 119, 120
ICBM, 37–39, 42
illiteracy, 52
illusion of truth, 14
imagined realities, 4, 171
immorality, 83
immortality, 2, 47, 70–73, 75, 77, 80, 164
immune system, 54, 58, 79
incest, 54
India, 34, 37, 47, 55, 59, 108, 119, 131
Industrial Light and Magic, 16
infant mortality, 55, 101
inferences, 103
influence behavior, 54
Inquisition, 64, 135, 138
insighters, 93, 95, 96, 106
intelligence, 12, 19, 29, 72, 88, 99, 119–121, 125, 141, 145, 148, 163, 165, 166
intelligence agencies, 19
interconnected neurons, 2
Internet, 87, 101, 111, 122, 175, 176, 183
In The Fruit Garden Of Pakistan, 44
introduction, 165, 181
invisibility, 2
Iran, 19, 20, 33, 35, 37, 47, 148
Iraq, 14, 20, 101

190   INDEX

ISIS, 37, 44, 107, 179
Israel, 18, 25, 34, 37, 52,
   108
italics, 8
Italy, 108, 181, 182
It is all About Connections, 66

J
Japan, 15, 36, 108, 148
Jews, 18, 143

K
kidnapping, 44, 108
Kim Jong Un, 35
Kissinger, Henry, 34
Kitt's Peak, 13
Korean peninsula, 42
Kurzweil, Ray, 121, 166

L
legacy, 70
legacy issues, 8, 170
leisure, 53, 120, 175
lethality of viruses, 111
liberalism, 163
lies, 11, 14, 28, 54, 73, 129, 131,
   165, 171, 174
life expectancy, 55, 101
life extension, 25
life span, 53, 69, 70, 79, 80
likelihood, 8, 22, 124, 143, 165
Lindbergh, Charles, 5
Lipstadt, Deborah, 18
literacy, 54, 101
Living Healthy Forever, 79
living standards, 128
Lone Wolf, 36
Los Angeles, 39, 40
loss of communications, 38

M
MAD, 34, 36, 37, 40, 47
Malthusian, 51
manipulate heredity, 153
manufactured diseases, 55
the man who saved the world, 41
Man Will Never Fly Memorial Society,
   17
Mao, 28
MAOA, 144
marketing, 54, 137, 162
Market Madness, 21
market place, 21, 22
market turmoil, 20
masochist, 129
Master Race, 157
mathematics, 135
Mavens, 94, 95, 100
McNamara, Robert, 34
media sources, 21
medical, 52, 102, 112, 114, 124, 132,
   137, 156, 164, 176, 177
Mein Kampf, 28
memory, 21, 29, 64, 66, 67, 71, 74,
   75, 77, 95–98, 100, 103, 120,
   125
Mengele, Joseph, 156
Methodologies, 169
Mexico, 54, 57, 108, 148, 163
Middle East, 24
Millennials, 143
The Millennium Project, 109
Ministry of Truth, 27
Minuteman, 41, 42, 46
miracles, 87, 164
model, 6, 15, 16, 66, 74, 108, 114,
   146
Molnya observation satellite, 40
moon, 16, 17, 123, 143
Moot Point, 84
moral code, 165
moral compass, 102

INDEX   191

morality, 84, 86, 100, 105, 175
mortuary, 112
Moscow, 40
Musk, Elon, 65, 121
mutual assured destruction, 34, 163
mysteries of human genetics, 153

N
National Gazette, 23
NATO, 34, 46
Nazi, 5, 14
Nazi Germany, 5
Nepal, 52, 129
network, 1, 21, 27, 42, 52, 88, 125
New York Stock Exchange, 22
Niger, 52
Non Proliferation Treaty, 34
NORAD, 41–43
normalcy, 109, 148
North Dakota, 41
North Korea, 19, 33–36, 42–44, 47, 48, 148
novelists, 4
nuclear, 3, 8, 13, 33–39, 41–44, 47, 48, 163, 170
nuclear weapons, 33

O
Opioid Crisis Response Act, 132
Opioids, 132
orgasm, 67, 130
Orwell, George, 27, 28
Our Computer Overlords, 119
overpopulation, 113
ovum, 54, 154

P
Pakistan, 19, 34, 37, 44, 47, 52, 108
panspermia, 161, 180

panspermia theory, 180
pants on fire, 11
Papyrus, Ebers, 131
Pascal, Blaise, 4
past, 1, 2, 7, 16, 20, 21, 35, 53, 56, 72, 92, 94, 98, 100–102, 111, 119, 121, 124, 131, 132, 138, 143, 164, 169, 170, 173, 174, 180
The path to SIMAD, 110
pattern recognition, 104
Penfield, Wilder, 97, 98
Peron, 28
personal medicine, 153
Petrov, Stanislav, 38, 40, 41, 43
pharmacies and health clinics, 52
photographic fraud, 21
phrenology, 98
Pinochet, 28
plausible deniability, 148
The Plot Against America, 5
Plug me in Poppy, 122
Poland, 181
policy analysis, 7, 173
political changes, 2
political chaos, 144, 165
political malaise, 148
political scientists, 137, 178
politicians, 11, 14, 54, 103, 123, 127, 137
politics, 122, 127, 144, 161, 170, 175, 179, 181
pollsters, 146, 147
polymath, 133
poor countries, 52, 53, 55, 177
Pope, 59, 87, 171
population, 23, 51–59, 78, 112, 113, 128, 132, 137, 145–147, 164, 175
population growth, 51–56, 137, 164
pornography, 21, 23, 123

192 INDEX

positive identification of individuals, 58
pre-crime, 29
The Precursor Real Time Delphi Study, 178
pre-detection, 45
predilections, 2, 164
pregnancy immunization, 55
President, 5, 7, 11–13, 16, 21, 22, 26, 28, 33, 34, 37, 42, 43, 45, 48, 69, 71, 114, 149, 171
privacy, 22, 115, 170, 175, 179
Prize, 41, 175, 176
probability, 39, 102, 104, 136, 172
probability of failure, 39
progress, 3, 45, 52, 58, 65, 70, 125, 127–129, 132, 133, 136, 165, 171, 172, 174
proliferation, 3, 8, 36, 46–48, 137, 163, 170, 179
propaganda, 4, 11, 12, 18, 19, 28, 170, 171
prophylactic measures, 155
PROSTASIS, 137
protection of nuclear wastes, 49
psychiatry, 153
psychological test, 99
psychology, 62, 77, 102, 130, 141, 165
public opinion, 19, 147
Putting The Genie Back In The Bottle, 48

Q

quantitative modeling, 163
quantum encryption, 125
quantum phenomena, 2

R

racial bias, 146

railroads, 171
RAND, xi, 47, 161, 166, 181
random processes, 58
rape, 54
rationalism, 135
Real Time Delphi, 3, 4, 109, 161, 163, 178, 181, 182, 184
The Real Time Delphi Method, 181
refugee, 179
reinterpretation, 4, 161, 170, 173, 179
reinterpretation/reinvention of facts, 170, 178
religion, 61–63, 68, 83, 84, 86, 87, 127, 131, 132, 164, 175
religions, 2, 64, 83, 85, 86, 115, 122, 164
Religion Tech, 86
religious dogma, 170, 179
remote detection of DNA, 180
Replika, 125
reset, 115
resilience, 128, 136, 148
rhetoric, 26
rigid airships, 5
risk, 22, 38, 101, 102, 115
rituals, 22, 131, 141
roadmap, 166
robot, 45, 164
Roosevelt, Franklin, 5
Roth, Philip, 5
Rot in Peace, 77
rumors, 4, 79, 161, 170, 173, 178, 179
Russia, 19, 28, 34, 37, 38, 41, 46, 47, 64, 84, 108, 109, 148
Russian, 19, 37, 46, 84

S

sadist, 129
sadness, 125

INDEX 193

safeguards, 38, 39, 150
Sagan, Carl, 34
Sanders, Sarah, 26
Saturday Night Live, 28
Saudi Arabia, 20, 108
scales of time, 2
scarlet fever, 156
scenarios, xii, 2, 4, 5, 8, 21, 26, 39, 40, 43, 45, 64, 68, 79, 83, 88, 91, 109, 116, 121, 128, 144, 163–167, 172, 174
science, xi, 4, 11, 12, 37, 61, 63, 65, 72, 73, 84, 85, 101, 103–106, 120, 127, 161, 164, 173, 175, 181
Scowcroft, Brent, 34
Second World War, 14, 18, 169
secret signs, 22
security, 19, 29, 45, 83, 108, 113, 141, 142, 165, 175, 176
seed of the future, 162
selection of the gender of unborn children, 55
selfish interests, 146
sensation amplification, 123
Shangri-La, 129
Shoemaker–Levy, 13
SIMAD, 109, 110
Singularity, 121
skullcap, 88, 122
slave, 123, 156
slavery, 59
sleeper facts, 161
smaller families, 52, 164
social marketing (SM), 54, 137
social media, 11, 19, 22, 29, 84, 110, 113, 138, 146, 147, 171
South China Sea, 8
South Korea, 36, 42, 181
Soviet, 13, 34, 36, 38, 39, 41
Spanish flu, 110, 112
speculation, 8, 33

Speeding up learning, 180
sperm, 54, 55, 154
Stalin, 28
starvation, 18, 53
Stasis is good, 137
stealth bombers, 43
stereotyping, 4, 141, 143
stockpiles, 33–35
The Story Behind Trump-Putin Day, 45
Strong Woman, 145, 149
submarines, 36–38, 40, 43
suicide, 44, 55
super intelligence, 58, 120, 125
Super Saltpeter, 56
Super Sari and her sisters, 124
Supreme Court, 21, 23, 28, 87, 115
sustainability, 57, 175
symbols, 29, 104, 143, 144

T

talent, 91–93, 100
The Talent for Decisions, 91
tattoos, 88, 122, 143
tax reform, 25
technology, xi, 2, 8, 11, 12, 29, 47–49, 52, 54, 55, 58, 65, 66, 77, 80, 83, 86, 108, 123, 126, 127, 142, 146, 163, 164, 171, 175, 182
Teller, Edward, 13
terrorism, xii, 8, 53, 108, 109, 163–165
terrorist attack, 88
Terrorists, 107, 108
tests for ethical behavior, 149
Tetlock, Philip, 6, 26, 93
third world, 52, 114
time lines, 2, 71
time-map analogy, 2
time traveler, 4, 6

194 INDEX

Todorova, Mariana, xii
Trade Off, 114
Transhumanism, 166
troll, 19
Truman, 145
Trump, Donald, 11, 12, 16, 18, 19,
 23, 26–28, 33, 35, 36, 42, 45,
 47, 48, 171
Trump Tower, 45
truth, 11, 14, 21–23, 28–30, 65, 68,
 86, 95, 104, 105, 161, 163
The Truth in Imagery Law, 22
Turing test, 121

U
Ukraine, 46
uncertainty, 2, 37, 78, 80, 81, 164
United Kingdom, 34, 108, 181
United Nations, 78, 129, 131
United States, 14, 17, 24, 27, 28,
 33–36, 38, 42, 56, 57, 62, 64,
 78, 83, 108, 181
universal happiness, 127
unproven beliefs, 178
unresolved issues, 3, 7, 8
use whatever means, 42
US Presidential election, 19

V
Vaccines, 54
Venezuela, 108, 181
video cameras, 104
violence, 26, 29, 68, 115, 144
Voltaire, 133–136, 172

W
war games, 34, 37, 38
warhead in orbit, 37
warheads, 34, 36, 46

War of the Worlds, 12, 66
wars, 2, 53, 65, 110
Washington Post, 11, 27
Watson, 119, 120, 124
weapons, 33–36, 38, 39, 43, 47, 49,
 105, 107, 108, 126, 134, 137,
 163, 175
weapons of mass destruction, 109
weapons policies, 36
weather patterns, 179
Wells, H.G., 12
Welles, Orson, 12
Wesleyan, 161
Wesleyan University, 161
What constitutes progress, 127
what might have been, 3, 14
Where is Morality, 105
White House, 26
Wikileaks, 19
wise men, 24, 25, 59, 105
Without Warning, 13, 14
women, 24, 51–54, 59, 78, 80, 94,
 122, 128, 130, 142
women in the labor force, 54
work, 6, 14, 21, 23, 26, 45, 47, 52,
 54, 70, 78, 80, 92, 93, 100, 102,
 110–112, 123, 124, 135, 142,
 161, 171, 172, 174, 176, 179
world population, 51, 62, 78
World population growth rate, 52
World War III, 40, 43
World wars, 2

Y
Yeltsin, Boris, 37

Z
Zeppelin, 5

9783030184360